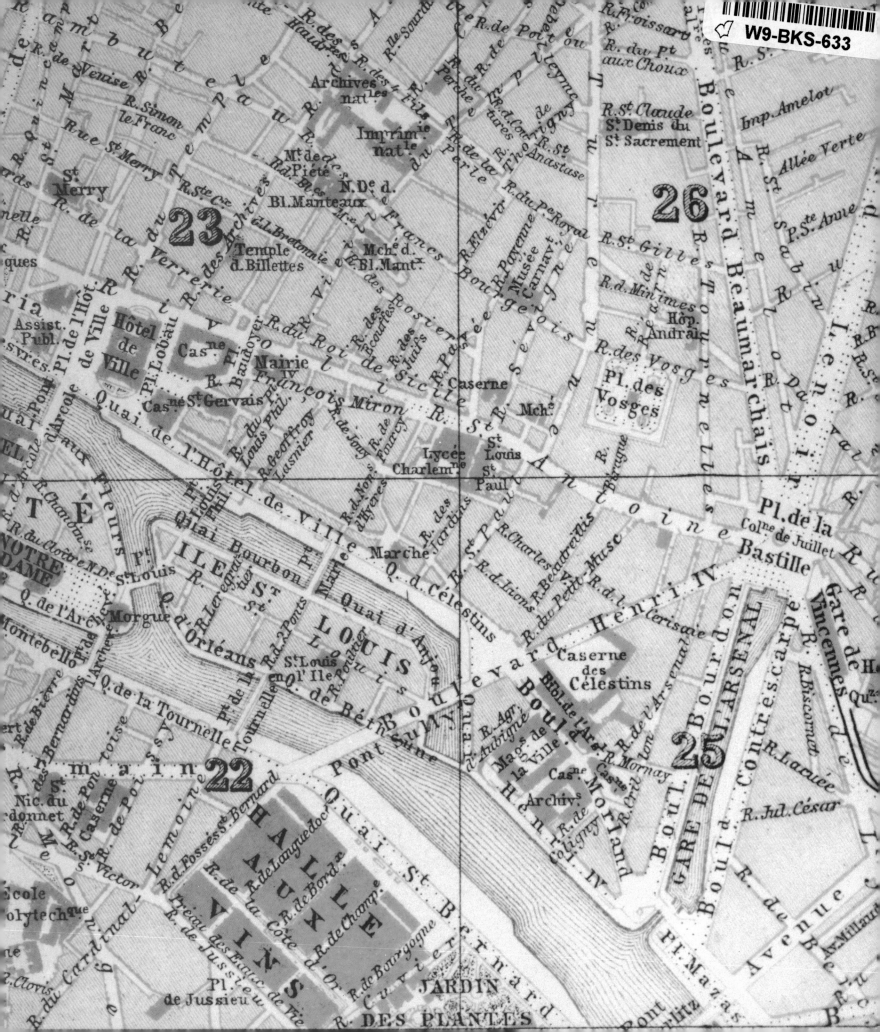

# THE STUDIOS OF PARIS

## THE CAPITAL OF ART IN THE LATE NINETEENTH CENTURY

John Milner

Yale University Press
New Haven and London · 1988

*In memoriam Brian Petrie*

Designed by Mary Carruthers
Set in Linotron Baskerville by Best-set Typesetter Ltd.,
and printed through Bookbuilders in Hong Kong.

Jacket design by Michael Harvey
Front and endpapers: annotated plans of Montmartre
and the Quartier Latin, two areas of Paris with
heavy concentration of artists' studios, from
*Plans of Paris*, Baedeker, 1894.

**Library of Congress Cataloging-in-Publication Data**

Milner, John.
    The studios of Paris : the capital of art in the late nineteenth
century / John Milner.
        p.        cm.
    Includes index.
    ISBN 0-300-03990-5
    1. Art, French—France—Paris.  2. Art, Modern—19th century—
France—Paris.  3. Artists' studios—France—Paris.  I. Title.
N6850.M48 1988
709'.44'361—dc19

# Contents

# Acknowledgments

This book was made possible through the generosity of the Leverhulme Foundation and the assistance of the University of Newcastle-upon-Tyne. I am grateful to my wife, Lesley Milner, for tolerating it, and to Kathryn Varley for typing it. I am grateful also for the assistance of the following: Bengt Danielsson, Tahiti; John Bensusan-Butt, Colchester; Jean-Paul Bouillon, Paris; Peggy Buchanan, Fort Worth; Marjory J. Cafone, Philadelphia; Gilles Chazal, Paris; Georges Cheyssial, Paris; Melissa Dalziel, Cambridge; Jacques Desoye, Bourg-la-Reine; Frances Dines, Wildenstein, London; Sandy Dubrow, Los Angeles; Dennis Farr, London; Jacqueline Fontseré, Moulins; Jean Forneris, Nice; Pascal Gauthier, Paris; Caroline Durand-Ruel Godfroy, Paris; Michael Goodison, Northampton, Mass.; Daniel Hennemand, Paris; Anne Herme, Roger-Viollet, Paris; Philip Jago, Melbourne, Australia; Moira O. Jones, Williamstown, Mass.; Christopher Lloyd, Oxford; Geneviève Lacambre, Paris; Edda Maillet, Pontoise; Françoise Maison, Compiègne; Barbara McCandler, Austin, Texas; Lisa Mirello, Pittsburgh; Melissa M. Moore, Minneapolis; Richard Ormond, London; Gilbert Pétridès, Paris; Benedict Read, London; Danielle Resche, Paris; Anne Roquebert, Paris; J.M. Schmitt, Colmar; Maria Helena Soares Costa, Lisbon; Christine Speroni, Strasbourg; Mary-Anne Stevens, London; Jean-Louis Thomas, Paris; Mme G. Volle, Albi; Philip Ward-Jackson, London; Christopher Zagradzki, Paris.

PHOTOGRAPHIC CREDITS

I am particularly grateful to M.A. Terrasse for permission to reproduce Plates 130 and 131, to Mme Chagnaud-Forain (128), to M.J.P. Bouillon (294), to Mrs B. Welsh-Ovcharov (28, 195), and to Mr Bengt Danielsson (287).

I also acknowledge the help of the following in providing photographs:
Armand Hammer Collection, Los Angeles 114; Art Institute, Chicago 76, 158, 189; Atelier 53 185; Bibliothèque Nationale, Paris 21, 30, 84, 95, 139, 141, 173–5, 183, 193, 200, 211, 256, 271; Trustees of the British Museum, London 5, 247, 258, 261; Brooklyn Museum, New York 47; J.E. Bulloz, Paris 73; Carnegie Museum of Art, Pittsburgh 187; Chambre des Députés, Paris 82; Chrysler Museum, Norfolk, U.S.A. 59; C.M.T. Assistance Publique Paris 197; Courtauld Institute of Art Galleries, London 241; Courtauld Institute, Conway Library 77, 85, 100; Courtauld Institute, Witt Library 72, 148, 194, 201; Jacques Desoye, Lanchère 138, 161, 179, 182; Durand-Ruel, Paris 66, 110; Editions Flammarion, Paris 62; Fine Art Museum, Boston, Mass. 97; Fitzwilliam Museum, Cambridge 132, 186; Galléie Pétridès, Paris 185; Gulbenkian Foundation Museum, Lisbon 37, 239; Harry Ransom Humanities Research Center, Austin, Texas 44; Hyman-Unwin, London 287; Kimbell Art Museum, Fort Worth 190; Lauros-Giraudon, Paris 19, 30, 61, 73, 227, 270; Lords Gallery, London 94; Marlborough Fine Art, London 167; Metropolitan Museum, New York 6, 8, 35, 63, 154; Minneapolis Museum of Fine Arts 135, 249; Musée

# PART ONE

## 1. Introduction

> Here is a piece of advice worth having. Never let your daughter marry an artist. You will bring her to sorrow if you do... An artist cannot be hampered by family cares. He must be free, able to devote himself entirely to his work.[1]

These are the words of Ernest Meissonier, the most honoured and successful artist of the late nineteenth century, whose aims and ambitions were as committed and determined as any of his contemporaries. Today he is a figure of greater obscurity. In a hundred years his reputation has largely vanished, despite all the splendour of his worldly success. In the histories of art he is rarely mentioned. There evidently lies a gulf between contemporary reputations and posthumous recognition. Painters and sculptors of the utmost diversity, commitment and professionalism have vanished by the hundred. Their works have been relegated from places of the highest honour to shadowy picture stores. With the passage of time their prices have plummeted from spectacular heights; their names are invoked as no more than a foil to the splendours of Impressionism and its heirs. Yet they were more than a background — they provided a highly visible and well-established foreground which time and criticism have largely erased.

Not only has our view of history changed but in doing so it has become vastly simplified, obscuring the intricate diversity of the period to provide an image of the time as one of heroic struggle. Yet life for the artist is rarely easy: as Meissonier implies, its demands are all-consuming, as often consumed by the need to succeed as by the fashioning of an image. In this dichotomy lie the struggles and the hopes of the artist, 'Nothing is really interesting to the artist', according to Meissonier, 'but that which he has not yet done'.[2] Yet the urge towards originality has to be reconciled with two sets of material factors — firstly the demands of the medium employed, whether oil paint or stone, but in addition, and equally subtle in its demands, there is always the need to survive and even to succeed with all the inherent difficulties, ranging from wayward models to relations with dealers and the pursuit of success through exhibition juries and the manipulation of the framework of patronage.

This book is about Paris during one of the most complex periods of its history, when its artists were numbered in thousands and when the annual Salon jury *reduced* its selection of works for display to a privileged 5,000–6,000 works. For an artist to assert his presence, and even to be seen at all amongst the multitude of warring styles and ambitions was a formidable task calling for resolute commitment and determination. Merely to survive as a painter was a difficult task; to succeed as a painter was an almost insuperable task, demanding cunning as well as talent, shrewdness as much as originality: an awareness of what was wanted had to be reconciled with what the artist wanted to achieve in his work. The demands of daily existence were not easily related to the demands of art and for each artist who found worldly success there were many hundreds who failed. Yet they too have their place in the history of art in Paris. In the

1. Meissonier's studio in Paris. The studio of a supremely successful artist.

words of Jules Breton: 'There are many humble painters who might have become great artists if Fate had placed them in circumstances more favourable to the development of their natural gifts, but who die unknown to the general public, their merits recognised only by a limited circle...'[3] Like Meissonier, the painter Breton thought marriage and family life potentially hazardous to either artists or their partners: 'High-minded and conscientious in the performance of their obligations, seeing themselves in the necessity of providing for the wants of the family, and devoted to their domestic duties, they are not free to enter the arena where alone fame is to be won.'[4] Only after the children grow up and leave home is he

> able to give himself up to studies long interrupted. Real progress, surprising at his age, leads to fresh successes. He has still a long future before him. It will only be a dream. All those emotions, like the warmth of a St Martin's summer, only serve to shatter still more an organization enfeebled by long continued vigils, and the artist breaks down while apparently in the full enjoyment of health.[5]

Whilst such practicalities are not an immediate influence upon the adjustment of tones, colours and lines upon a canvas, they are nontheless persistent, penury being no more attractive to the artist than to the practitioners of any other profession. 'I will lay it down as a general proposition,' asserted an anonymous essayist as in *The Studio* magazine of 1899, 'that no man makes a success in painting or sculpture, however great his talents may be, unless those talents happen to be associated with worldly wisdom and commercial astuteness,' for 'genius in painting...cannot succeed in a practical sense unless it be associated with businesslike qualities. I did not say these qualities and genius must necessarily be combined in the same person, I meant that genius must have these aids at its disposal, whether supplied personally or vicariously.'[6] This invokes the whole apparatus of recognition, promoted by journalists and dealers. The journalist agrees:

> The commercial man, the dealer, and the patron really make the painter. His art does not make him. Leaving out imbeciles and duffers on the one hand, and a few giants on the other, when you come to capable painters there's not all the difference between them that interested parties would have you believe. It's just a question as to how much capital in money and in brains has been put into them. The critics, dealers, and patrons have really entered, unconsciously for the most part, no doubt, into a kind of partnership. They hallmark certain men, dead or living, and these men get on the official list, so to speak...[7]

In fact there are two 'official lists', one drawn up at the time, and evident in the successful reputations of the day, and the other drawn up in the intervening hundred years. This book approaches the first of these. These were the artists visible to the talented young artists of the day; they reveal much of the structure of the hive that comprised the art world of Paris at the end of the nineteenth century, its preoccupations, tastes and conflicting developments. They permit a study of those practicalities and ambitions that combine in a commission, in which the demands of painting or sculpture meet the demands of survival and success.

The profession of artist reached a high point in the 1880s and 1890s, which a subsequent stress upon originality, aesthetic theory and the supremacy of the artwork's demands have relentlessly undermined. As artistic conventions have fallen before the brilliant but convulsive achievements of twentieth-century art, so too has the profession of artist suffered decay and transformation. This process was already at work in the late nineteenth century. Paris, which drew so many artists to its multitude of both splendid and sordid studios (Plates 1–2) was at the heart of this process, providing both the structure of support and of selection, both the means for sustaining convention and destroying it. By 1900 success had begun to change its meaning and its means.

2. Cheap studio accommodation for the unknown artist at *Le Chateau*, Rue Croulebarbe in the Gobelins district. Demolished c. 1930.

To walk in Paris from the northern hill of Montmartre, down across the great boulevards to the slow and and light-filled river, to pass the colossal Louvre, beyond the Ile de la Cité dominated by Notre-Dame, and on through the Latin Quarter into Montparnasse is to see much of the Paris that existed a hundred years ago. It is readily recognisable in the paintings which it inspired. It is also to witness the city as a living organism in its wealth, its poverty and its self-esteem, its complex system of streets and its spectacular revelations. Such a walk south through the heart of Paris shows north-facing skylights throughout, a physical indication of the Paris of those thousands of artists who congregated in its palatial studios and in its makeshift backstreet studios. Paris, the common factor of artists famous then but now forgotten, and of those whom subsequent history has lifted from obscurity, had a pull that was scarcely to be resisted. The resulting network of ambitions and talents had a structure which selected the successful, providing frameworks for tuition and subsequent advancement or failure. The relationship between Paris and its artists is visible in its geography, in whole streets devoted to studios, in the distinct areas they favoured, in its monuments, its collections and its art. To examine that relationship is to evoke the place as much as the time.

In *Trilby* the novelist George du Maurier presented a suggestive image of Paris: 'he would see discoloured, old, cracking, dingy walls, with mysterious windows and rusty iron balconies of great antiquity — sights that set him dreaming dreams of medieval French love and wickedness and crime, bygone mysteries of Paris'.[8] But to attain success the artist needed more than dreams: he had also to be a man of the world.

# 2. The Louvre

The Louvre is one of the great palaces of the world. In 1793 the Musée de la République was established there and it began its great career as a museum. Its colossal galleries, which now house one of the richest and most spectacular collections of art in the world, have more than once come under direct attack. The scene of bloody events in the French Revolution, the Louvre was again stormed by the mob in the Revolution of 1830. Subsequently under Napoleon III it was extended into almost symmetrical form, with its great arms stretching along the river front and along the Rue de Rivoli to join the Palais des Tuileries. The latter faced the Tuileries Gardens that still provide one of the great vistas of Paris stretching to the Place de la Concorde, where the guillotine had been so active, and beyond to the Champs Elysées and the Arc de Triomphe.

During the vicious fighting which gripped Paris after defeat in the Franco-Prussian War of 1870–1, when the Commune arose in Paris, central areas of Paris were devastated. Over 15,000 Parisians were killed in the midst of the city streets. The Second Empire of Napoleon III gave way to the Third Republic amongst scenes of carnage and desolation in the city. The Commune destroyed much and was ruthlessly suppressed. The great new boulevards which Haussmann designed for Napoleon III and his newly embellished city became the scene of slaughter and bloodshed. The Vendôme Column in the Place Vendôme was demolished with the active participation of the painter Courbet; the Hôtel de Ville, The Ministry of Finance, the Palais du Quai d'Orsay were destroyed by fire and the Louvre library was burnt. The Palais des Tuileries was attacked, fired and gutted in the fighting (Plate 3). The charred shell of the building which had been the permanent residence of Napoleon I, Louis XVIII, Charles X, Louise-Phillippe and Napoleon III remained a wrecked relic of the bitter conflict for thirteen years'.[1] A young art student of the 1880s recalled how 'my way lay

3. Giuseppe de Nittis, *The Place du Carrousel and the Ruins of the Tuileries Palace in 1882*, 1882, oil on panel, 45 × 60 cm., Musée d'Orsay, Paris.

across the Place du Caroussel, where the blackened ruins of the Tuileries Palace still stood as a grim reminder of the events of 1870'.[2] Meissonier too observed the ruins (Plate 4) and through them the smaller triumphal arch, the Arc de Triomphe du Caroussel, which echoes in shape the distant Arc de Triomphe:

> We passed the blackened Tuileries. In the midst of this colossal wreck, through which the car of victory appeared in the distance, on the Arc du Caroussel, we were suddenly struck by the sight of the words Marengo and Austerlitz, the names of two incontestable victories which appeared, shining and intact.[3]

If the Louvre, at the very core of Paris and its history, stimulated patriotic thoughts in Meissonier, it was its collections of art which stimulated both him and the artistic population of the city. With the restoration under the Third Republic of damage suffered during the Commune, the Louvre assumed its modern form: the Tuileries Palace was demolished and in 1889 the ruins removed, some of them to the Tuileries Gardens, where sculptures by Maillol now stand. The great wings of the Louvre enclose a vast public space extending the Tuileries gardens from the centre of the Louvre itself

4. J.-L. Ernest Meissonier, *The Ruins of the Tuileries Palace after the Commune of 1871*, 1877, oil on canvas, 135 × 95 cm., Compiègne Museum. The inscription refers to the battles of Marengo and Austerlitz. Beyond the ruined Salle des Maréchaux the quadriga of the Arc du Triomphe du Carrousel is visible.

through trees and paths to the Place de la Concorde, the long formal garden embellished by sculpture and recorded in the paintings of Pissarro, Monet and Vuillard.

The Louvre had special significance to painters and sculptors: it was far more than an effect of light in the bustling and elegant city centre. In its historical associations and its vast collections, the Louvre presented a formidable challenge and inspiration. Here the artist had available for the closest inspection revered masters of the Italian Renaissance, of Holland, Flanders and France. Here through the controlled but encouraged process

5

5. James A. McN. Whistler, *The Long Gallery at the Louvre*, 1894, lithograph, 21.5 × 15 cm. A copyist is at work on a large canvas. Published in *The Studio* magazine, 1894.

of copying direct from these paintings, an artist could learn and could accept the challenge of the art of the past. Here too the artist could hope, if ambitions were reckless, that one day his own works might hang, albeit after his death, as the ultimate recognition of his abilities. The Louvre's collection of French art was of particular significance in this respect: here the great traditions and achievements were handed down from Goujon, Poussin, Boucher, David and other more recent artists. The latter now include Delacroix, Ingres and even the Communard Courbet. The relationship between the Louvre and artists was a dynamic and continuing one and it was rare for painters, although Monet and Pissarro were among those who were, to be content to observe the fall of light upon the austere cut and sculptured stone of its exterior. Degas learnt much from the Louvre without undermining his modernism, and Renoir too acknowledged his debt to its seemingly endless parade of paintings and sculpture from the earliest times to the nineteenth century: 'It is in the Museum that one learns to paint. : . One must make the paintings of one's own time. But it is there, in the Museum, that one develops the taste for painting, which nature alone cannot provide.'[4]

The impact of the art of the past was more than a historical exercise, for the paintings and sculpture continued to effect the eyes and imagination of artists. To visit the Louvre was an exploration not to be hampered by too strict a determination to see the art displayed there in terms of the period and society which produced it. These aesthetic experiences were immediate and contemporary, sharpened for the practising artist by an astute awareness of techniques and methods. Rodin rejected too historical a view: 'Let us force ourselves to understand the masters — let us love them — let us go to them for inspiration; but let us refrain from labelling them like drugs in a chemist's shop.'[5]

To study in the Louvre was not a rare practice — it was built into the artist's education. Jacques-Emile Blanche was one amongst the throng of copyists there: 'I limited myself to painting at the Louvre. My copy of Mantegna's *Parnassus*, at which Gustave Moreau and Baudry both watched me work day after day, and which people offered to buy, still hangs in my house at Auteuil.'[6] In the Louvre the artist was in a public space, open to the passing criticism and insolence of the crowd (Plate 5). Artists themselves were part of that crowd, examining works of art with the professionalism and experience that a wine taster brings to rare wine or a cabinet-maker to the structure of a fine piece of furniture. The Louvre was a vast source of reference and learning, offering direct experience of a different order from work in progress at the art-school or evoked through the words of critics. The control of effects in drawing, tone, colour and composition could be studied in the original and largely as their artist had left them. For the practising artist to visit the Louvre was as much a professional activity as for a composer to listen to music. Here he could study the structure and aims of art, from the inside, as it were, defining in the process new directions in his own discipline. His process of looking at art was likely to be professional and critical. Degas depicted it in his pastel of the painter Mary Cassatt at the Louvre (Plate 6). That look is a link, an examination of imagery, handling and colour by a trained and experienced eye. What is learnt contributes to painting. Degas displays the paintings hung on the wall like a library available to the researcher who seeks information of significance and use in her own work. It is a kind of scholarship.

Thus, the Louvre provided simultaneously a challenge and an inspiration. Its vast and overwhelming panorama of painting and sculpture stretched from ancient times up to the decorations of Delacroix in the Galérie d'Apollon. Here above all was an assertion of quality. Many artists accepted the challenge. Degas and Rodin were amongst them, aware both of the achievements of the past and of a commitment to modernity. To resolve this dichotomy was a formidable undertaking but it was central to the examination of tradition and convention that underlay the multiplicity of tendencies that comprised art in Paris in the 1880s and 1890s, from the apparent formulae of the Ecole des Beaux-Arts to the rebellions of the Impressionists and the Symbolists. To visit

7. James Tissot, *In the Louvre*, *c.* 1885, oil on canvas, 46.5 × 32.5 cm., Rhode Island School of Design, Providence, Rhode Island.

6. Edgar Degas, *Mary Cassatt in the Louvre*, 1880, pastel on joined paper, 94 × 51.5 cm., private collection, New York.

the galleries of the Louvre, in parts densely hung with paintings up to the ceiling, was itself a process of selection and exploration, a mining of the past with modern eyes. Through the windows lay contemporary Paris and the life of the bustling city (Plate 8). Since the death of Delacroix in 1863, the challenge of modernity had been spelled out by the poet Baudelaire and others who shared his views. The painter of modern life ignored the Louvre, and all it represented, at his peril. Its collections were at once a challenge and a threat to originality.

8. Jean Béraud, *A Windy Day on the Pont des Arts*, oil on canvas, 39.7 × 56.6 cm., Metropolitan Museum, New York. The domed Institut is visible across the bridge.

# 3. The Institut

Whilst the Louvre was open to all, at once both the pinnacle of posthumous recognition and publicly accessible, a little way along the river Seine and on the opposite bank, with the Louvre very much in view, stands the domed Institut, housing a highly exclusive body of expertise with the five assemblies of the French Academy and administering the affairs of the Sciences and the Arts. Since 1795 the Académie des Beaux-Arts met here to oversee developments in painting, sculpture, architecture and music. There were forty members. Each new member was appointed by the votes of existing members and approved by the government. Membership was normally for life and appointment to the Academy comprised the highest public honour available specifically to artists. Its influence upon exhibitions, teaching and recognition was far-reaching. Insofar as its aims stressed the continuity of traditions, it is not surprising that its authority was repeatedly challenged by independent groups of artists (Plate 9). Amongst the fourteen seats allocated to painters during the period 1880–90, none were occupied by artists celebrated a hundred years later. The Institut stood for the ultimate in professionalism and no hint of radical changes in painting was permitted representation. Here the most celebrated and honoured artists of the day deliberated the future of French art with scant reference to the growing plethora of independent groups. It was at once the highest recognition for the authority of living artists and a body which promoted a system of patronage which to many appeared anachronistic and inappropriate. This tension did much to enrich debate and, paradoxically, to promote the emergence and development of alternative exhibition opportunities.

The Academy, originally founded along with the Ecole des Beaux-Arts in 1648, organised the Salon exhibitions from 1667. Supressed by the Revolution in 1793 it was replaced in 1795 by the Institut Nationale des Sciences et des Arts with its five constituent Academies, of which the Académie des Beaux-Arts was one. Its definitive form established in 1819, it appointed professors to the Ecole des Beaux-Arts and determined the winners of the Prix de Rome. Although in 1863 much of the Institut's power over the Ecole des Beaux-Arts was removed, in 1874 a system was introduced whereby the Institut awarded prizes and diplomas to contemporary artists. The fourteen painters of the Institut represented, in terms of professional activity, the top of the tree; they were vigorously committed to continuity and a sense of tradition (Plate 10). To many they were the arbiters of taste, the men who determined success by their work and by their position. The honour of election to the Institut was often accompanied by further indications of success. Although increasingly challenged and eroded, the authority of the Institut was a sign that painting and sculpture survived as a profession determined to preserve the particular processes of teaching, recognition through prizes and medals at exhibitions and recommendations for commissions, which militated against amateurism. It became a symbol of authority increasingly under threat and at odds with those developments in art that menaced its principles by stressing modernity and originality, but it was a vigorous force in the art life of Paris both in its teaching and rewards, representing coherence in a period of widespread experimentation.

Amongst its longest serving members were Gérôme (from 1865 to 1903) who was an active and vehement opponent of Impressionism, Bonnat (from 1880 into the twentieth century), Hébert (from 1874 to 1908), Bouguereau (from 1876 to 1905), Meissonier (from 1861–91), who fetched by far the highest prices of his day, his pupil and follower,

9. Lourdey, *Caricature of Bouguereau painting allegories,* *c.*1900.

9

## THE 14 MEMBERS OF THE ACADEMIE DES BEAUX-ARTS 1879–1905

|  | from 1860 | from 1867 | from '65 | from '50 | from '79 | from '64 | from '49 | from '70 | from '64 | from '63 | from '74 | from '61 | from '69 | from '76 |
|---|---|---|---|---|---|---|---|---|---|---|---|---|---|---|
| 1879 | | | | | | | COGN-IET. | | H. LEH-MANN. | | | | | |
| 1880 | | | | | | | | | | | | | | |
| 1881 | EMILE SIGNOL (1804–1892) | NICOLAS-LOUIS CABAT (1812–1893) | JEAN-LÉON GÉRÔME (1824–1904) | JOSEPH-NICOLAS ROBERT-FLEURY (1979–1890) | ELIE DELAUNAY (1828–1891) | CHARLES LOUIS LUCIEN MULLER (1815–1892) | | PAUL BAUDRY (1828–1886) | GUSTAVE BOULANGER (1824–1888) | ALEXANDRE CABANEL (1823–1889) | | JEAN-LOUIS-ERNEST MEISSONIER (1815–1891) | JULES-EUGÈNE LENEPVEU (1819–1898) | WILLIAM-ADOLPHE BOUGUEREAU (1825–1905) |
| 1882 | | | | | | | | | | | | | | |
| 1883 | | | | | | | | | | | | | | |
| 1884 | | | | | | | | | | | | | | |
| 1885 | | | | | | | | | | | | | | |
| 1886 | | | | | | | | | | | | | | |
| 1887 | | | | | FRANÇOIS-LOUIS FRANÇAIS (1814–1897) | | | | | | | | | |
| 1888 | | | | | | | | | | | | | | |
| 1889 | | | | | | | | | | | ERNEST HÉBERT (1817–1908) | | | |
| 1890 | | | | | | | | | GUSTAVE MOREAU (1826–1898) | | | | | |
| 1891 | LUC-OLIVIER MERSON (1946–1920) | J.-J. BENJAMIN — CONSTANT (1845–1902) | | | | | LÉON BONNAT (1833–1922) | JULES BRETON (1827–1906) | | JEAN-JACQUES HENNER (1829–1905) | | JEAN-PAUL LAURENS (1838–1921) | FERNAND CORMON (1854–1924) | |
| 1892 | | | | | | | | | | | | | | |
| 1893 | | | | | | | | | | | | | | |
| 1894 | | | | | | | | | | | | | | |
| 1895 | | | | | JULES LEFÈBVRE (1836–1911) | EDOUARD DETAILLE (1848–1912) | | | | | | | | |
| 1896 | | | | | | | | | | | | | | |
| 1897 | | | | (1833–1900) A. VOLLON | | | | | | | | | | |
| 1898 | | | | | | | | | | | | | | |
| 1899 | | | | | | | | | | | | | | |
| 1900 | | | | | | | | | | | | | | |
| 1901 | | | | | | | | | AIMÉ MOROT (1850–1913) | | | | | |
| 1902 | | | EMILE-AUGUSTE CAROLUS-DURAN (1837–1917) | | | | | | | | | | | |
| 1903 | | | | | | | | | | | | | | |
| 1904 | | | | | | | | | | | | | | |
| 1905 | | | | | | | | | | | | | | |

10. Members of the Académie des Beaux-Arts at the Institut showing who held seats at a given moment and who replaced whom.

the military painter Detaille (from 1892 to 1912), the painter of rural scenes Jules Breton (from 1886 to 1906) and Jean-Jacques Henner celebrated and popular for his suggestively erotic studies of ginger-haired nudes. In addition there were Benjamin-Constant, portraitist and depictor of Arabian themes, Jules Lefèbvre and J.P. Laurens, all highly active teachers and the authors of many commissions and Salon pieces, Gustave Moreau, the tutor of Matisse, and Cormon amongst whose specialities was the depiction of prehistoric scenes. These were men of power in the art world whose work was widely influential and well-known in their day. To assess the structure of opportunities and recognition prevailing in the period 1880–1900 requires reference to their authority and their work.

For a talented young artist whose career was beginning at this time their names would have figured large in the relentless competition for survival, recognition and success. To ignore them was to fall back upon alternative and often ephemeral opportunities. It was to ignore the structure wilfully in favour of an extremely difficult path. Only with the emergence of alternative Salons, and the increasing but still rare possibility of one-man exhibitions in the galleries of commercial dealers, did this become a viable possibility.

Although the Ecole des Beaux-Arts had gained some independence of the Institut, the relationship between them remained close. To enrol at a private teaching academy in Paris usually meant studying under a master who was either a member of the Institut (for example, those of Bonnat, Benjamin-Constant or Cormon) in which case it was undertaken often as a preliminary to application to the Ecole des Beaux-Arts, or studying, as at the Académie Julian, by working from plaster-casts and from the life-model with regular critical visits by Academicians.

In this way the influence of the Institut was felt at every level, providing opportunities and preventing opportunities, preserving traditions of professionalism and manipulating the machinery of success. Its fourteen members, having themselves reached the pinnacle of recognition, elected compatible replacement members, and so endeavoured to preserve a grip upon the process of recognition for those who followed. In a city housing thousands of artists it was inevitable that their authority should be challenged. Financial necessity alone dictated as much for those whose approach was not acceptable. On the other hand for those whose art was compatible and preferred, financial necessity argued compliance, for here lay the main possibility of promotion in a competitive, precarious and difficult career.

# 4. Beginnings

The studio to which I had been recommended was perched high up in the Passage des Panoramas, and in it I found Monsieur Julian, a typical meridional: dark eyes, crafty and watchful, a seductively mendacious manner, and a sensual mind. We made friends at once — he consciously making use of me, I unconsciously making use of him. To him my 40 francs, a month's subscription, were a godsend.[1]

This characteristically wry description by George Moore, who was soon to abandon his career in art for that of novelist and playwright, describes his arrival at the Académie Julian, the most popular and successful commerical academy preparing artists for the Ecole des Beaux-Arts or exhibition at the Salon. For Moore 'Julian threw open a door of Parisian life'.[2]

Later, after meeting Manet and Impressionist painters he became skeptical of the value of teaching systems such as that employed by Julian: 'That great studio of Julian's is a sphinx, and all the poor folk that go there for artistic education are devoured... After two years they all paint and draw alike, every one has that vile execution — they call it execution — *la pâte, la peinture au premier coup...*'[3]

Jacques-Emile Blanche, who also began his art tuition at Julian's, responded with similar disillusionment: 'My leanings were towards Degas, Manet and Renoir, who drew me away from official teaching, and such painting classes as were held at the famous Julian Academy'.[4] But Julian's Academy was nevertheless an immensely successful enterprise in its own terms and many artists looked upon it with affection and gratitude reserving a good deal of respect for Julian and his methods.

Founded by Rodolphe Julian in 1873, the Académie Julian flourished for many years and was attended by a vast number of painters including Bonnard and Vuillard as well as Matisse, Derain and Léger. Julian ammassed a fortune from the numerous studios he established. On occasions he even subsidised his students. His first teaching studio was opened in the Passage des Panoramas off the Boulevard Montmartre in 1868 in a former dance studio. Many others followed for men and for women in various parts of Paris.[5]

11. Rodolphe Julian, *An Academy of Painting*, c. 1875 (Salon 1876), whereabouts unknown.

Julian himself was a painter and would sometimes draw at his own academies. His work was exhibited at the Salon des Refusés in 1863 and at the Salon proper from 1865 before he turned his attention to the teaching which earned him the Légion d'Honneur in 1881. His successful strategy was to hire models and arrange weekly visits from celebrated artists of the day who would criticise students' work. Bouguereau, Lefèbvre and Boulanger were visiting tutors along with the influential painter Tony Robert-Fleury.

The ages of students varied widely. A hopeful young British artist, Shirley Fox, enrolled at Julian's Academy in the 1880s at the age of 12, the youngest ever to enrol there except for the painter Rochegrosse. 'Julian', wrote Fox, 'at this time had two studios for men, one in the Passage des Panoramas, near the Bourse, the other in the Rue d'Uzès, a small street close by, running out into the Rue Montmartre.'[6] At the latter the visiting tutors were Bouguereau and Tony Robert-Fleury who alternated over periods of one month making tours of inspection on Saturdays. Julian himself supervised the day to day running of his studios, establishing the life-model's pose for the week on Monday mornings: 'He used generally to seat himself on a high stool on the outskirts of the students and make a careful pencil study of the model in a large sketch-book which he brought for the purpose.'[7]

For Julian his academy was a paying financial concern with some students continuing to use his services for many years. For his visiting tutors it was similarly a useful source of income made available by virtue of their position and renown. For his students, it provided an invaluable introduction to the discipline of drawing and painting from the life-model, contact with other artists, informed criticism both from Julian and respected tutors, and through them the possibility of advice and expertise in the preparation for application to the Beaux-Arts (Plate 11). Aesthetic considerations aside Julian's Academy was for many years an invaluable start for a career as an artist, guaranteeing a model, tuition, experience and contacts for little outlay and without difficult entrance requirements. Progress was competitive but open to all.

The newcomer was broken in gently at Julian's Academy — he was, after all, a customer: 'Although no ragging of newcomers took place there, such as prevailed at the Beaux-Arts, it was customary for all *nouveaux* to pay a *bienvenue*, or footing, which usually took the form of a bowl of punch together with a supply of little cakes known as *brioches*.'[8]

12. John Cameron, *At Julian's*, c. 1895.

Students began by drawing from plaster casts before graduating to the life-room (Plate 12). The great stove and the life-model were at the core of Julian's Academy and teaching. Life-studies dominated the walls and the racks of stacked paintings in the studio. Seated on low stools or standing further back at light-weight easels, Julian's students learnt the severe disciplines of analytical observation by drawing and painting from professional models. The criticism from Bouguereau or Robert-Fleury was often severe (Plate 13), although students also learnt from each other. According to George Moore 'In the studio were some eighteen or twenty young men and among these were some four or five from whom I could learn; there were also some eight or nine young English girls. We sat around and drew from the model.'[9] Work continued until mid-afternoon: 'At 4 o'clock there was a general exodus from the studio; we adjourned to the neighbouring café to drink beer'.[10] Once outside the studio the rich street-life of Paris was attractive and immediate in its impact 'I watched this world of Parisian adventurers and lights-o'-love. And this craving for observation of manners, the instinct for the rapid notation of gestures and words that epitomize a state of feeling, of attitudes that mirror forth a state of soul, declared itself a main passion.'[11]

For a young woman entering Julian's Academy the experience was directly comparable with that of male students: 'Julian says that his women pupils are sometimes as strong as his men pupils. I would have worked with the latter but they smoke, and otherwise there is no difference,'[12] so recalled the painter Marie Bashkirtseff, for example, who enrolled at the age of 17. 'It seems to me', she wrote in her Journal in 1877, 'that a year of Julian's Academy would provide a good base.'[13] She drew daily from 8 am. until noon and from 1 pm. until 5 pm., a demanding and disciplined eight hours of drawing each day for the committed student. Marie Bashkirtseff put in immense labours in the studio. Furthermore she had considerable respect for the visiting tutors, and established a much closer relationship with both Julian and Tony Robert-Fleury: 'It is on Saturdays that M. Tony Robert-Fleury comes to the studio, the painter whose *Last Day of Corinth* was purchased by the State and placed in the Luxembourg Museum. Furthermore from time to time the premier artists of Paris come to give advice to *us*.'[14] She was very alert to Robert-Fleury's every word and desperately eager to gain his approval, particularly after receiving his praise after only six days at Julian's, although to be singled out in this way caused bitter jealousy amongst her colleagues and this she came to dread: 'I have aroused jealousies, because none of them have known anything like it, those students of one, two and three years who do academic nudes and who paint in the Louvre.'[15]

Periodically assessments were carried out by the visiting tutors together, and it was a matter of importance to be selected amongst the first six of the anonymously submitted works. 'The Competition will be judged tomorrow; I am so afraid of being badly placed' confided the young Bashkirtseff to her journal.[16] She need not have worried as she clearly had a facility for drawing. Robert-Fleury warned her against this facility, how-ever, urging her to pass beyond it to more demanding achievements. In her case at least the visiting famous artist was more than an esteemed figure adding tone and respectability to Julian's Academy, for he became closely involved in her own artistic development and in her more worldly progress.

For Bashkirtseff, Julian was a respected figure, both effective and useful, who 'without being a powerful painter…is a perfect tutor'.[17] Julian knew where his talents lay and was highly successful at exploiting them for the good of aspirant artists. If his academy was a commercial concern, it nevertheless played a vital role in relation to official systems of tuition. The sheer competitiveness of art in Paris was reflected in the process of assessment and thereby selection which took place in his studios. Those whom the visiting tutors placed in the first six were subsequently placed in a further competition for a medal. Bashkirtseff in her day won it and had to parade the studio on a hobby-horse constructed as a Mr Punch. This was a standard studio ritual which invoked

13. John Cameron, *Bouguereau and the English student, c.* 1895. Bouguereau assumes the student's seat whilst delivering his weekly criticism.

14. Marie Bashkirsteff, *The Meeting*, 1884, oil on canvas, Musée d'Orsay, Paris.

15. At the Académie Julian, life-class in sculpture.

16. Mme Thoret's drawing studio for young ladies in 1890. Strict discipline was maintained and drawing was from casts.

hatred from her fellow students. As her success grew, she became increasingly un-popular: '"Expect," Julian said to me in a low voice, "expect to be hated here, for I have never seen anyone make such progress as you have in five months".'[18]

Beyond such successes lay a closer relationship with Robert-Fleury who invited such students to his studio to advise them on their career and on entry for the Salon. Julian however firmly discouraged too early an attempt to exhibit. Three years after entering his academy, Marie Bashkirsteff was impatient 'And the Salon is approaching! I go to discuss all this with the great Julian and we are agreed, especially him, that I am not ready.'[19] This occurred four months before the opening of the Salon and despite the utmost commitment and driving ambition. Two years earlier she had declared 'I swear...that in 4 years I shall be famous'.[20] Julian however was firm and determined that she should either make a great impact at the Salon or not exhibit at all. His advice to Bashkirtseff reveals a glimpse of the chasm that existed between the established structure of tuition, progress and success and that which increasingly challenged and threatened it. One can understand the confusion and stress this caused the talented and ambitious student: Bashkirsteff recorded in her Journal in 1880: 'Julian says that I draw ten times better than Manet, and he adds that I do not know how to draw' (Plate 14).[21]

Julian's was but one of the commercially run academies catering for students and for older artists preparing for the Beaux-Arts, or working independently with need of a model and tuition (Plate 15). Madame Thoret's drawing academy for female students was another (Plate 16): it was densely packed and highly disciplined but likewise promoted life-drawing as an essential discipline for the young artist. For women freedom of movement in Paris often necessitated a chaperon. Bashkirtseff loathed having to visit the Louvre in the company of a chaperon whose enthusiasm for art did not match her own, and even the highly self-confident and unconventional painter Rosa Bonheur in her maturity found the social conventions of Paris tedious. She lived at Fontaine-bleau, and 'what bored her most was going to Paris, for it meant the discarding of trousers, smock and felt hat, as well as the putting away of cigarettes which she constantly smoked'.[22]

In Montparnasse, to the south of the river Seine, the Atelier Colarossi attracted many students, and here too life drawing was the central activity. It was a much appreciated facet of Parisian art education: 'A year or two at Julian's, the Beaux-Arts, or Colarossi's, is worth a cycle of South Kensington, with all its correctness and plaster casts.'[23] Certainly both the Julian and Colarossi studios attracted many foreign artists. The Germans Corinth (in 1884) and Nolde (in 1899) and the Spaniard Zuloaga attended the Académie Julian for example. On the other hand, artists, particularly landscape

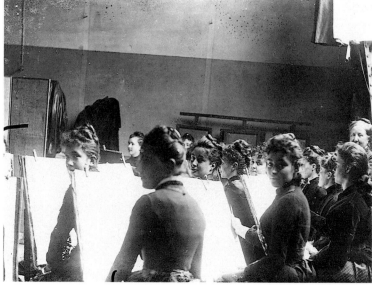

painters for whom the life-class was less immediately relevent, were increasingly attracted to the example of painters working direct from nature in the Fontainebleau forest and by the example of those Impressionists who had abandoned formal teaching in their youth. 'I recall', wrote Camille Pissarro in a letter to his son Lucien in 1884, 'that at the Académie Suisse there were students who were remarkably skilful and could draw with surprising sureness. Later on I saw these same artists at work; they were still skilful, but no more than that. Just think of Bastien-Lepage! and Carolus-Duran!!! No, no, no, that is not art.'[24] Bastien-Lepage in his short career was heralded by many contemporaries as a genius. He became a dominant influence upon Marie Bashkirtseff in her own brief but frustrated career. Carolus-Duran became one of the most fashionable artists of his day and a visit to his studio was an event in high society. In 1904 he took Gérôme's chair at the Institut.

In stark contrast to Julian's disciplined methods, the young Jacques-Emile Blanche was encouraged by the independent approach of Renoir and Manet, who, he asserted, believed 'that I should be allowed to paint just as I wish'.[25] When the powerful critic Albert Wolff, who vigorously attacked Manet's work, provocatively informed Manet that he pointed the way to many younger artists, he was subsequently greeted on several occasions by Manet holding out his arm like a sign-post pointing the way. To many the sophisticated innovations of Manet and Impressionist painters, strange as it may now seem, threatened to engulf the professionalism of art in amateurism and unintelligible originality through the directness of their approach. Their individuality and the authenticity of their vision was at odds with the main structure of tuition, exhibiting and recognition. Alternative structures and approaches were steadily demanding respect and acceptance: they were met with outspoken and determined opposition.

The experiments and courses of Horace Lecoq de Boisbourdran were a case in point. A believer in the importance of memory-training for artists, he envisaged his courses running as an optional extra alongside more traditional studies. The Institut member Jean-Jacques Henner was enraged by these experiments: 'He swamped me with brochures, and as I had never given him my opinion of them, he assumed that I agreed with his views! He wants students to draw without having the model before their eyes, even though the greatest masters have so much trouble drawing from nature!'[26]

Lecoq was a painter of portraits and religious themes who had exhibited at the Salon between 1831 and 1850. He was made a *chevalier* of the Légion d' Honneur in 1865 and like Julian saw teaching as his prime activity. Less directly related to the professional career structure, Lecoq's teaching was experimental and he carefully studied the results of his experiments which were undertaken at the Petit Ecole, the Ecole de Dessin et de Mathématiques which in due course became a School of Decorative Arts, and provided an alternative to the Ecole des Beaux-Arts in Paris. Fantin-Latour, Legros, Tissot and Lhermitte were amongst his pupils; Rodin, Dalou and Whistler were impressed by his methods and continued to make use of them in their mature careers.

'A master', wrote Lecoq, 'teaches by his work, a professor by his instruction and method'.[27] As he considered himself a professor he rarely took up a brush or charcoal to alter students' work and scrupulously prevented them from seeing his own work for fear of imitation. Although his method was highly controlled and disciplined, he saw its potential for developing the students' own characteristic qualities. His maxims stressed this: 'Art is essentially individual. It is individuality which makes the artist.'[28] He believed that 'All teaching, that is real teaching, based upon reason and good sense, must make it its aim to keep the artist's individual feeling pure and unspoiled, to cultivate it and bring it to perfection.'[29]

Beginning with copies of straight lines drawn from memory Lecoq's pupils moved on to copying complex shapes, shading and modelling until they could recall images from memory that were clear enough to produce drawings of objects in full relief. He considered this 'a sort of gymnastics course'.[30] Any technique or style was permitted for the drawing which necessarily assumed a knowledge of anatomy for the understanding of human form. Such exercises aimed greatly to increase his students' powers of visual analysis, concentrating as much upon the process of looking as upon drawing. Legros attained a high degree of proficiency in this. For Lecoq and his pupils this was far from a mere mechanical exercise for it stressed the relation of memory to imagination. Experiments in colour-memory followed, working up from two flat complementary colours placed side by side on grey paper, via several colours with a complex inter-relationship to the direct observation of colours in still-lifes set up in the studio. His system comprised carefully graduated stages each of which was to be completed before moving on to the next.

Advanced study was from the living model moving in the open air. Hours of observation resulted in colour studies executed from memory in the studio on the next day. Here the selective power of memory came into play based upon a rigorous training in looking. 'Personal impressions of this kind', wrote Lecoq, 'derived directly from nature, immensely favour the development of individual feeling and the birth of original talent.'[31] It provided a rich alternative to the disciplines of conformity inherent in other systems, for Lecoq valued individuality in his students: 'it will prevent their being reduced to eternally paraphrasing the same Old Masters'.[32] Composition in particular was necessarily original in that it responded more to the dictates of selective percep-tion and memory than to precedents. For this reason Lecoq also rejected the idea of photographic truth. 'Truth in art', according to Lecoq, 'is not photographic truth',[33] a statement reflected in the ideas of Rodin, who also used moving models, as much as in Van Gogh's copies from memory after Delacroix and Rembrandt.

Lecoq was so concerned to protect his students' individuality that he was wary of encouraging them to visit galleries: 'the habit of going to picture galleries too soon,' he wrote, 'a habit impossible to prevent in Paris, has its dangers for very young students',[34] and he despised prizes: 'The distribution of fine prizes in money and honours may do much to stimulate and encourage artistic output, it can do nothing to raise its quality.'[35]

Fantin-Latour recalled expeditions to the country on Sundays for bathing and open-air memory-studies of models and of each other. The models were often naked and observation of the effects of colour, light and shade from a figure moving through undergrowth or in the dappled light beneath trees was extremely demanding whether for painters or sculptors. 'The models I had hired for the occasion,' wrote Lecoq, 'had to walk, run, sit or stand about in natural attitudes, either naked like the fauns of old, or clothed in draperies of different styles and colours.'[36]

Thus, Lecoq de Boisbaudran, like Julian, was primarily a teacher, but his working context and approach was quite different. Julian's was closer to that of the Ecole des Beaux-Arts which many of his young clients sought to enter, whilst Lecoq's was an alternative and supplementary system much valued by Rodin, Dalou, Fantin-Latour and Legros. For a few it was of the greatest importance, with its stress upon disciplined sight, imagination, memory and individuality. Looking, as much as making, was the role of the artist, and an activity whose exploration demanded discipline and training. 'The only thing is *to see*'[37] commented Rodin in conversation with Paul Gsell, an exaggeration with which Lecoq would have had sympathy. Like Pissarro in his criticism of facile drawing ability, both Lecoq and Rodin believed in innate ability which more traditional teaching systems were unable to provide and might even destroy. 'The profession of the artist', said Rodin, 'is not meant for the mediocre, and to them the best counsels will never succeed in giving talent.'[38]

On the other hand, to succeed or even to survive as an artist meant to seize upon opportunities beyond the confines of the studio. In the search for opportunity it was to the Ecole des Beaux-Arts in Paris that young artists were drawn. Perhaps it was all to the good that Rodin was rejected three times and found differing kinds of training fruitful to his own development, but he certainly tried to gain admission and there were few who did not.

16

# 5. The Ecole des Beaux-Arts

On Monday mornings in the Rue Bonaparte at the heart of the left Bank of the Seine, the sculptured heads which preside over the gates leading to the great courtyard of the Ecole des Beaux-Arts looked out upon a model-market (Plate 17). 'Groups of models, mostly Italian, were seen to be lounging about the outer gates, the women and children in national costume.'[1] They were looking for work in the great studios. Some became well known as perfect types of Bacchus or Job; the Italian children made perfect *putti* to occupy a lesser role in a major composition. And good models were vital to the smooth running of the studios: 'Gathered at the big gates was a great crowd of models of all sorts, men, women, and children, fat, lean and of all possible sizes.'[2] By the late 1890s they could expect to earn 30 francs per week. George du Maurier immortalised one of them in *Trilby*:

> I'll just take a bite of you don't object; I am a model you know, and its just rung twelve — 'the rest'. I'm posing for Durien the sculptor, on the next floor. I pose to him for the altogether.
> 'The altogether?' asked Little Billee.
> 'Yes — l'ensemble, you know — head, hands and feet — everything — especially feet. That's my foot,' she said, kicking off her big slipper and stretching out the limb. 'It's the handsomest foot in Paris. There's only one in all Paris to match it, and here it is', and she laughed heartily (like a merry peel of bells), and stuck out the other.[3]

In the great studios themselves the model's job was exhausting, boring and demanding with long hours of vacuous stillness and frequent criticism from the painters and sculptors. In Gérôme's teaching studio at the Ecole des Beaux-Arts the floor was sloped to permit those at the back to see the isolated model whose form alone was the focus of their labours. The model was locked for hours in an interior world of reflection, motionless amongst the dense crush of artists and their paraphernalia. It is small wonder that models were often lively upon their escape, eager to remain popular with artists in order to continue their employment but eager also to escape the studio's confines, its barely changing north light and its stove where,

> A veritable forest of easels each bearing a canvas or drawing, almost filled the room, while immediately around the model's table were seated upon very low stools, a semi-circular row of students, their drawings supported on stools with backs to them, somewhat resembling a *priedieu*. The air looking towards the light was blue with smoke and dust, and a strong odour of paint and stale tobacco greeted the nostrils. The walls in several places were inches thick with the scrapings of palettes, some of them apparently dating from very ancient times.[4]

Many of the models became 'the contented companions of students and artists' outside the studios.[5] Successful models could hope for a regular income: 'All the great painters have their exclusive model or models, paying them a permanent salary... They are never seen in the academies, and rarely or never pose in the schools.'[6]

The Ecole des Beaux-Arts had existed since 1648 and was the most venerable art-teaching academy in France. The present building by Debret and Duban dates from 1820–38 but was extended with a new wing in 1860–2. In 1885 the adjacent Hôtel Chimay was incorporated into the Ecole des Beaux-Arts to provide workshops. It also became the site of important retrospective exhibitions. It housed a museum of copies

17. John Cameron, *Monday morning, Rue Bonaparte, c.* 1895.

18. Edouard Cucuel, *Gérôme teaching at the Ecole des Beaux-Arts*, 1899.

and Paul Delaroche's 7 metre high hemicycle painting in encaustic depicting seventy-five revered artists of the past. The Beaux-Arts carried its glorious past with it into recent times, a past highly respected by its chief painting tutors, each of whom directed a large teaching studio. In the 1880s these were Gérôme, Cabanel and Lehmann who was subsequently replaced by Hébert. Gérôme, Cabanel and Hébert were all long-standing members of the Institut.

Gérôme, according to the Shirley Fox, was 'a typical specimen of the old "Imperialist", he was like his work, neat, correct and impeccable (Plate 18). Upright as a dart, his spare figure and clear cut features arrested the attention, and his manner, abrupt, sharp and incisive, marked him at once as a ruler among men.'[7] Scrupulously punctual, Gérôme was also a demanding tutor 'more commanding of respect than affection',[8] with a tendency to treat all students alike and encourage the production of similar work. His criticisms, given on Mondays and Wednesdays, had him 'storming and scolding mercilessly when his pupils failed to follow his instructions'.[9] These sessions were no easier for the model who had to maintain the pose 'however difficult and exhausting. Often he is kept on a fearful strain for two hours.'[10] Gérôme visited regularly twice a week for over thirty-nine years.

Cabanel was perhaps more flexible 'gentle and sympathetic. . .much more ready to allow his pupils to follow their own bent, modifying and adapting his advice to their individual requirements.'[11] Cabanel had been a favourite painter of Napoleon III before the Franco-Prussian War and had executed mural decorations for the Hôtel de Ville as well as a portrait of Napoleon III which hung in the salon of the Empress in the Tuileries Palace of the Louvre. The Commune had destroyed both buildings and with them these paintings and in the process deprived Cabanel of this highest of patrons. He had won many honours and Salon medals, and for many years had directed the Salon with Bouguereau. He had been a professor at the Ecole des Beaux-Arts since 1863, and many Salon exhibitors acknowledged him as tutor. His studio was perhaps an obvious place to aspire to be taught. George Moore, for example, commented that on arrival in Paris 'my plans, so far as I had any, were to study painting in Cabanel's studio'.[12] Yet even fashionable painters on occasions doubted the value of their years at the Beaux-Arts. Bastien-Lepage who studied under Cabanel was one of them: 'I learnt my trade at the Ecole and I do not wish to forget it, but in reality, I did not learn my art there'.[13]

Bastien-Lepage was in the custom of starting work at 4 am. The Ecole began its day later, but a 7 am. start in summer and an 8 am. start in winter were too much for George Moore, for whom it 'required so painful an effort of will, that I glanced in terror down the dim and grey perspective of early risings that awaited me.'[14] He gave up the struggle. Methods too were strictly taught. Gérôme would not tolerate impasto which 'will make the colour-merchant happy'[15] and insisted 'that his pupils, before starting to paint, lay on a red or yellow tone, and that they keep their brushes scrupulously clean'[16]. Impressionist tendencies received withering criticism as 'the result of stupidities that certain intriguers have put before your eyes'.[17] As at Julian's Academy, which reflected Beaux-Arts teaching, study began in the Antique Room (Plate 19), drawing from casts, and only subsequently from the life-model. All progress was highly competitive, relying upon a regular system of assessments to determine the best works. A curious and elastic feature of their procedure was that on occasions non-members of the life-class, and even non-Beaux-Arts students, could submit drawings to the anonymously displayed competition 'which took place on the last Saturday of each month in the life class, and if sufficiently well placed, one was qualified to make a start from the living model on the following Monday.'[18] In this way the tutor chose the preferred six works each month, ascribing a double first, marked with two figure ones, to a work on each occasion. Inclusion in the first six permitted inclusion into the hallowed studios of Gérôme, Cabanel, Lehmann or Hébert. There was also an end of year competition to which any works of the last twelve months could be submitted. This display, held in the large hall

19. The glazed court at the Ecole des Beaux-Arts for the study of classical sculpture from casts.

facing the Quai Malaquais was opened as an exhibition to the public. But the most important and prestigious competition at the Beaux-Arts remained the Prix de Rome, which provided for students to study at the French Academy in Rome at the Villa Medici for three years together with a state bursary. Very occasionally it was won by non-Beaux-Arts students. Competition was fierce for this 'blue ribbon of the French art student'.[19] The selection occurred in several distinct and demanding phases. After a 'painted sketch' trial, the survivors were submitted to a second trial for the contest proper, which reduced the candidates to ten students who were entered 'en loge' for the definitive contest (Plate 20). These 'loges' were in a building divided into small studio cubicles. Here the ten competitors were locked in for a day to produce a compositional drawing on a set theme, usually classical or biblical, and were then required to produce a finished painting which followed this study closely. It was a competition that carried great kudos, and the highest accolade for a young artist. Paul Baudry, who from 1870 to 1885 was a celebrated member of the Institut, had found it gruelling as a student in the late 1840s and had won only on his fourth attempt in 1850.[20] The Prix de Rome was as difficult to achieve as it was desirable, a substantial boost to recognition for an artist at the outset of an independent career, and was recorded in subsequent Salon catalogue entries.

20. Alexis Lemaistre In 'les loges', the cubicles for the drawing competition at the Ecole des Beaux-Arts, 1889.

21. The Atelier Bonnat at the Ecole des Beaux-Arts, *c.* 1888.

22. Clive Holland, *A Massier*, photograph from before 1902.

The Beaux-Arts atelier, or studio-teaching-system with a celebrated artist directing each studio, was set up in 1863. It was going strong in the 1880s, processing large numbers of largely forgotten, determined and talented students both French and foreign, who populate the group photographs of the Atelier Gérôme, the Atelier Bonnat, Atelier Gustave Moreau and others (Plate 21). Almost lost amongst them are many of the figures who in subsequent years developed their training to accommodate their individuality, new methods of painting or sculpture and the demands of modernity. Seurat, who studied under Lehmann, and Matisse, who studied under Gustave Moreau, are two examples amongst many.

The atelier system survived further modifications in 1883 and found reflection in the establishment of commercial teaching studios working under renowned artists throughout Paris. Within each Beaux-Arts studio, the students enjoyed a degree of autonomy: 'Although free to come and go at will and do just as much or little work as we pleased, we were nevertheless to some extent under the control of law and order. An imposing-looking *gardien*, magnificent in uniform and cocked hat, was ever present to watch over us.'[21] Although the studios were in the charge of particular professors who paid twice weekly visits at most, the professors concerned themselves very little with the day-to-day practicalities of studio life which were controlled by a *massier*, a kind of chief student elected by his fellows (Plate 22). The model's pose was also established by a vote and students positions were in principle allotted according to the sequence of marking in the last assessment, although the *massier* was normally given first choice of view-point. It follows from this that the functioning studio operated like an exclusive, largely independent and fiercely competitive club, in which the *massier* was a figure of importance and power.[22] During breaks in the pose, new models attracted by the Beaux-Arts' payments, would parade before students who voted upon which of them to hire. The model chosen was booked by the *massier*: 'Every Monday morning from ten to twenty present themselves, male and female, for inspection, in *puris naturalibus*, before the critical gaze of the students of the different ateliers'.[23]

For the newcomer, *nouveau* or *rapin* (Plate 23), initiation into the studio involved appalling rites as well as extra duties. As at Julian's, the newcomer was obliged to pay for refreshments for the whole studio upon his first arrival, refreshments from which he was usually excluded (Plate 24). Subsequently he was obliged to arrive very early at the studio to sweep it, tidy it and light the stove in preparation for the day. A *nouveau* remained a *nouveau* for a whole year and had many menial duties. A newcomer studying sculpture, for example, could expect to arrive early, sweep up, fetch clean water, mix clay and keep it fresh and each week break up some forty figures and restore them to the clay bins. He suffered every kind of ignominy and provocation until the arrival of the next *rapin* and his eventual acceptance by the group and participation in its rituals.

Many newcomers were appalled by the violence and degradation involved in this regime which endured for many years. Paul Baudry had been involved in fights in the drawing class in which 'stools, wood, easels and boxes flew all over the place'.[24] In this respect studio life had changed little since Horace Vernet had painted an atelier, showing horse, dog, fencing and drumming in the studio. In addition, physical violence was not rare in initiation ceremonies inside and outside the Beaux-Arts. They were dreaded, with good reason, by newcomers. In 1852, a newcomer could be strapped to a ladder (Plate 25):

> This consisted in tying him securely by his head and limbs to a ladder, and preceded by one of their number blowing on an old hunting-horn, he was borne by four students along the suburb, the remainder following in solemn procession. Now and then the ladder and *nouveau* would be placed against some convenient blank wall, and left there for a while, exposed to the jeers and laughter of passers-by.[25]

Meissonier's recollections were horrifying too: 'One of my friends very nearly hurt himself seriously, nay, mortally. He had to jump from a considerable height, out of a loft, from which the ladder had been carefully removed, after the floor beneath had been piled with the studio stools, turned legs upward.'[26] It was most dangerous to respond aggressively for 'nothing so delights the students as for a *nouveau* to lose his temper'.[27] Meissonier agreed:

> The student who took the first joke in evil part, was done for. In one studio there was a young fellow who would not submit to persecution with a good grace. Morning after

23. Edouard Cucuel, *A Nouveau*, 1899.

24. Edouard Cucuel, *The Atelier Gérôme going out for a drink at the Nouveau's expense*, 1899.

25. George du Maurier, *Taffy à l'échelle*, 1894, illustration for du Maurier's novel *Trilby* based upon du Maurier's experience at the Atelier Gleyre, with Whistler in monocle fleeing at left.

morning he found his canvas spoilt and his tools broken up. He got so furious at last that coming early one day to the studio, he slashed every single canvas across, smashed every stool, and standing proudly at bay, knife in hand, behind the ruins he had wrought, he forced his tormentors to retreat.[28]

Such riotous activities were still common at the Beaux-Arts in the 1880s: 'References to our personal appearance were many and insulting, and any particularly brilliant sally would be greeted with roars of laughter. Then would follow discussions as to what should be the treatment awarded to us, and some alarming suggestions were made.'[29] New students could face the relatively gentle but ignominious paintbrush rite whereby two newcomers were forced to strip naked and fence with brushes on the model's dias (Plate 26). One brush was loaded with red oil paint and the other with blue, the winner being determined by a count of the marks implanted on the opponents' bodies.

Over and above such torments, the smooth-running and competitive system of teaching and selection which operated at the Beaux-Arts was not universally admired. The most frequent criticism was that it encouraged conformity along with skill, and that its commitment to competition distracted students from the development of individual ability. Lecoq de Boisbaudran was outspoken on this issue:

Even if the Prix de Rome is not surpressed, and I do not suppose it will be for many years to come, it is at least possible to reduce its evils very considerably. First the reign of the old competitions must be publicly declared at an end, and the competitors must be persuaded that they need no longer be the slaves of convention, but are free to express with absolute sincerity whatever impressions they receive from nature.[30]

Dalou, who had studied with Lecoq and subsequently at the Beaux-Arts, believed that his time there was counter-productive as he 'lost all serious and sympathetic direction'.[31] Bastien-Lepage found its tuition equally unrewarding and stifling in its commitment to the conventions of the past: 'When I arrived from my village I knew nothing about anything, but I was certainly not seeking this heap of formulas with which they pervert you. You want to paint what exists, and they invite you to paint the Unknown Ideal, that is to say, more or less to imitate the paintings of old.'[32]

Whilst the atelier system provided the backbone of French art-education, based primarily on drawing and painting from the life-model, its large classes did not promote close contact or cordial relations with the professors who directed the studios and assessed the work produced in them. But it did attracted acolytes to celebrated artists who in turn, for relatively little contact in teaching, could earn useful amounts of money. For this reason, private or commercial teaching studios independent of the Beaux-Arts flourished in the 1880s and 1890s, some of which, inspired perhaps by the early success of Courbet's *Atelier Libre*, provided for a more flexible relationship between tutor and student and even a degree of collaboration. The example of the Atelier Benjamin-Constant is instructive. An English art student from Julian's , by the name of Rawlins, originally set up a studio in Montparnasse, south of the Seine, by gathering a few interested friends together to share the cost of a life-model's fees and studio accommodation. As more artists began to attend this informal co-operative, Rawlins opened a second studio in the area, and in doing so had established in effect a small and successful business. As this flourished too, Rawlins began to plan more adventurously and decided to approach a celebrated name to head a third studio. He approached Benjamin-Constant, established painter of important portrait commissions and Salon paintings of Arabian themes. The latter agreed to participate, but specifically on terms equivalent to those at the Beaux-Arts, in that the teaching studio would carry his name and 'If you will provide a studio, close at hand, which I can visit "in my slippers", when and how I like, then I will consent'.[33] In this way both Rawlins and Benjamin-Constant profited. A studio was found almost adjacent to Benjamin-Constant's own in the

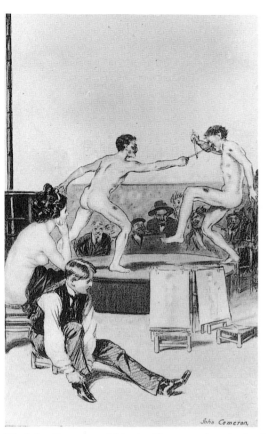

26. John Cameron, *Inititation Ceremony: the paint-brush fight.*

27. Benjamin-Constant with the students of the Atelier Benjamin-Constant *c.* 1888.

Impasse Hélène in Montmartre (Plate 27). After its eventual closure Benjamin-Constant began to visit Julian's Academy as tutor.

Very many artists studied in such independent and commercially run art schools which were essential if the vast number of artists in Paris in the 1880s and 1890s were to receive tuition. Each had its hierarchy of tutor and *massier* and was fee paying.

The Academician Fernand Cormon ran an atelier in the Boulevard de Clichy area of Montmartre which had a reputation for freer teaching systems and which was called an *atelier libre*. Toulouse-Lautrec, Emile Bernard, Anquetin and Vincent Van Gogh studied under Cormon there, and no sign of imitation of Cormon's own Salon or decorative paintings is evident in their own work although Cormon apparently sought Lautrec's assistance on a decorative scheme in 1884. Two photographs of the studio taken in 1885 show Bernard and Lautrec among a group of over thirty students with the usual plaster casts in the background and a starkly naked middle-aged male model (Plate 28). In the first photograph Cormon plays out his role as tutor seated at the easel and posing as if adjusting a student's painting, his students gathered respectfully around him. The second is an informal snapshot taken after Cormon's departure from the room (Plate 29). The studio dog has appeared and a feigned experiment in mesmerism, popular at the time, is underway. The art-school skeleton joins the group and a top-hatted student has his arm around the model who flagrantly displays his physique. Together the photographs reveal the importance of the master but also permit a glimpse of the studio life which was an important aspect of such ateliers, where much was learnt by the exchange of ideas between students.

Lautrec had previously studied under Bonnat, whose private studio closed after his appointment as professor at the Ecole des Beaux-Arts in 1883. Bonnat was strict and in 1882 severely criticised Lautrec's drawing: 'Your painting is not bad, it is fashionable but really it is not bad, but your drawing is throughly atrocious.'[34]

Lautrec had originally dreamed of studying under the most fashionable of portrait-painters Carolus-Duran whose private studio evolved in a way similar to that of Benjamin-Constant. At the Salon of 1869, Carolus-Duran's elegant and restrained

28. The Atelier Cormon, 1885–6. Cormon is at the easel, Emile Bernard and Toulouse-Lautrec (foreground left) are present. The male model is visible upper left and casts at right.

29. The Atelier Cormon, 1885–6. The master is absent.

*Woman with a Glove* (now in the Louvre) had made his reputation. As a result of this an American art-student, Robert Hinckley, approached Carolus-Duran for instruction. Like Benjamin-Constant he agreed on condition that Hinckley find a studio and administer it. By 1874 when John Singer Sargent enrolled at the Atelier Carolus-Duran there were over twenty students. The more prestigious the artist lending his name and selling his wisdom, the more students wished to attend and the higher could be the fees charged. This system ensured further close links with the members of the Institut and their principles. It was a sign of success and source of income and the most renowned studios were not easy to enter. Acceptance in itself conferred kudos, as well as high hopes, upon such students. Benjamin-Constant was elected to the Institut in 1893, Cormon in 1898 and Carolus-Duran in 1904.

Carolus-Duran's visits were formal and impressive and his teaching stressed accuracy of observation. He was a fanatical admirer of Velasquez and advised a close study and control of tones in a painting. The main planes of a head were to be applied directly to the canvas with a broad brush, establishing three or four planes for forehead, nose and so on. These planes, sitting side by side as in a mosaic were only subsequently modified to depict detail and smaller planes.[35] In the Atelier Carolus-Duran on the Boulevard Montparnasse, students clearly received valuable practical advice at the hand of the master and this was an immediate advantage in such a system when it was working well. A disadvantage was dependence upon a single tutor with its danger of invoking imitation.

Amongst the broad mass of Salon exhibitors in the later 1880s, Cabanel was clearly the most popular tutor, followed in order, by Lefèbvre, Gérôme, Bonnat, Bouguereau, J.P. Laurens, Cormon and Benjamin-Constant. They were all members of the Institut. If their names are little known today, it is clear nonetheless that their fame and influence was widespread and far-reaching in their day amongst the mass of artists whose conflicting hopes and ambitions were fighting for recognition in the studios of Paris.

# 6. *Paris as a Dwelling Place for Artists*

> To the right, Paris, gigantic Paris, spreads away to the horizon her great seed plot, sown with innumerable houses, so small in the distance that one might hold them in the palm of one's hand. Paris, vision at once monstrous and sublime, colossal crucible wherein bubbles increasingly that strange mixture of pains and pleasures, of active forces and of fevered ideals![1]

So wrote Paul Gsell looking over Paris from Rodin's studio at Meudon. The painter Jules Breton used the same image: 'A thousand elements flow from all sides into this crucible, which is constantly in operation, and in which the pure metal is separated from the dross.'[2] Into this crucible flocked artists from all over France and Europe, as well as Russia and America. For the great majority, art and Paris were synonymous, and Paris with its studios, museums, galleries and patrons responded. In 1886 The persuasive and influential critic of *Le Figaro* Albert Wolff wrote of Paris as 'the Capital of Art': 'It is in art that Paris, after its disasters, has found the renewal of its high European standing... The Seige of Paris scarcely ended, foreign merchants were rushing towards the capital to search there for the masterpieces of the French School of which Europe and America had been deprived since 1870.'[3] He continued, generously admitting that not all great artists live in Paris, that 'nowhere else can we assemble so great a gathering of men who

30. Pierre Bonnard, *Street Corner seen from above*, 1899, lithograph in four colours, 36 × 21 cm., from the series *Quelques aspects de la vie parisienne*.

have marked out the luminous phases of art.'[4] Yet the experience of the artists' life in Paris frequently impressed the unknown artist too: 'Paris has ineradicably impressed itself upon us. We have lived its life: we have been part of its throbbing, working, achieving individuality.'[5] But fame and splendour were scarce, and life for the unknown artist could be hard in the extreme. Van Gogh was one such artist in Paris trying to convince himself that 'in one word, with much energy, with sincere personal feeling for colour in nature, I would say an artist can get on here notwithstanding the many obstructions'.[6]

By contrast Albert Wolff was aware that any artist in order to succeed financially, which Van Gogh never did, had to respect his clientèle, become an adaptable and clever man of the world:

> In our epoch the painter is no longer the labouring artisan who locks himself away in his studio behind a closed door living in a dream. He has thrust his head foremost into the bustle of the world and participates in the activity of elegant Paris; he has his day when his studio is transformed into a salon where he receives the elite of polite society.'[7]

What Wolff said of the artist's own studio applied equally to the teaching studio, for beyond their walls lay the active city, increasingly beguiling artists as a subject in itself, as a central theme of the painting of modern life, but also as the source of opportunity, recognition and income through sales. For both of these reasons the life of the boulevard was a subject of fascination, and some artists, as Wolff suggested, were society figures, 'The boulevard alone', wrote Jules Breton, 'can develop that brilliant but superficial faculty which we call *esprit*. . .'[8] There were so many artists in Paris that they impinged upon the society which they observed and to which they catered. Artists had an ill-defined social status, enjoying almost simultaneously the company of the highest and lowest echelons of society: 'One evening we would spend at. . . the Rue de la Gaité, in the company of thieves and housebreakers, and on the following evening we were dining with a duchess or a princess in the Champs Elysées.'[9]

Thus beyond the confines of the still studio light lay the flickering activity of the Parisian street, as active by night as by day, an invitation to the artist to abandon his solitude for the multitude. Manet, Degas, Monet, Béraud, Raffaëlli and many others were to take this step in their paintings of the city, making Paris more aware of its own appearance, its light and its life, the multi-faceted organic coherence and movement of the city, the communal living identity of its populace.

It attracted the attention of numerous writers too. Zola, for example, frequently described the life of the city street.

> Through the three open gates could be seen the vibrant life of the swarming boulevards, ablaze with light in the fine April night. The rumbling of carriages stopped short, doors slammed, and people entered in little groups, waiting at the barrier before climbing the double staircase behind, where the women, their hips swaying, lingered for a moment.[10]

Paris was as poor as it was rich, as sordid as it was sensual, and artists of the 1880s and 1890s reflected all of these aspects, just as they operated at every level from wooden shacks in Montmartre or from the magnificent studios of the Avenue de Villiers. In the process they reflected the splendour and the poverty, the action and the stillness, accidental fleeting effects as well as the established grandeur of the city's vitality and structure. Where they lived and worked reflected their role and standing in the city. They supplied its needs and in substantial part they supplied its image. The streets of Paris beyond the studio window were unsurpassed as a source of both inspiration and opportunity (Plate 30). The studio was part of the street and the street part of the studio. The relationship was symbiotic.

# 7. *The Studio as Such*

The poet Baudelaire had lamented the passing of a great era in French art with the death of Delacroix. After Delacroix, Baudelaire saw a vacuum emerging, in which artists could no longer effectively challenge the art of the past, of the great Italian, Dutch and French masters, a period in which the imagery of past eras would no longer remain viable for the contemporary artist. In his essay *The Painter of Modern Life* published in 1863, the same year as his last eulogy of Delacroix on that artist's death, the poet and critic had called for an art that abandoned great biblical and classical themes and turned its attention instead to the superficial beauties of contemporary life, to the look of the city in particular, and to the activities of its inhabitants, calling for the artist to become a 'man of the crowd' of which he was a part but of which he was also the observer. The press had once depicted Delacroix and Ingres fighting in front of the Institut; in the period which followed a different conflict ensued in which the depiction of contemporary life from the artist's own experience was often at odds with a system of teaching and patronage, particularly through the Salon and the influence of the Institut, which stressed the continuation of older traditions. In many respects Ingres had appeared as a paragon of the professional artist respectful of the past, for whom finished drawings and composition were separate and distinct aspects of the evolution of a painting. His approach continued to retain respect, particularly amongst artists who had studied attentively at the Beaux-Arts. Degas, Seurat and Puvis de Chavannes were amongst them. Even for Jules Breton, Ingres was a figure in whom 'we seem to see the highest dignitary of the World of Art'.[1] Delacroix on the other hand continued to appeal to younger artists by the emotional immediacy of his work and his adventurous handling of the medium of paint in which the application of pigment was left very much in evidence. Puvis de Chavannes and Degas were also admirers of Delacroix: 'On a painting of considerable size, a Lion-hunt... Delacroix was working with concentrated engergy, striping his canvas with parallel hatchings.'[2] For the painter, the performance of the act of painting was of as much importance as the image which resulted. Delacroix's richness in this respect exerted a powerful fascination upon generations of younger painters. The colossal Delacroix memorial exhibition at Martinet's Gallery on the Boulevard des Italiens in 1864, provided an overwhelming wealth of works crowded to the ceiling. Delacroix's murals for a chapel in the church of Saint Sulpice on the Left Bank were readily available for artists to see, as were his decorations in the Salon d'Apollon in the Louvre itself. For many younger artists he remained a hero whose abilities were increasingly recognised. For Jules Breton, Delacroix 'whose head looked like a sick lion's, is a genius who must always remain alone'.[3] In 1885 the Ecole des Beaux-Arts mounted a major Delacroix exhibition which attracted 12,000 visitors in its first week and which launched the subscription appeal that resulted in Dalou's elaborate and dynamic Monument to Delacroix which now stands in the Luxembourg Gardens in Paris.

Delacroix was a literate and highly articulate artist, a dandy in the terms of his own day and a paragon of individual talent, increasingly recognised as both a worthy heir to the traditions of French art, and as an innovator. Curiously his influence was deeply embedded in the work of those who sought the depiction of modern life or worked from direct observation and experience.

In 1852 his studio had already attracted attention. In an illustration published that year, the cluttered interior of an immense room is illuminated by a vast north-light

31. E. Renard, *The Studio of Eugène Delacroix at 54 Rue Notre Dame de Lorette*, 1852, wood engraving, 20.5 × 24 cm., published in *L'Illustration*, 1852.

window in wall and roof, which could be adjusted by a large blind and curtains (Plate 31). A small stove, essential feature of every studio with its high heat loss, stands before it, its stove pipe forming an immense arc across the room to release maximum heat. Amongst the profusion of paraphernalia, of paint boxes, palettes and easels there is only one comfortable chair and a sofa, for the studio is a workshop primarily, and only incidentally an area for the display of the paintings which fill the wall to the left and the five easels. At the right, gigantic steps await the next large commission. On the right-hand wall and beyond are plaster casts, including casts of limbs hanging on the chimney-breast. This is the professional studio par excellence with a wealth of studies, finished paintings, stored works, architectural decorative works, and a framed painting on the easel perhaps ready for dispatch. This is where the action of painting occurs and it has the air of a kind of one-man factory in which, for all the clutter, nothing superfluous is included, where the artist can pursue the procedures both of painting and of selling his work.

Delacroix's last studio was unique and is now preserved with a few of his works and possessions as the Musée Delacroix. Hidden away off the Rue Furstenberg in the Latin Quarter, the two-storey building inhabits a still and secluded yard at the centre of the city (Plate 32). Above the ground floor, stands the studio itself, smaller than that in the Rue Notre Dame de Lorette, but similarly dominated by the north light with roof-light above it. Less like a factory and more like a study, the studio is purpose-built and developed as part of the architecture of the building, its big window having a moulding and keystone in a slight forward projection of the wall. Below this window, and to either side above the smaller windows, are inset casts of antique relief sculptures. Before it is a spacious yard. Here is the ideal studio for the painter. Purpose-built, it is out of the busy

29

32. The studio of Eugène Delacroix, Place Furstenberg, now the Museé Delacroix.

activity of the street yet immediately accessible for artist and clients. Nothing is superfluous or intrusive. Essentially functional it is nevertheless a work of architecture that is simple, aloof and restrained in its proportions and ornamentation. It can be seen as a model against which to view studios of very different kinds, for here worked, and died, one of the most distinguished and celebrated artists of his day, at the height of his career, an artist whose work earned the respect of future generations in a subtle and pervasive way. This is perhaps the explemplary courtyard studio.

By the starkest contrast, the unknown aspiring young artist could only hope for such a studio by achieving recognition after years of often hopeless and unacknowledged toil. His room hardly merited the name studio at all and was often makeshift accommodation on the fifth floor or higher and without a lift (Plate 33). It was likely to be situated in the furthest reaches of Montparnasse in the south of Paris, in an area only recently established as part of the city itself:

33. Clive Holland, *A Studio Interior*, photograph from before 1902.

> The room is very much like those of scores of other students. It combines within its four walls the sitting room, studio, bed-chamber and kitchen, with — as was once wittily remarked — the peculiar features and disadvantages of all these. It is fairly commodious; for rooms, except mansardes, rule large hereabouts... In the corner of the room stood a stove, on which the owner does (or some obliging model does for him) his cooking, stews his afternoon tea when giving an informal five o'clock, and brews his matutinal coffee. The bed occupied one corner; a bachelor's bed, which looked as though it was never properly 'made', and the untidiness of which was after midday disguised by a travelling rug thrown across it. In a word this *chambre garnie* was very typical of scores of others in the Quarter.[4]

They were usually taken for terms ranging from three months to a year, the terms generally expiring in July.[5]

If the disadvantages of living at the top of a tenement block were obvious, there was, however, the possibility of a north-facing roof light and many such studios survive in Paris. Yet its bodily comforts were likely to be poor, without running water in particular. It also had the advantages of being near to the facilities of the city street, of models available where such studios congregated and local cheap eating houses,

30

although even here, the newcomer risked ridicule or being cheated: 'A *nouveau*, by Madame's regular *clientèle* was always regarded much as one would suppose a missionary is by cannibals'.[6]

In Montparnasse in particular it was occasionally possible to find studios in purpose-built but ramshackle accommodation constructed from wood and glass, or abandoned and reassembled exhibition buildings hidden away in streets and yards sealed off at one end or accessible through a sequence of yards near the slaughter houses (Plate 34). The polygonal complex La Ruche became in time the most celebrated of these but there were others and they could be made highly useful and effective workshop studios. Many have now been demolished, but these *cités d'artistes* were a useful and effective resource, similarly, to the north of Paris in Montmartre, again on the furthest edge of the city in the midst of the construction of new buildings, there existed the Maquis, a warren of wooden sheds, more like an allotment than a studio complex where painters and sculptors shared accommodation with rag-pickers and chickens. Here it was possible to work even in poverty which, if it was of any use at all to the artist, provided a driving and often desperate incentive to work to succeed. Meissonier, the most expensive artist of his time, was emphatic about this: 'No, no, it is a mistake to suppose that poverty is a necessary experience for the artist.'[7]

34. *Cité d'artistes*, Montparnasse.

35. Edgar Degas *Portrait of the Painter James Tissot*, c. 1866–8, oil on canvas, 151.4 × 112.1 cm., Metropolitan Museum of Art, New York. Purchased from the Rogers Fund 1939.

# 8. *The Image of the Artist*

Just as artists were drawn to Paris, in return Paris was celebrated for its artists, and their public image took a particular form. Ingres, who in old age lacked physical charm, embodied the image of the respectable man: he dressed with dignity and restraint in unobtrusive city clothes of quality. Delacroix's flowing hair and elegant clothes struck the note of the inspired and formidable dandy to many who met him. Millet in his clogs and peasant clothes was a striking contrast. For the most part the black top hat and frock-coat of city dress sufficed for many selling and exhibiting artists of the 1880s and 1890s. Degas was indistinguishable as an artist and so was Tissot to judge from Degas' portrait of him in his studio, top hat on the table, cane in hand. For others, Harpignies is one example, beard, velvet painting cap and large floppy bow-tie were comfortable indications of the artist's profession (Plate 36). The ambiguity of the artist's standing in society is reflected in their appearance, some wishing discreetly to blend into the busy activity of the boulevard or café, others asserting their role. In the studio the smock was merely useful, as was the hat which was so often an apparently indispensible requirement for painting. According to one source the Beaux-Arts student was distinguished by his 'long hair, his whiskers, his Latin-Quarter "plug" hat, his cape, blouse, wide corduroy trousers, sash, expansive neck-tie and immense cane'.[1]

36. The painter Henri Harpignies (1819–1916).

The painting of the artist in his studio was a theme used more than once by Degas. These paintings are portraits of friends posed informally in front of their work and thereby indentified with it, exemplifying their professional activity: their elegant appearance is not an arbitrary element of the paintings. As in the work of a realist writer, Degas provided supporting evidence which set the figure into the context of a professional activity, the artist either actively pursuing painting or relaxing. This is also the case for Degas at the racecourse, ballet or even in the brothel. Clothes, pose and context, together with the precise delineation of features and an apparently fleeting view of the model, are assembled into a composition (Plate 35). Tissot appears languid and conversational in a pose inserted into an almost symmetrical composition, with a framed old-master or copy occupying the focal point. Both the framed old-master and the concern for control, evident in draughtsmanship and composition are signs of his Beaux-Arts training. On the other hand Degas, like the realist writer Zola, is concerned to depict modern life with an originality and apparent directness that is in fact the result of sophisticated artifice.

When Degas portrayed painters, he was in effect depicting his own profession of course, which gives these paintings particular interest. The *Portrait of Henri Michel-Lévy in 1879* portrays the act of painting in two ways (Plate 37). Firstly, Degas is willing here to leave his own processes evident in the unresolved cross-hatchings of brushwork in the collapsed figure at bottom right. This looseness of handling is particularly emphatic in his depiction of Michel-Lévy's own works, themselves perhaps unfinished as they hang on his studio wall. In the foreground, pride of place is given to the open paint box, tubes of colour, palette and brushes. In a sense Degas' depiction of Michel-Lévy's paintings, as with Tissot's, is a homage to their work, just as these portraits indicate respect for their sitters. Each has an irregular dynamic composition. In the later portrait, the collapsed lay-figure, an artist's flexible dummy used in the model's absence, provides a visual shock, for a painted lay-figure can be as credible a depiction of a human-being as the bearded painter himself: Degas sustained this ambiguity precisely. She is in reality no more than a studio prop, however, and can be seen in the unfinished large canvas which occupies the left edge of Degas' canvas. The artist, elegantly dressed despite the

33

37. Edgar Degas, *Portrait of the Painter Henri Michel-Lévy*, c. 1879, oil on canvas, 41.5 × 27.3 cm., The Calouste Gulbenkian Museum, Lisbon.

38. A model relaxing from the pose with lyre and cigarette, photograph from *c.* 1900.

lack of a jacket, stares dispassionately at the viewer, or Degas, from the midst of his work.

Models, of course, were crucially important to late nineteenth-century painters engaged in elaborate compositions. It was difficult to work on the figure at all sensitively without access to a model. As we have seen they were numerous and important in the community of artists. Their anonymity in the majority of figure paintings — although a few became famous — allowed the painter a good deal of freedom to study human anatomy, and even to alter it, without the exigences of likeness or character analysis intervening. The contribution of this long-suffering and nameless mass of people is difficult to realise. For Meissonier, as for many others, 'a model is an intelligent lay-figure of which we can alter the type at will'.[2] At times they suffered considerable discomfort as well as ignominy in their efforts to fulfil painters' and sculptors' needs to envisage Hercules, Venus or the muses, admitting to merely human existence only temporarily during the rest when their mythical poses were exchanged for those of relaxation, a toga-clad figure with lyre at her feet and a cigarette (Plate 38).

39. Gustave Courbet, *The Painters Studio, A Real Allegory Summing up Seven Years of my Artistic Life*, 1855, oil on canvas, 361 × 598 cm., Musée d'Orsay, Paris.

They must often have needed the rest and their work could be bizarre: 'In order to pose his model in the act of plunging into the river [he] had rigged up a tackle, which, depending from the ceiling, caught the model at the waist, after the manner of a fire escape belt, and thus half suspended her.'[3]

Cool studio light falling upon flesh has inexhaustibly challenged painters to capture its elusive colours upon the human form's anatomy. To paint the nude was naturally to invoke the life-room and its central place in French art education. For a painter as analytical as Seurat, the demands and attractions of the life-room were not in the least incompatible with techniques inspired by and developed out of Impressionist painting. In that still and opalescent studio light, Seurat found the familiar opportunity for analytical observation of the light-bathed figure away from distractions, where he was able to refine both his vision and technique (Plate 41). The model for all her anonymity was the source of endless discoveries in terms of the processes of both looking and making. In the Beaux-Arts manner, but with a revolutionary technique, Seurat built up his large canvas from colour-studies. The model's pose was more important than her identity. It is possible that in the large version of *Les Poseuses* of 1888 she appears three times, a natural consequence of having hired a satisfactory model for this painting of Seurat's studio, in which a few framed studies hang on one wall whilst on the other, Seurat has executed what is in effect a curious and slanted copy of his own great outdoor scene of urban figures relaxing on the Ile de la Grande Jatte. In the silence of the studio the model is posing quite motionless in three positions, the human body revealed in three elevations, back, front and side.

Some artists, Rodin included, liked the model to move and even the academician Jean-Jacques Henner, found this useful: 'You must never have a model take up a pose. It is necessary to wait for chance to present one to you. When it strikes you and interests you, you are sure to have arrived at something good.'[4]

In contrast to the bustling city street, the artist's studio was his own space for concentrated study and experiment. This is clear even in Courbet's painting of himself in a great studio, a painting which he called a 'real allegory' and into which he introduced the figures that inspired him (Plate 39). He depicted himself working with panache upon a landscape, observed by a child and a model. When this painting was

40. Paul Gauguin, *Portrait of Vincent Van Gogh*, Arles, 1888, oil on canvas, 73 × 92.7 cm., Rijksmuseum Vincent Van Gogh, Amsterdam.

exhibited in the Courbet retrospective exhibition at the Ecole des Beaux-Arts in 1882 it aroused much admiration. The very fact of the exhibition was a sign of the increasing acceptance of the revolutionary Courbet's art after his death. Henner for example was greatly impressed by the painting, declaring that 'the female nude has never been better painted'[5]. Jules Breton, who knew Courbet, was worried by his directness in other works: 'if on the one hand his vigour may have served to stimulate art, on the other hand he has propagated the most detestable abuses – the use of the palette-knife, which may be attended with the most serious dangers.'[6]

Courbet's subject was in fact the process of painting, both practical and inspirational, the act which forms the pivot of this enormous canvas which was finally accepted by the Louvre. The model who looks on has a special significance: she is no longer simply the subject that the artist is observing, she is depicted as a living person who has stopped modelling and has abandoned the pose — Courbet after all is at work on a landscape, the painting within the painting. Still naked, the model has not yet stepped back amongst the clothed in their daily life, she is caught between the two, observing an activity to which she contributes but in which she does not directly participate.

A closely similar pose was used by Gauguin in 1888 to depict the painter at work, this time not a self-portrait but a portrait of Vincent Van Gogh painting sunflowers (Plate 40): the arms adopt the same position with the palette tipping away at bottom centre. Against a background as flat and ambiguous as that of Courbet, Gauguin focusses upon the act of painting. Van Gogh looks intently at the sunflowers, his surprisingly small brush working on the painting, summing up succinctly the duality of the process which demands an equivalent made of static pigments for the experience of vision that constantly shifts and changes.

The self-portait necessarily depicts the artist, but in a sense usually depicts his self-

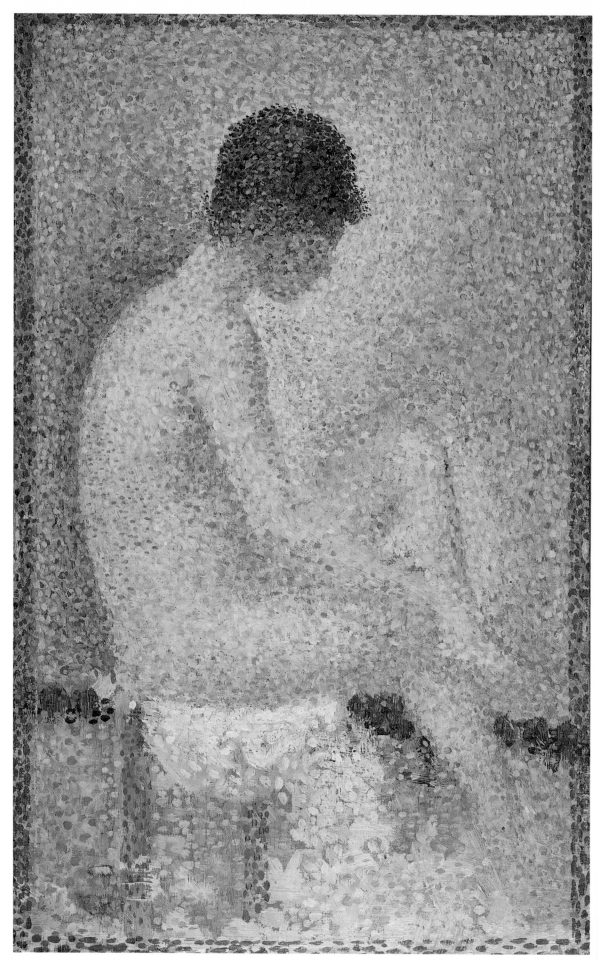

41. Georges Seurat, *Seated Model in Profile*
1887, oil on panel, 25 × 16 cm., Musée
d'Orsay, Paris.

image with some degree of psychological intensity and rarely depicts the act of painting. To imagine Courbet's viewpoint when portraying himself painting, points to one of the obvious difficulties of this and the visual ambiguities and artifice it involves, difficulties which Lautrec and a photographer friend wittily pointed out in a photomontage of Lautrec at work on a self-portrait (Plate 42).

In their tuition the academies provided a means of achieving control in painting through distinct phases of work, each of which could be mastered in turn. Thus an initial compositional sketch would capture the overall concept, to be followed by drawings from the model, sometimes nude first and clothed later, permitting control of pose, line and chiaroscuro. Undetailed colour studies followed massing in the composition as a whole and in more detail for particular parts, and only then the large canvas was approached. These methods were developed with great originality and skill by Degas, Seurat and others. A cause of dismay to less innovatory academicians, were the procedures adopted by those Impressionists who painted directly from observation without recourse to studies; this appeared an arrogant and rash approach, although even Meissonier, who never behaved this way, could see some degree of achievement in such works: 'The tendencies of modern painting are deplorable in every respect. The absence of thought is remarkable; but combined with this nullity of invention we often find a technique and a knowledge of effect truly astonishing. Many modern painters are not composers, they are experts of the brush.'[6]

42. Maurice Guibert, *M. Toulouse makes the portrait of M. Lautrec-Maufra*, c. 1890, photomontage.

# 9. *Plein-air Practicalities*

> Some women and a man are relaxing in a forest, in the sun. Isn't that sufficient? There, that's enough to make a master-piece.[1]

The novelist Emile Zola is here describing a work reminiscent of Manet's *Déjeuner sur l'herbe* which had caused such excitement at the Salon des Refusés in 1863. Implicitly, the character in Zola's novel is demanding an art of modern life, just as Manet's painting, despite a reference to Raphael in its composition, was emphatically and even outrageously a scene of contemporary life. Manet's subsequent *Olympia* equally outrageously updated a theme from Titian. To graft themes of modern life onto hallowed compositional achievements of the past was provocative, but it also pointed to a difficulty for the painter concerned to depict contemporary themes and experience. The role of composition was problematic. The more painting endeavoured to capture the appearance of the passing, shifting scene, the less useful were traditional compositional methods, both in terms of the final layout of the painting, and in terms of the process by which this composition was evolved. This was a problem of urgent importance to realist painting and to Impressionist painting after it. The very process of constructing a painting was problematic henceforth, for insofar as painting reflected authentic experience more or less directly, so it not only abandoned, for example, the classical deities of old, but it also had to find new ways of organising the painting. A Daumier lithograph sums this up and incidentally points to the importance of landscape painting in the finding of solutions (Plate 43). Here he shows the *plein-airiste*, the painter who works out of doors directly from the landscape, behind him a second *plein-airiste* looks not at the landscape in which they both sit, but at the solutions the first painter has found in the face of the problems posed. As Daumier's caption puts it: the first copies nature, the second copies the first. Both use the easily portable and collapsible three-legged stool with paints in a box on the ground.

43. Honoré Daumier, *Landscape Painters: the First copies Nature, the Second copies the First*, 1865, lithograph, published in *Charivari*, 12 May 1865.

44. Constant Dutilleux, *Corot at Arras*, 1871, photograph, Gernsheim Collection, Harry Ransom Humanities Research Center, University of Texas at Austin.

Painters had made studies outside for many years. Corot may be seen in photographs encumbered with parasol as well as paints, brushes, canvas, easel and stool for working in the open air in the 1860s (Plate 44). The light was more brilliant than the regulated and even north light of the studio which was specifically designed to reduce the effects of the sun's movement and cut out direct sunlight. Consequently a fast working method was demanded and typically such studies formed the basis of paintings executed in the studio under less maddening conditions. A gust of wind, for example, could devastate Corot's arrangement of parasol and canvas, although parasols not only protected the painter from direct sunlight and heat but offered a primitive means of controlling light on the canvas.

Fontainebleau forest provided a much frequented site for painters, particularly for the Barbizon painters who had a direct impact upon the beginnings of Impressionist technique, although many others worked there too. Rosa Bonheur lived and made studies on the northern edge of the forest and avoided the Barbizon circle. Jules Breton, who knew Daubigny, also worked in this forest: 'Every morning we set out to make the conquest of some new motive, and our umbrellas were seen like a crop of gigantic mushrooms, dotting the field in the sunshine.'[2]

Although Breton later concluded that 'light out of doors is unfavourable to painting',[3] he clearly found the process stimulating: 'No more lugubrious subjects, for we were digging away at outdoor painting'[4] which was 'guided by an impulse of clear and rapid perception'.[5] This was a process of exploration of visual impressions with minimal reference to conventions of composition or to the art of the past, and the activity was refreshing in its immediacy: 'Each day Nature revealed new secrets to us, and our eyes, eager to search into her mysteries, found ever new delights.'[6] Paris was still within easy reach thanks to the burgeoning railway system: 'Enchanting suburbs of Paris, we thought there was nothing in the world to equal you'.[7]

As we have already noted, Lecoq de Boisbaudran had also used outdoor themes to train the eyes and memory of his students as a basis for paintings executed later in the studio. He had found,

a most beautiful spot, a sort of natural park. The deep shadows thrown by the great trees in full leaf contrasted sharply with the blaze of light with which the open glade was flooded. A pond full of reflections lay at their feet. It was a perfect place, offering endless backgrounds for the human figure, with every possible effect and range of light and shade, exactly satisfying the purpose I had in view.[8]

Here Lecoq paraded his naked models for his students to study and observe. As he said, 'The sight, odd enough for outsiders, was full of interest and instruction for my students.'[9] What inevitably interested Lecoq most as a tutor was the figure seen in this context:

Once our admiration rose to the highest enthusiasm. One of our models, a man of splendid stature, with a great sweeping beard, lay to rest upon the bank of the pond, close to a group of rushes, in an attitude at once easy and beautiful. The illusion was complete — mythology made true lived before our eyes, for there before us was a river-god of old, ruling in quiet dignity over the course of his waters![10]

Lecoq promoted the use of memory to devise compositional motifs and believed that memory complemented imagination in this way. For Impressionist painters, if Degas is excepted, the evolution of a painting was often rapid and remained closely dependent upon direct observation. The Beaux-Arts procedure, involving distinct phases of work leading up to a composition, was very largely abandoned and composition became more instinctive, rapid and less calculated, occurring on the motif rather than in the studio. The loose handling and apparent lack of finish, the characteristic Impressionist brushmark or *tache*, was a consequence of this. In effect Impressionist painters did not

45. Pierre-Auguste Renoir, *Monet Painting in his Garden at Argenteuil*, 1873, oil on canvas, 46.7 × 60 cm., Wadsworth Atheneum, Hartford, Connecticut. Bequest of Anne Parish Titzell.

46. John Singer Sargent painting out of doors, photograph from *c.* 1883–5, Collection Ormond Family, London.

dispense with preliminary studies, rather they intensified those studies to stand for themselves, as completed works, telescoping the meticulous traditional process into a brilliant fast form of painting in which the depiction of a coherent and credible daylight, achieved by means of a network of visible brushmarks, provided a new kind of unifying structure for the painting. As a result, composition became informal or dramatic in a way determined by visual experience and selectivity rather than precedent. *Monet Working in his Garden at Argenteuil* by Renoir is an example (Plate 45). Astutely observed, it has, in fact, a compositional structure in which the fence and houses remain parallel to the picture plane but this appears casual and informal, even though it establishes a distinct set of rhythms with the tree and large house counter-balancing the figure of the artist and his easel. Monet is depicted in a common-place setting and the drama, in so far as there is one, is distinctly suburban. Narrative as such has disappeared along with earlier kinds of subject matter and composition. What is painted is familiar and does not require classical or historical erudition to be interpreted. By taking up a light-weight easel with paints lying casually on the garden grass, a considerable revolution in painting technique has been achieved, and the studio and its seclusion has been largely abandoned. In wilder landscape, which often attracted Monet in particular, such a process was highly inconvenient and often required an assistant to carry equipment. In the garden, it was easier to accomplish and visually as rich. Manet used this as a theme late in life. Bonnard, who tended to work in the studio from memory, also found it a fruitful source.

*Plein-air* techniques of this kind spread very rapidly in the 1880s and 1890s. Just as Manet had been excited by the revelations of Impressionist technique when painting with Monet in 1874, so Sargent followed his example on similar expeditions in 1888

47. John Singer Sargent, *Paul Helleu painting out of doors with his wife*, 1889, oil on canvas, 66.3 × 81.5 cm., The Brooklyn Museum, New York.

(Plate 46). His picture, *Claude Monet Painting at the Edge of Wood* shows Monet seated on a sketching stool working directly on a canvas about 1 by 1⅓ metres in dimension; and wearing his painting hat. Sargent's technique is loose and flowing, allowing the brushmarks to provide much of the movement in the painting, so that he pays homage to Monet also in the handling of his paint. Such convivial painting sessions beyond the suburbs were not uncommon. They required impromptu equipment sometimes. Sargent's depiction of the French painter and printmaker Paul Helleu is an example, although it was in fact painted in England (Plate 47). Helleu and his wife, together with the invisible Sargent, have pulled up their rowing boat onto the river bank so that the two men can each paint a rapid canvas. Helleu in straw hat looks down upon his painting which is propped against a fishing rod planted amongst the reeds. He is using a small, light-weight, rectangular palette and all of seven brushes to keep the colour clear. In such a context, the act of painting is a kind of rapid virtuoso performance. Sargent, working on a similar sized canvas to that of Helleu, is perhaps to a degree in competition with him, although his subject in a sense is the act of painting and he has taken great care to depict the position of Helleu's fingers applying just the right amount of pressure as the mark is made.

For longer periods of painting out of doors on occasions when the light and weather might change swiftly, the conveniences of the studio were again useful and desirable. Daubigny, who died in 1878, found his studio-boat *Le Botin* invaluable, it provided the solitude, equipment and comforts of the studio, and incidental fishing facilities, whilst permitting some control of light, shelter when necessary and instant access to the landscapes and river-views that attracted him. For a painter of water it was invaluable and Monet, for whom the reflection of light on water provided a recurrent stimulus that generated painting after painting, a studio boat following Daubigny's model was of

great practical usefulness. Manet depicted Monet painting on his boat in 1874, with his wife relaxing beneath its striped awning (Plate 48). These extraordinary floating studios were ideal for the *plein-air* artists for whom the city studio had not only inconveniences but drawbacks and dangers for the artist. Monet's commitment to the direct painting of daylight drove him out of the studio until his later years at Giverny where his studios were of great importance but where he also continued to paint regularly out of doors: 'Even though not vigorous, he would set off for the motif for the session, carrying towards it in his arms pens, brushes, canvases, easels, boxes of colours and brushes — often assisted by his daughter-in-law Blanche.'[11]

Sometimes the *plein-airiste* carried weights to hang from his light-weight easel, for it could act like a mast and sail in a wind, particularly if it bore not only the wet canvas

48. Edouard Manet, *Monet working on his boat at Argenteuil*, 1874, oil on canvas, 82.5 × 100.5 cm., Neue Pinakothek, Munich.

43

but a parasol. Such were the inconveniences of working directly outside on the final canvas in one session, and even Monet sometimes adjusted his paintings in the studio. The rewards on the other hand, were considerable, for immediacy was preserved in the completed painting and the light of day was carried into the darker spaces of human dwellings: 'In the midst of this St Vitus dance of Nature in the paroxysm of an hysterical attack, I remember...in some private exhibitions some works of this school whose strangeness attracted me — white lakes quivering in opalescent lights, where real breezes blow from the silvery sky and bend the yellow reeds,' commented Jules Breton.[12]

To a degree the inconveniences could be minimised by a kind of knapsack for paints, stretchers and canvas as was used by Pissarro and Cézanne (Plate 49), and of course full daylight exists immediately outside the studio, as brilliant in the boulevards of Paris as in the Fontainebleau forest. The *plein-air* painting of the city street was an important contribution to the painting of modern life, the landscape *plein-airistes'* grasp of light permitting the depiction of the boulevards' bustling occupants as mere light effects, as insignificant in themselves as the numberless flickering leaves of a tree.

Lautrec made extensive use of the studio as well as sketches to evolve his large compositions, despite their appearance of being dynamic events directly observed at the Moulin Rouge and elsewhere. But he also respected daylight with its full range of colours and worked in the garden of his studio (Plate 50). A little like Monet's boat the studio with its garden combines the advantages of both, even in the midst of Montmartre.

# 10. A Society Studio

As well as an arena for work, the studio, especially for the successful artist, was a social arena. To visit the studio of Carolus-Duran was an event for high-society. 'He was been very successful,' wrote a commentator, 'for years he was the spoilt darling of the public, or, to be more correct, one of its spoilt darlings; for the public has had many in the past five and twenty years.'[1] His studio in Montparnasse was crammed with paintings from floor to ceiling, the majority standing ready in heavy and elaborately moulded frames for quick dispatch to patrons, collectors and museums. Amongst copies after Rubens and paintings inspired by Velasquez, hung the portraits which made him both famous and wealthy. He held open day at the studio on Thursdays at the unconventional time of 9 am. to 11 am. in what Albert Wolff called 'the most curious studio in Paris'.[2] Carolus-Duran's demeanour was gracious and the early opening time of his studio was a challenge to the elegant and wealthy, for according to Wolff 'a Parisian woman never rises before midday except on Thursdays to visit Carolus-Duran'.[3]

Clad in a short velvet jacket he would pass through he throng of admiring visitors, clasping their hands briefly before moving on. He wore 'shoes the elegance of which was worthy of the softest carpets in Paris'.[4] Some visitors never reached the artist, whilst and important American client would have to wait her turn in the master's crowded diary of portrait sittings. Wolff described Carolus-Duran slipping money into the pocket of his velvet jacket, but his attractiveness was clearly supreme, as Marie Bashkirtseff found: 'Carolus-Duran approaches to speak to me — this man is a charmer'.[5] The writer Edmond de Goncourt described him in his journal with acidic skepticism as: 'This artist with the puff of wind in his hair his romantic appearance, hidalgo, guitarist, fencer, with this love bracelet on one arm...'[6] He played the guitar or the organ regularly after the departure of his clientèle from his studio at 11 am. precisely. As Wolff noted, 'He would sit in front of the organ and call forth from it several plaintive chords; then he would take down a guitar as accompaniment to an Andalusian song'.[7] Lunch followed.

Carolus-Duran was so successful that he could afford to tantalise his clientèle and they loved him for it. His rules were strict, access to his studio was limited and he never haggled over prices.

The studio was a major sales area for him, a setting which showed off his paintings to advantage, in great numbers and without the comparisons and competition of the Salon. Here the evident charm of the man himself and the luxuriousness of his studio complemented the impact of the paintings themselves. He was presenting himself as a painter with whom a commission could be safely lodged, an honorable, established and fashionable man of business whose merchandise would reliably serve its purpose as both portrait and status symbol: 'It is impossible', wrote a visitor in 1896, 'to deny the fascination, both mental and personal, of this refined and accomplished scholar, who has read everything, seen everything, heard everything worth reading, seeing and hearing.'[8] The ambience of the studio reception was reflected in the paintings, for the 'love of his for all that is rich and luxurious is seen very forcibly in the wealth of stuffs and silks, brocades and plushes, laces and jewels with which he adorns his women's portraits'.[9] This did however involve a risk, for the removal of a work from so sympathetic and supportive a context could reveal its weaknesses: 'As with many others, we have seen the painting in the studio of the artist: it had certain brilliant qualities; it has not lost them on the way (to the Salon) but their impact is reduced.'[10]

Such worldly success was accorded to extremely few of the artists active in Paris. Their fame could not have arisen without the existence of the Paris Salon, which though

49. (*facing page, top*) Camille Pissarro and Paul Cézanne prepared for *plein-air* painting, photograph, from *c*. 1877.

50. (*facing page, below*) Toulouse-Lautrec painting the portrait of Berthe la Sourde outside the studio, photograph from 1890.

open to all, was so enormous that to make one's mark there was an incredibly difficult and, for most, a hopeless undertaking. Conversely, success at the Salon was the golden route to recognition. It was determined by the selection committee or jury, the preference of such powerful critics as Albert Wolff, public response and by the officially awarded medals and honours. To challenge accepted values of either jury or public in this context was to invite rejection, ridicule, or worst of all, simply to be ignored.

# 11. Salon Stars and Hopefuls

> What service do we render to our kind? We are jugglers, mountebanks, dreamers who amuse the people in the market place. They scarcely deign to take an interest in our efforts. Few people are capable of understanding them. And I do not know whether we really deserve their good will, for the world could very well get on without us.[1]

51. Edouard Cucuel, *The Last Moments and the Unfinished Picture*, 1899.

This conundrum the sculptor Bourdelle discussed with Rodin. If the artist was an entertainer, as he describes, the Salon was decidedly his auditorium and marketplace.

The annual Salon attracted vast numbers of painters and sculptors and a very large public. There is no clearer indication of the sheer mass of people painting, sculpting and printmaking in Paris, not to mention designing architectural projects, than a Salon catalogue to which must be added numerous contributors to alternative Salons and group exhibitions. The opening of the Salon was a great stimulus to action: 'In sumptuous studios, in wretched garrets, amid affluence, amid scenes of squalor and hunger, artists of all kinds and degrees have been squeezing thousands of tubes and daubing thousands of canvases in preparation for the great day'[2] (Plate 51).

The Salon also produced numerous publications including lavish *de luxe* volumes in the 1880s and 1890s, expensively bound with gilt decorations and prestigious illustrations together with a critical essay and list of prize and medal winners. Clearly the response to the Salon was sufficient to sustain the market for a considerable publishing venture in its wake. 'The Salonnier is a hero', wrote the critic Paul Mantz in the *de luxe* volume for the Salon of 1889.

> When the city is filled with joyful sounds, when humanity assures itself in the caressing sunlight, he thinks only of his duty. In vain the month of May displays her long awaited pleasures around him in fresh greenery. For the most part he is unaware of the celebration of new leaves on the trees or the singing of the birds. Do not speak of spring to this slave, this martyr: he is doing the Salon.[3]

The Salon had for almost a century been a government responsibility, from 1791 when the French Revolutionary government took control until, with a short break after the Revolution of 1848, control was eventually handed over to the Société des Artistes Français. The critic Paul Mantz welcomed the increasing freedom of access to the Salon for a widening range of artists during the intervening period. During the years following the French Revolution of 1789, according to Mantz, selection was too exclusive:

> As for free artists who had never sought a candidature or who were considered unfavourably, there is no question that they were considered non-existent. Unknown artists could have talent: they were perhaps the important figures of the future. The Academy knew nothing of them, and the halls of the Louvre were closed to them. This meant hardship for those who were not academicians![4]

52. A Salon Jury with Cormon, Tattegrain, Dantan, Lefèbvre, Tony Robert-Fleury, Maignan and others, photograph of c. 1885.

He saw a great improvement in the years up to 1889: 'Thanks to our forefathers, the artist is set free. If he wishes to express new ideas and to confide to us his unknown dreams, he has the right to choose his language. The painter and the sculptor have arrived at the fullest independence.'[5]

The Salon, an annual event since 1864, had steadily evolved its selection procedure towards this situation. By 1850 all previous exhibitors were invited to elect the Salon jury. In 1852 half the jury was elected and half appointed by the government. In 1857 the jury was given over to the Academy. Subsequently, medal winners were reserved a role in the jury, although it was wholly elected again in 1870. These complexities were resolved by the Marquis de Chennevières who by 1880 was dismayed at the quality of works exhibited at the Salon. He was outspoken: 'What a chaotic collection of useless artists! What a graveyard of mediocrities! What a muddle of insignificant painters!... What does one have to have done in order to merit exclusion from such an exhibition?'[6] In 1881 the Salon was given over to the artists of the Société des Artistes Français and exhibited annually at the Palais des Champs Elysées, a change formalised in 1884. Artists themselves had been dissatisfied and this provided a key element in the change. In 1879 a petition whose signitories included Bastien-Lepage and Roll had accused the Académie of bias and had proposed that all previous Salon exhibitors should have the right to elect the jury (Plate 52). In this way Manet, for example, was awarded a medal against the wishes of the academicians, and a powerful body of artists emerged who were relatively independent of the Academy but who declined to exhibit as small independent groups, as, for example, the Impressionists were doing. Amongst such figures were Bastien-Lepage, Roll, Besnard and Carrière.[7]

The organisation of the annual Salon was a colossal undertaking involving immense administrative work and the control of considerable sums of money, not to mention the high degree of emotional charge which surrounded the selection and hanging of several thousand works. Although a falling off of attendance occurred between 1881 and 1884 during the first four years under the Société des Artistes Français, visitors nonetheless swarmed to the Salon in impressive numbers. In 1881 there were 314,302 visitors followed by 343,874 in 1882, 298,497 in 1883, and 289,293 in 1884, immense attendances for art exhibitions. The Salon was a social event with high potential as a market place, and the Salon accorded a degree of respectability to the works exhibited as Renoir pointed out to his dealer Durand-Ruel in 1881:

> I am going to try and explain to you why I exhibit at the Salon. In Paris there are scarcely fifteen collectors capable of liking a painter without the backing of the Salon. And there are another eighty thousand who won't buy so much as a postcard unless the painter exhibits there. That's why every year I send two portraits, however small... This entry is entirely of a commercial nature. Anyway, it's like some medicine — if it does you no good, it won't do you any harm.[8]

Benjamin-Constant similarly believed that the Salon was an aid not only to glory but to survival: 'The Salon is our only means of publicity, through it we acquire honour, glory, money. For many of us it provides our livelihood, and without it more than one of the great masters that we admire today would have died wretched without anyone knowing.'[9] Gérôme was convinced that the Salon meant survival

> for a host of young artists who have only this means of establishing a relationship with the public, with art lovers and for selling their works. In order to sell, it is first of all necessary to have acquired a certain notoriety, and this can only be achieved by showing what one has done. Painters are not rich; they have to live. How will they live if they do not earn money? *Primo Vivere*: that is my motto. The painter eats, drinks, sleeps, clothes himself, like everyone else. You cannot work for glory alone.'[10]

The Salon represented opportunity. As submission day approached even 'the upper decks of the omnibuses were crowded with artists carrying their pictures' (Plate 53).[11]

On the financial side, in 1884 total receipts at the Salon were 352,000 francs, comprising 12,000 francs interest on investments, 11,000 francs from refreshments, 31,500 francs profit from catalogues, and 289,000 francs from entrance charges. Outgoings totalled 280,000 francs leaving a useful profit after deductions of 54,000 francs for medals and diplomas, 12,000 francs for charity and 14,000 francs to modify the Salon garden for the showing of sculpture amongst its shrubs and flower beds.[12]

Despite often adverse criticism of works from the press, this immense undertaking flourished with only a slight decline during the later 1880s, functioning vigorously as an arbiter of success and recognition. It displayed vast numbers of works and provided not a few honours to artists in the process. Takings in 1887 amounted to 323,000 francs. The catalogue listed an enormous exhibition of 5,318 works including 3,563 paintings and 1,092 sculptures. Such displays also helped artists to achieve numerous public honours. By 1887 the Légion d'Honneur had been accorded to 202 painters, 105 architects, 83 sculptors and 29 printmakers but only 60 musicians.[13] This occurred despite the complaints of such critics as F.G. Stephens who maintained that 'with but a few breaks in the movement the standard of the Salon is yearly declining', and that 'the Salon no longer fully represents French art.'[14]

Gargantuan paintings and myriad smaller works jostled for position and fought for the attention of the viewer and potential purchaser. The very scale of the exhibitions was a cause of wonder. The *Art Journal* in 1886 estimated a total of 14,209 yards of painting alone, of which military subjects and 900 antique subjects each consumed 3,279 yards, followed by 500 landscapes and 300 domestic subjects each occupying 2,186 yards, 100 portraits, 200 interiors and an unspecified number of other works occupying approxi-

53. Edouard Cucuel, *The Upper Decks of the Omnibus were Crowded*, 1899.

mately 1,093 yards each. The total exceeds 8 miles of paintings. In this context the visitor needed real determination and extraordinary physical stamina to see any works other than the most spectacular and celebrated productions. The trials of the Salon Jury may also be imagined: they had, after all, *reduced* the total of works exhibited from those submitted.

Amongst major purchasers was the City of Paris. In 1887, 80,000 francs was spent on purchases from the Salon, including 30,000 francs on sculptures to be cast in bronze.

As if to prove finally that the Parisian public's taste for art was in fact insatiable, a second Salon was established in 1889 and was exhibiting from 1890. Its origin lay in a disagreement caused by the Universal Exhibition of 1889 in Paris when many artists believed that the numerous medal winners in the display of art on that occasion should be accorded the usual Salon privileges. Meissonier was a prime mover, taking Dalou, Carolus-Duran, Cazin, Roll, Puvis de Chavannes, Alfred Stevens, Sargent, Boldini, and many others over to the new Salon of the Société de la Nationale des Beaux-Arts which exhibited at the Champs de Mars and was referred to as the Salon des Champs de Mars. Bouguereau, Bonnat and Gérôme were amongst those who resisted the move. The new Salon was ostensibly more liberal and did not give prizes. If one imagines in addition to this, numerous vigorously independent salons, of which the Salon des Indépendants founded in 1884 was the most significant, as well as the Salon des Cent and the Rosicrucian Salon, one begins to glimpse an essential feature of the art-life of Paris which was a busy as an ant heap and less well structured.[15]

'Apart from my art, which I began out of fantasy and ambition, which I have continued out of vanity and which I now adore; apart from this passion, for it is a passion, I have nothing but an atrocious existence! Misery of miseries.'[16] Marie Bashkirtseff, confiding these words to her diary on 27 June 1880, was still studying at Julian's Academy when she began to seek admission to the Salon where there was a chance at least of immediate success and 'Il faut arriver phenomène' said Julian.[17] Zola's hero in *L'Oeuvre* agreed for 'he acknowledged the usefulness of the Salon as the only battlefield on which an artist could assert himself at one blow.'[18]

Bashkirtseff considered that women were taken less seriously than men at the Salon, pointing to their absence from positions of influence — on the jury, at the Institut or as professors at the Ecole des Beaux-Arts, but she nevertheless felt rising excitement in the months after Christmas leading up to the opening of the Salon on the first of May. Sending-in day was in March with works to be received at the north entrance of the Palais de l'Industrie up to 6 pm. It was an excited and anxious crowd that gathered there, some artists delivering large works and travelling in smart carriages, others on foot with small works and all were subject to the comments of the crowd.[19]

It was extremely useful to have the support of an influential artist, particularly a jury member. 'It is quite clear,' said Tony Robert-Fleury who admired Bashkirtseff's paintings,

> that there are things twenty times worse than yours at the Salon, but nothing is at all certain because this poor jury sees 600 works pass before it in a day, and sometimes they refuse out of distaste what they have seen in a bad mood: but you have this going for you, which is important, [your painting] is of an agreeable tonality. And then I have Lefèbvre, Laurens, and Bonnat who are absolutely amongst my friends.[20]

In fact her painting was accepted and well placed, but it was still with anxiety that she attended the *Vernissage*, the preview of the Salon for artists, critics and the art world in general, by invitation on 30 April 1881: 'Finally we found my work, which is in the first room, to the left of the Salon of Honour, on the second row. I was delighted at its position and very astonished that the painting looks so well there. It is not good, but I was expecting a real horror. . .'[21] She had to accept with good grace the accidental omission of her name from the catalogue.

54. Henri Gervex, *The Jury for Painting, Salon des Artistes Français*, 1885, oil on canvas, 294 × 384 cm., Musée d'Orsay, Paris.

The jury had been kind to her in its vast labours. To serve on the jury, or selection committee, was both an arduous task and an honour (Plate 54). After all appointment to the jury was by vote open to all previous exhibitors and therefore a real vote of confidence. If Bastien-Lepage is an example, they took their work seriously: 'the universal suffrage of painters had designated him to be part of the committee charged with organising and directing the Société des Artistes Français and the annual Salon. No-one took his mandate to heart more seriously.'[22] The jury comprised forty artists, and membership reflected admiration and respect amongst a wide body of painters. In 1885 the top seven in the vote for the jury were Bonnat (with 1,168 votes), Lefebvre (1,166 votes), J.P. Laurens (1,118), Harpignies (1,109), Tony Robert-Fleury (1,077), Bouguerreau (1,059), Henner (1,028). Further down the list came Cabanel (992), Cormon (913), Detaille (862), Puvis de Chavannes (858), Benjamin-Constant (829), Roll (812), Carolus-Duran (771), Gervex (755) and Jules Breton (669 votes). In part, voters may have hoped that their tutors would be sympathetic, particularly as the catalogue would list the tutor of each exhibitor.

Artists who had previously been awarded a first or second class medal on two occasions were *hors concours* and by-passed the jury. For the remaining majority,

55. Arranging the hanging of the Salon, 1903. The works are to be hung closely packed together.

selection by the jury also largely determined the allocation of a good or bad place in the hanging of the exhibition:

> Those painters non-exempt from the selection by the jury are voted for by that body, and, according to the number of votes obtained, are allotted a reception number. Those obtaining unanimous favour are given a no. 1, which ensures a 'line-centre', and probably a medal to follow. Others not quite so popular receive a No. 2. This also gives a right to a place on the line. Finally some are received with a No. 3 or no number at all. These last can claim no special place and are apt to be 'skyed'.[23]

Thus, selection and hang went hand in hand and the position in which a painting was displayed indicated succinctly the opinion of painters elected by the mass of previous exhibitors (Plate 56). To be 'skyed' was to have a work hung close to the ceiling where it was almost invisible. Insofar as it implied criticism, it was a fate to be dreaded. Henner suffered this indignity early in his career after submitting to the Salon, according to his own account, under pressure from Manet and Degas: 'For three or four months, I imagined to myself that the effect would be superb. My illusion was soon shattered on the opening day of the Salon when I saw that they had placed me very high up in a corner. That enlightened me on the opinion of the jury.'[24] Jules Breton suffered the same discouraging experience, finding his painting 'hung under the ceiling. Impossible to recognise in this melancholy group, looking still more melancholy hanging up there, the gay peasants I had pictured to myself with the sunset flush that now seems to me a flush of shame.'[25] Zola described the experience in *L'Oeuvre*: 'it was hung so very high up that he could barely recognise it, it looked so tiny, clinging like a swallow to the corner of a frame, the huge ornamental frame of a tremendous canvas ten metres long representing the Flood'.[26]

In the selection artists were dealt with alphabetically, starting with a different letter each year (Plate 56). A picture accepted was almost certain to be hung. At the end of the main selection the jury reviewed the rejects, a process called *repêchage* or 'fishing again'. Undertaken with some reluctance and weariness it was nevertheless 'a time when a

51

56. *The Painting Jury Voting*, Salon of 1903.

friend at court is of the utmost value'.[27] The satirical writer Gyp caught the mood in a short play which described first of all the Salon jury at work, followed by the public opening and then a ghostly visit by old masters. During the *repêchage*, the following conversation is typical:

> And this portrait?...this awful portrait! I too ask that we fish it out again...
> Why?...
> The painter is a very pretty woman, very charming, who dresses superbly...
> And who has had a word in your ear?...
> You said it...Come on, let's see, a move in favour?
> Impossible!...it would cause an outcry...It's an insanity.[28]

According to Gyp, by lunchtime the attractions of art would lose their fascination:

> You say 'it has qualities'... Alright, I reply 'Show them to us'...
> But boys, let's go and eat, I beg of you...
> Numerous voices: Let's go and eat![29]

Zola described a similar scene, commenting that 'from four o'clock onwards they were a disorderly rabble'.[30] For all of these reasons, the *Vernissage* was a day of anxious excitement. Last touches were made and varnishing done with wide brushes continued in the midst of the crowd whilst steps passed precariously between the paintings and the people. The varnish which gave added lustre to the paintings also gave the day its name, Vernissage. It encompassed, as Edmond de Goncourt noted, 'a whole world of painters and their wives, making an effect with a late arrival, like the arrival of Heilbruth, and like the arrival of Carolus-Duran.'[31]

Fra Angelico, in Gyp's fantasy visit to the Salon by the old masters, found it all uninspiring: 'I find', he concluded, 'that the standard of painting has considerably declined this year at the Champs-Elysées.'[32] As Edmond de Goncourt implied, many of the visitors to the *Vernissage* in fact went there not to see the paintings, but see each other:

> Then which painting are you looking for?
> None!...paintings are all the same to us![33]

This was also clear to Zola: 'With the passage of the years it had become established in Paris that "varnishing day"...was an important day in the social calendar. Now it was one of those acknowledged "events" for which the whole town turned out in full force'.[34] But if the Salon was for many a social event (Plate 57–9), for painters, sculptors and print-makers it was all the more an immense market-place with many thousands of visitors. For all the difficulty of making an impact amongst its serried ranks of thousands of artworks, it provided recurrent opportunity for sales with a chance of recognition and success. Théodore Duret, a critic who supported the Impressionists, urged Pissarro not to disdain the Salon: 'you will be seen by fifty dealers, patrons, critics, who would otherwise never look you up and discover you...I urge you to exhibit; you must succeed in making a noise, in defying and attracting criticism, coming face to face with the big public. You will not achieve all that except at the Salon.'[35] The crush of potential purchasers was immense; Zola described it: 'By this time it ws almost impossible to move at all. All the benches were full and the crowds blocked the alleyways, so that the slow progress of the visitors was punctuated with stops and starts marked by the most popular bronzes and marbles...while over the seething tide of humanity in the garden, the din from upstairs, the tramping of feet on the cast-iron floors, roared on and on like the beating of a gail against cliffs.'[36]

The Salon was followed by a period of exhaustion and anticlimax: after 'the Salon and the lunches at Le Doyen's and other restaurants with *café-concert* in the Champs-Elysées, the artists tired of strolling through the rooms of the Palais de l'Industrie, the gardens filled with sculpture, and the walks between clumps of rhododendrons interspersed with statues and busts'[37] and they frequently turned their attention to travel.

In general, critical opinion was often adverse and unsympathetic even to Salon stars. Artists could be criticised for originality or for conformity. Furthermore artists, necessarily biassed in this matter, were often dismayed by the art they saw accepted and showed many signs of disillusionment with the Salon even whilst exhibiting there. Bashkirtseff provides the view of one young hopeful artist in 1878 'There is Bastien-Lepage, but the others?... It is knowhow, custom, convention and the art academy; a lot of convention, enormous amounts of convention. Nothing true, nothing vibrant,

57. André Rouveyre, *Vernissage 1900*, 1900, including the painters Carolus-Duran, Carrière, Besnard, Dagnan-Bouveret, Jean Béraud, la Gandara and Jacques-Emile Blanche.

58. The Buffet at the Salon on Varnishing Day, 1898.

59. James Tissot, *The Painters and their Wives*, *c.* 1885, oil on canvas, 146 × 101.7 cm., The Chrysler Museum, Norfolk, USA. The setting is Ledoyen's restaurant near the Palais de l'Industrie which was built on the Champs-Elysées for the 1855 Exposition Universelle.

nothing that sings...'[38] She excepted Bonnat 'because he has truth'.[39] Bonnat was well on the way to becoming one of the most respected Salon stars of his day. In 1882, Degas who viewed the Salon and the machinations it engendered with a skeptical eye, was intrigued by Bonnat's *Portrait of Puvis de Chavannes*. He wrote to the collector Henri Rouart on 2 May 1882: 'Sunday great varnishing day. An astonishing Whistler, excessively subtle but of quality! Chavannes, noble, a bit of a rehash, has the bad taste to show himself imperfectly dressed and proud, in a large portrait done by Bonnat.'[40]

A more widespread disillusionment was indicated in 1885, when 'By professional as well as amateur opinion, the display of pictures...was not of very high order, and the interest they awakened among the great body of artists was exceedingly faint.'[41] There was even difficulty distributing the medals. No medal of honour was given in sculpture, and in painting Bouguereau's *Byblis* won the medal of honour with only 77 votes out of a total of 407 votes cast by 950 potential voters. The *Art Journal's* critic noted 'the enormous and increasing size of the pictures, suggesting astonishment as to the ultimate destination and the purchasers of canvases of ten times twenty, and seldom less than twelve feet in length.'[42] This, of course, was one means to attract attention and was often combined with lurid subjects, the 'presence in great numbers of terrible pictures of a revolting character, M. Bonnat having painted this year for the decoration of the Panthéon, the most ghastly, namely, the *Martyrdom of St Denis*' (see Plate 231).[43] It is hardly surprising that in this market-place of art, painters and sculptors who were witnessing competition at its fiercest and most direct sought spectacular and eye-catching effects, often on a gigantic scale. F.G. Stephens regretted this: 'Wrecks and livid corpses cast ashore are, of course, to be expected, but there is a huge picture of the *Deluge* which will cause the blood of even the most hardened critic to curdle a little.'[44] Religious subjects were declining, however, 'probably due to the government having ceased to purchase works in this category, and the decreased wealth of religious communities'.[45] On the increase were subjects of 'Oriental magnificence' and 'Peasant-life portrayed in the manner of, but at a long interval from the works of Millet, are everywhere.'[46] Parallel to this the posthumous value of Millet's own paintings was rising fast. Jules Breton was one of those painters pursuing comparable themes, exhibiting in 1885 'two works in which the poetry of nature and the dignity of the labourer are harmonised in a way that leaves nothing to be desired.'[47] Mythological themes thrived ensuring continued employment for the colony of models. One reviewer appended a list of 'monstrosities' at the Salon which featured four of the Salon stars of the day — Aimé Morot's *Episode in a Bullfight*, Benjamin-Constant's *The Sheriff's Justice*, 'a mass of mangled corpses', Mercié's *Michel Angelo Studying Anatomy*, and Jean Béraud's *Asylum at Charenton*.[48]

Further crises over medals continued in 1886 when no first class medals were awarded specifically in painting although Bouguereau was awarded the Salon's medal of honour. It is possible that the Salon which had responded slowly and reluctantly to paintings of modern life and which was increasingly challenged by alternative salons and group exhibitions was undergoing a period of reduced confidence and self-criticism. The Salon des Indépendants had been operative for two years by 1886, the year which also saw the last of the Impressionist group exhibitions. As the *Art Journal* noted that year 'The tendency of the younger school of French artists during the last fifteen years has been towards depicting the everyday life of our great cities and rural districts in its naked truth, and often in its intense ugliness.'[49] This was by no means the concern solely of Impressionists and of Neo-Impressionists. Gustave Doré who died in 1883 had executed a series of 'horrible paintings of "Paris as it is"'.[50] Raffaëlli and De Nittis were also attracted to such subjects, as were many others, amongst them Jean Béraud whose brush 'he does not scruple to use as a scalpel' (Plate 60).[51]

This situation continued after the Salon split of 1889–90 and the founding of the Salon de la Nationale des Beaux-Arts under Meissonier, as more and more alternative means of exhibiting and progressing became available. As the Parisian art world

60. Jean Béraud, *St Mary Magdalen before the Pharisees*, 1891, oil on canvas, 97 × 130 cm., Musée d'Orsay, Paris. The reference is to Luke Chapter VII, verse 48. Béraud has portrayed contemporary figures, featuring Liane de Pougny before Renan and others.

became increasingly diverse and brilliant in different and unorthodox ways, so the Salon became increasingly anachronistic and felt its dominance in the market and in the taste of its clientèle slipping away. 'It is simply a race for the Grand Prix and accompanying medals,' wrote a critic in 1896, 'Art itself has only a secondary importance.' The forty or so rooms of the Palais de l'Industrie appeared 'full of noisy incongruity' (Plate 61).[52] The Salon stars of the 1880s, important men of the Institut, were losing both their appeal and their authority by the mid–1890s: 'We may avoid Gérôme' with his 'cold and hard productions, clumsily treated, and quite remarkably puerile in conception.' A similar critical fate awaited others, for 'nothing better can be said of *Irene* or *Les Otages* by M. Jean-Paul Laurens, with his everlasting fondness for bric-a-brac.' Furthermore, 'we may pass over those paintings of M. Bouguereau, whose *La Vague* is not worth considering, and also those of MM Bonnat and Jules Lefèbvre.'[53] On the other hand, there was praise for Lucien Lévy-Dhurmer's *Notre-Dame de Penmarc'h* (see Plate 123). Impressionists, Post-Impressionists, Symbolists and others were all making their mark and the monolithic authority of the Salon was decisively undermined:

> we know well enough beforehand what to expect from such men as Benjamin-Constant, Bonnat, Bouguereau, J.P. Laurens, Gérôme, Detaille, Clairin and Tony Robert-Fleury, and we don't expect them to give us anything new. Their art is always the same, as far removed from life as it is from dreamland, as far from truth as from the ideal — an art steeped in antiquated conventionalities, with no trace of life about it.[54]

The great market-place had grown, diversified, spawned offspring and collapsed in the midst of apparent vigour. By 1896 there were some 5,000 artists exhibiting in the two main Salons alone. When innovations of technique were added to a large canvas to attract attention, the result was seen to be

> sheer exaggerated egoism, overwhelming conceit, sheer fatuity, born of the frantic craving for notoriety, which actuates them one and all, and prompts them to all kinds of noisy futile eccentricity, simply to attract notice, simply that their pictures may not be passed unheeded in the throng of so many others, conceived and executed in something of the same fashion, and with the same object in view.[55]

\*　　\*　　\*

If the Salon formed a link between the authority of those artists at the Institut and the broad mass of thousands of exhibitors, it nevertheless enjoyed a degree of formal independence: it elected its own juries and its colossal market-place represented vast sales potential, albeit in the context of formidable competition. The Ecole des Beaux-Arts on the other hand staged major exhibitions of artists who were dead, but it did so with such originality and independence that these retrospectives were a force in modifying contemporary views of art; they could challenge the values promoted by the Institut, and even promote the posthumous reputations of artists who were at odds with the Institut in their lifetime. From this point of view alone the Courbet retrospective which opened in May 1882 was a remarkable event and it was followed in January 1884 by a major exhibition of Manet's work. The catalogue of the Manet exhibition contained a preface by Zola and the exhibition comprised 116 paintings plus pastels, watercolours, lithographs and drawings totalling 179 works in all. This represented a recognition of Manet's importance. The committee of fourteen which organised the exhibition comprised the politician Antonin Proust, as well as the painters Gervex, Guillemet, De Nittis, Roll and Alfred Stevens, the collector Faure, the dealers Durand-Ruel and Georges Petit, and the writers Emile Zola, Philippe Burty and Théodore Duret. In addition to the major Delacroix exhibition in 1885, the Ecole des Beaux-Arts' memorial exhibition devoted to Bastien-Lepage was crowded day after day. In 1886 there followed an exhibition devoted to Paul Baudry (389 works) and in 1887 to J.F.

Millet (218 works) with again profits enough to pay for a monument. Such exhibitions could challenge the Salon by challenging conventions dear to many Salon painters.

61. Jules-Alexandre Grün, *Vendredi au Salon des Artistes Français*, 1911, oil on canvas, 360 × 616 cm., Musée des Beaux-Arts, Rouen.

Thus, for the practising artist in Paris opportunities were growing to exhibit outside the traditional confines of the Salon. The Salon des Indépendants, formed in 1884, dispensed with a jury altogether; with both Signac and Seurat as founder members, its early years did much to promote Neo-Impressionist painting.[56] The Salon des Cent in the Rue Bonaparte on the Left Bank brought alternative exhibitions practically to the front door of the Ecole des Beaux-Arts and was particularly strong on Symbolists and prints. Dealers were multiplying in number too, so that independent group exhibitions and the substantial one-man shows devoted to living, practising and saleable artists were no longer a rarity. With the decline of the official Salon the great open market-place gave way to smaller specialised enterprises. There was even a Salon des Humor-istes which in due course attracted royalty to its *Vernissages* in the persons of the British King Edward VII and King Leopold II of Belgium as well as celebrated statesmen such as Clemenceau and public figures such as the artist-tragedienne Sarah Bernhardt. Amongst the strangest of the new independent salons was the Rosicrucian Salon, master-minded by the exotic Sâr Mérodack Péladan who proclaimed a hatred for realism and a devotion to all that was spiritual in art. At the openings of the Salon de la Rose + Croix, music by 'the superhuman Wagner' and fanfares composed by the young Erik Satie were played. Péladan followed what he called 'magical law' and refused to exhibit work by women. In practice the majority of his displays were distinctly Symbolist in flavour and featured German, Belgian, Dutch and British artists who fitted his exclusive mystical criteria, amongst them Emile Bernard, the Belgian Fernand Khnopff, the Swiss Hodler, and the Dutch-Javanese painter Jan Toorop, as well as the sculptor Bourdelle. The Salon of the Rose + Croix, organised by the Ordre de la Rose + Croix Catholique du Temple et du Graal (the Catholic Rosicrucian Order of the Temple and the Grail) headed by Péladan exhibited in Paris from 1892 to 1897.

57

L'ESTAMPE
et
L'AFFICHE
REVUE D'ART
directeur Clément-Janin
rédacteur en chef André Mellério
abonnement 6 fr
se vend à Paris
chez Edouard Pelletan
Aux Editions d'Art
125 boulevard St Germain

# 12. Vicarious Exposure

Those who could not attend the Salon, and many of the hundreds of thousands who did without acquiring a painting, could easily acquire reproductions of celebrated works by the major figures of the day. The sale of reproductions not only spread the fame of these artists, it could also raise considerable sums of money for dealers, artists, distributers, printers, engravers and photographers. The Goupil Gallery, important dealers in both old masters and contemporary art in Paris, had paid Ingres 24,000 francs for the reproduction rights on his *Odalisque*, a painting which he sold in the original for 1,200 francs. Such vicarious selling of works could be an important source of income over and above sales of originals, and as they travelled easily they spread images of the artist's work across continents and around the world, something an exhibition in itself could never do, however successful. Thus, Rosa Bonheur was but one artist among many who found it worth her while to spend long evenings signing reproductions of her paintings. Increasingly lavish art periodicals carried reproduction prints of several renowned artist's work in each issue, occasionally incorporating unsigned original lithographs amongst their mass-produced pages. Dealers too could promote works this way and publish reproductions for sale. Occasionally dealers were also the publishers of periodicals, which might be used, according to editorial discretion, to promote stock. By reducing the artwork to a mass-produced image in this way, ownership of the resulting prints became universally available; by replacing the original product it provided an advertisement for it but it also undermined many of the qualities of the original by neglecting its physical scale, handling, colour and medium in order to produce objects accessible to mass ownership.

Insofar as this involved increasingly sophisticated printing techniques that emulated or used fine-art printing processes ranging from engraving to etching and lithography, this development rendered ambiguous the status of the original fine art print in particular. Lithography especially is a process susceptible to large print-runs and it is a testament to the vitality and success of late nineteenth-century Parisian poster-artists, that their products became popular collectors' items despite their large print-runs (Plate 62). Conversely, the posters of Bonnard, Vuillard, Lautrec, Steinlen, Mucha and many others introduced a vigorous input from practising painters into public advertising for display on street-hoardings. This was as far from the hallowed halls of the Salon as one could go.

Curiously, the rise of the widely and publicy available lithographic poster coincided with a broad revival of the artist's print, which had been much encouraged in Paris by the foundation of the Society of Etchers (Société des Aquafortistes) whose members included Félix Bracquemond, Manet, Whistler, Legros and others. The etching process did not normally permit a long print-run. The process, which involves waxing a copper plate, then scratching a drawing through the wax with a pointed burin, and emersing the plate in acid to bite the line into the metal, is slow to set up. After the wax is removed ink is applied to the plate and then wiped off to leave ink in the furrows bitten by the acid. A sheet of paper is placed on the plate and the whole inserted into the etching press which forces the paper into the furrows to pick up the ink. It is necessary to re-ink for each print which is laborious. All of this slow, meticulous work results in a distinctly limited edition, so that etching remained closer to the concept of an original art-work than to a widely available reproduction.

Etchers were often specialists, producing a large variety of prints and sometimes extending their activity to the printing of other artists' plates. Delâtre at his print

62. (*facing page*) Pièrre Bonnard, *The Print and the Poster* (L'Estampe et L'Affiche), lithograph in three colours, 80 × 60 cm. A poster advertising the periodical edited by Clement Janin and André Mellerio.

63. Edgar Degas, *Mary Cassatt and her sister Lydia in the Etruscan Gallery at the Louvre*, 1879–80, etching, aquatint and electric crayon (third state), 26.7 × 23 cm., Metropolitan Museum of Art, New York (Rogers Fund 1919–19.29.2).

workship in Montmartre was one such etcher involved in printing as an expert trade. Other artists such as Charles Jacques and Félix Bracquemond simply concentrated on etching as their specialist medium. There were numerous instances however of painters turning to etching. The example of Manet and Whistler was followed by many by the 1880s and 1890s including Camille Pissarro and Edgar Degas, who experimented with it, and Helleu and Anders Zorn for whom etching was a major medium which did much to propagate their art at reasonable prices (Plates 63–4). In this period a wide range of printing processes were vigorously exploited and explored, from Degas' monotypes, which allowed a run of only one or two prints, to Charpentier's intaglio prints in which no ink was used at all, the image being simply embossed on the paper. Even photography could be viewed as a printing process, and the development of the 'fine art' photograph is related to the expansion of print-making. Photographic processes also revolutionised reproductions in art-periodicals which radically altered their appearance and appeal by adopting photographic illustrations and thereby sounded the death knell to the careers of hosts of engravers for whom reproducing the artworks of others had until this time been a vital and an apparently inexhaustible source of work and income.

When working on wood, the engraver turned his block on end, exposing the cross-section of the grain, the end-grain. This allows the cutting tool, cupped in the plam of the hand, to move smoothly in any direction, cutting fine lines as well as broader areas from the block to provide the white parts of the print whilst the uncut remainder takes the ink. The long-standing vogue for Japanese woodblock prints, of which Bracquemond had been an initiator, employed a different process, emulated by Henri Rivière, whereby the side-grain could be employed. A cruder relative of this method, was the woodcut technique by which the side-grain was cut away, preserving the awkward and rough appearance which resulted from the resistance to cutting provided by the hard and soft grain of the wood and its changing direction. In Paris, Félix Vallotton made extensive use of the woodcut which was characterised by a dramatic contrast of solid black and white readily adaptable to reproduction in periodicals (see Plate 156).

The flourishing and richly diverse developments of the print served to propagate artists' work; they could be assembled into exhibitions in themselves, but they also complemented exhibiting as a process promoting recognition and success. They supplied a public demand relatively cheaply: whilst individual prints were cheaper to acquire than paintings, the sale of a whole edition of prints could make more money than a painting. This business technique of selling more objects cheaply in order to increase profit assumes a wide market amongst the less wealthy. In fact there were many collectors who acquired prints or who specialised in them, but there was also a large potential market amongst buyers who would scarcely consider themselves serious collectors.

There was a price to be paid for this tactic which coincided with the rising power and popularity of photography. The print could be viewed either as an original art-work or as the result of a process of reproduction. No clear dividing line exists between, at one end of the spectrum, a commercial reproduction printed from a photograph and distributed in thousands of copies universally available, and at the other extreme, the one-off monotype, because every intervening stage exists. The status of the print called into question the value of a unique artwork. Curiously this problem could exist also in relation to sculptures cast in bronze which could similarly be reproduced and issued in editions. Reproduction demolishes uniqueness, and a broad market established prices in a way quite distinct from that employed when a dealer discussed with an individual client the price of a painting or sculpture. A sign of the commercial value of prints, however, was the increasing attention paid by dealers to the publication and commissioning of print portfolios. The astute dealer Ambroise Vollard provides one example amongst many who were offering such portfolios for sale in the later 1890s, whilst some dealers specialised in prints.

From this point of view the most ambiguous print technique was lithography which in its original form involves drawing with a special crayon on a stone slab. The drawing could be very loose or precise, soft in effect or sharp, allowing spontaneity or lengthy consideration of the marks made. Although the printing process, which makes use of incompatibility of grease and water, was complex enough to require the assistance of a specialist lithographic printer, once set-up it was capable of very large print-runs, with consecutive printings permitting a wealth of colour in subtle optical mixtures. For Whistler, Fantin-Latour and Redon, it was primarily a medium to be explored much as they explored etching, and they did so in brilliant, innovative and different ways. Yet the process permitted runs long enough to illustrate periodicals with original prints. The *Studio* magazine published lithographs by Whistler in this way (see Plates 258 and 261).[1] They were not signed individually by the artist, which would have increased their value, but they were still original lithographs, albeit with a very long print-run. Once this point was reached, no distinction could be sustained between an original artwork and a reproduction, for reproduction was inherent in the process the artist employed.

64. Anders Zorn, *Portrait of Auguste Rodin*, 1906, etching.

61

TOUS LES SOIRS A 8 HEURES
32, RUE RICHER
FOLIES BERGÈRE
TRAVAUX DE VOLTIGE · BALLETS
PANTOMIMES · OPERETTES
O. MÉTRA ET SON ORCHESTRE
PRIX UNIQUE 2fr. à toutes places non-louées
IMP. J. CHÉRET. 18. R. BRUNEL. PARIS

Amongst the most original artists to concentrate on lithography was Jules Chéret (Plate 65). Whilst he also painted, his most prolific and celebrated works were his posters, some of which were enormous. These were unapologetic advertisements of events and products. Chéret was an advertiser of everything from skating-rinks to night-clubs. His attenuated, carefree and effervescent figures were executed with a lightness of touch and an explosive rhythm that transformed the ubiquitous hoardings of Paris. His was an art of the street and his posters were not rare. But they were certainly collected and his use of interwoven areas of hazy colour showed an innovative brilliance of technique that was not lost upon painters, among them Georges Seurat and Toulouse-Lautrec. Like Chéret, Seurat employed small spots of colour that blended in the eye; Seurat did so in oil-paint, Chéret with the medium of lithography. For Seurat the large unique canvas was evolved according to a modified version of the processes of the Beaux-Arts. In Chéret's case, the poster was mass-produced and as public as only a poster can be, instigated by the determination of a commercial patron to sell his products through advertising.

If for Chéret painting was a secondary source of income, for Toulouse-Lautrec painting was never relegated to second place in his working life as an artist. Yet it was largely in terms of advertising that Lautrec employed his own extensive innovations in lithographic technique, using sprays of colour, liquid lines and flat areas of colour in an intensely dramatic and decorative interplay. Bonnard, Vuillard, Ibels and Steinlen, amongst many others, including Alphonse Mucha and Grasset, brought to advertising the innovations and daring of the studio, transforming the art of poster-design in the process. This was not possible without lithography. It provided work, income and fame for the artist as well as fame for the commodity or person advertised; originality lay in the design whilst the poster itself was mass-produced and as emphatically public as the client and printer could make it. It transformed the streets of Paris as exhibitions of painting and sculpture could never do. In undermining the uniqueness of the single hand-made object, the art work of the poster extended the print revival immeasurably and in doing so reached an immense audience, not in the studio or gallery but in the boulevards. Art lowered itself to the commercial poster, but the poster was collected as art.

65. Jules Chéret, *Aux Folies Bergère*, 1875, poster, Musée de la Publicité, Paris.

# 13. Sales

The artist relied, in the midst of the fiercest competition, upon recognition. For a few wealthy individuals, Manet and Cézanne amongst them, such recognition was not an urgent financial requirement, but it persisted as a determination to make public the achievements of the studio. According to Meissonier 'No artist would paint if he knew he was never to show his work, if he felt no human eye would ever rest upon it.'[1]

As soon as the artist sought recognition a host of middle-men seemed to be required. Unknown artists were dependent to an extreme degree upon intermediaries to advance their case: to confront the public directly was difficult and expensive to arrange; this was an expert field for which few artists found either the will or the means to face the administrative and human problems involved. The Salon provided a point of regular public contact that was vital but it hardly reduced competition to manageable proportions. Group exhibitions, as the eight Impressionist exhibitions revealed between 1874 and 1886, were a powerful force for establishing a presence outside of the Salons but they were open to dissention and ridicule in the press and from the public. They were also a financial risk.

For the majority of artists seeking success the support of dealers and critics was indispensable. Operating between artists and their public they could make or break reputations, ruin careers or make a fortune for an artist. Paris had critics of every kind, vigorously articulating the reasons for an art that was Realist or Academic, Impressionist or Symbolist, but a few were immensely powerful and their opinions much respected. 'In the *Figaro*,' wrote Jacques-Emile Blanche, 'Albert Wolff, the critic, or a man like Octave Mirbeau, had power to make the fortune of a poor beginner from one day to another by merely publishing an article on the Salon. What happy days for the artist who was their protégé.'[2]

The critic, acting essentially as a specialised journalist, had links with literary salons as well as artistic circles, and was frequently a celebrated figure of Parisian society. It is not surprising that their portraits are numerous. Dantan's painting of the *Interval at the Comédie Française* evokes the mélange of successful writers amongst them Albert Wolff as well as Emile Zola and the younger Alexandre Dumas, together with painters including Meissonier. The scene of hectic social activity and excitement in the theatre, attracted Renoir and Degas too in their desire to pursue the painting of modern life. Zola's critical eye summed it up in his novel *Nana* in 1880 in his description of a less renowned theatre:

> The whole of Paris was there, the Paris of letters, of finance and of pleasure. There were a great many journalists, a few authors, a number of speculators, and more courtesans than respectable women. It was a singularly mixed world, composed of all the talents, and tarnished by all the vices, a world where the same fatigue and the same fever appeared in every face.[3]

For the artist to gain recognition from such a world of intellectuals and wealthy pleasure-seekers, the assistance of well-connected critics and dealers was crucial. Contacts had to be established; recognition was essentially a process of exchange — not simply a product bought and sold, but a two-way process whereby acceptance made demands upon the artist in his work, whilst the possession of the work conferred upon its purchaser implications of taste or kudos.

On the death of an artist of standing, it was normal practice to hold a sale of the studio contents. This provided income for the sale room, usually the auctioneers of the Hôtel Drouot, and potentially considerable sums for an artist's widow or dependants. It also assessed the demand for an artist's work on the open market without the special pricing which might be undertaken by dealers. For the dealers it provided opportunities to observe market trends and to purchase works for stock, speculating upon a painter's reputation in the years following his death. In terms of market forces, the death of an artist of repute was an important event. In closing his career, it simultaneously limited the availability of his work, so that buyers henceforth sought purchases in a limited pool. In the case of an artist successful in his day, this served to increase the value of his works. The studio sale which followed a well-known artist's death was an important event, perhaps the last major opportunity to buy cheaply, or to speculate on the future financial value of works. For dealers the most difficult decisions involved an assessment of changes in taste which might radically effect future sale prices. The timing as well as the pricing of sales was vitally important. The studio sale permitted sizeable stocks of works to be bought more or less wholesale if the dealer speculated upon a substantial increase in an artist's fame and the desirability of his works after his death. Such reflections, discouraging in the extreme to painters and sculptors, were important to dealers and even to collectors. The studio sale therefore represented a sensitive and revealing moment, providing insights into the success of artists as did similar sales of private collections of contemporary art.

At the Courbet sale of 1881 the *Artist's Studio* sold for 21,000 francs but a painting by him of *Fighting Stags* realised 49,100 francs. This compares with the asking price of 10,000 francs for Manet's *Olympia* in the Manet sale of 4–5 February 1884. Salon stars could reach, on occasions, very high prices indeed. At the sale in 1886 of the Morgan Collection, works by Vibert were sold at 62,500 francs and 125,000 francs. Whilst Impressionist prices remained relatively low the Charles Guasco sale of 10–11 June 1900 sold a Pissarro for 8,200 francs and a Sisley for 15,350 francs but a painting by Gustave Moreau for 53,000 francs. A Sisley sold the same year, however, had reached 43,000 francs at the Tavernier sale on 6 March. By sharp contrast Cézanne's *Temptation of St Anthony* was purchased for 800 francs and Seurat's *Seine at Courbevoie* for only 630 francs. By 1912 Impressionist paintings were, for many reasons, much more attractive to the market. Manet's *Music Lesson* reached 120,000 francs, and Renoir's *Allée cavalière au Bois de Boulogne* 95,000 francs, whilst Puvis de Chavannes' *Hope* (L'Espérance) was sold for 65,000 francs. The rise of Impressionist prices was well underway and speculation in their work would have been highly remunerative.

Occasionally artists held auctions of their own works during their lifetimes although to sell by auction could be unnerving and was potentially disastrous. The dealer in contemporary art was far more sophisticated in his efforts to find the right purchaser for particular works, and such dealers as the Goupil-Boussod-Valadon firm (of which Theo Van Gogh was an employee), the great Impressionist dealer Durand-Ruel (who by no means restricted his field to Impressionism), Georges Petit, Ambroise Vollard and Bernheim-Jeune, played a crucial role in connecting the artist with his purchasers, working out deals with artists and purchasers alike and operating internationally.

Vincent Van Gogh, who knew much about dealers' practices, especially through his brother Theo but partly from his own experience, acknowledged the importance of dealers but equally realised that an aspiring artist first had to be recognised by the dealer himself. The important dealers, according to Van Gogh 'do little or nothing for young artists. The second class contrariwise sell those at low prices.'[4] At the opposite extreme to Van Gogh's obscurity, Meissonier was also dismayed at the art market in which he saw 'tradesmen buy, and painters swarm, as in a sort of artistic rabbit-warren, full of nameless works, ephemeral as their authors.'[5] A very successful artist could choose exactly when to sell, by starving an eager market lose none of the power to sell, and perhaps even raise prices by inadequately supplying the demand. The successful Rosa Bonheur seems to have had few problems with dealers: 'A money offer could never hasten her. She would dispose of as many pictures as would furnish her the funds she was in need of, and then, as soon as she had some ready cash on hand, she would return to her studies.'[6]

By the mid–1880s there were many exhibition opportunities available in Paris other than the Salon. Group exhibitions and one-man exhibitions were numerous. Dealers played a vital role in this, although periodicals of literature and art also made available their offices for exhibitions, and on occasions Vincent Van Gogh and several friends exhibited in Montmartre restaurants.

Such exposure could be nerve-wracking as Edmond de Goncourt recorded in the case of his friend the painter De Nittis. After describing the artist's wife driving five or six times past the door to see if anyone was going to the exhibition, de Goncourt describes the artist: 'seized with the discouragement which, for a man of imagination, usually precedes the contact between his work and the public, he passes the day with his door shut, lying on the divan in his studio in a black slumber'.[7] The combined pressures of supplying work to a dealer and managing to extract money from him whilst retaining his confidence in difficult times, could be equally stressful. Degas and Monet, for example, wrote frequently to Durand-Ruel for money. 'For want of big money', wrote Degas in 1884–5, 'send me small...Damnable life. I am finishing your devilish pictures',[8] or forthrightly in the summer of 1884 'I will stuff you with products this winter...and you for your part will stuff me with money'.[9] Yet the dealer Durand-Ruel, after some

66. The Grand Salon at Durand-Ruel's appartement, 35 Rue de Rome, photograph from after 1885. Door panels by Monet. This view is from the dining room.

severely difficult times in the 1880s eventually succeeded and by 1892 was evidently wealthy. Edmond de Goncourt noted in his *Journal* that year that,

> Durand-Ruel's home is a strange habitation for a nineteenth-century picture dealer. A huge flat in the Rue de Rome, full of pictures by Renoir, Monet, Degas etc., with a bedroom with a crucifix at the head of the bed, and a dining room where a table is laid for eighteen people and where each guest has before him a Pandean pipe of six wineglasses. (Plate 66)[10]

Jacque-Emile Blanche excepted Durand-Ruel from this condemnation of unsympathetic dealers who profited from Impressionist painting: 'Prices had been rising since the 1880s and 1890s, but the Impressionist painters were still faced with the problem of making ends meet, because the dealers, with the exception of Durand-Ruel, would not give way, but went on paying scandalously low prices for their work.'[11]

Edmond de Goncourt provided a hint of dealers' practices at Boussod-Valadon if his *Journal* for 30 March 1889 is to be believed. Like Durand-Ruel, the Boussod-Valadon firm of dealers were well aware of the wealthy American market. Boussod had apparently bought a painting by the late J.F. Millet for 12,000 francs and hoped to sell it to an American collector for 35,000 francs. A visitor asserted that it was not by Millet and called in Millet's widow who did not recognise the painting. When Millet's son was consulted he said that he did not remember it although it was painted in his father's manner. The visitor recommended that Boussod consult the widow, who again said that she did not recognise it as Millet. Boussod contacted her in order to buy a selection of Millet's drawings for 4,000 francs but also requested a letter authenticating the painting. By now in some doubt, she provided the letter and sold the drawings.

Boussod's painting was now authenticated. A few days later the painter Chaplin burst into Boussod's gallery exclaiming 'How happy I am to find this wretched painting again!... But there is a signature which has to be removed, for this Millet is by me!'[12]

Many different kinds of contracts were evolved between painters and dealers. When in 1888 Monet submitted ten works to Theo Van Gogh at Goupil's, they were exhibited in a separate room at 19 Boulevard Montmartre and well received by certain sympathetic critics, including Gustave Geffroy. Theo Van Gogh bought the ten Monet paintings at prices from 1,000–1,300 francs according to size (total cost 11,900 francs) but agreed in addition to pay Monet half of any profit on reselling them. The painting *The Beach at St Juan-les-Pins*, for example, was bought from Monet for 1,300 francs, sold to a certain Boivin for 3,000 francs, yeilding a profit of 1,700 francs, half of which went to Monet (total for the painting 2,150 francs).[13]

By contrast, Gauguin's friend Daniel de Monfried, acting as Gauguin's agent in 1899, sold Vollard nine paintings for 1,000 francs; Gauguin was dismayed and considered that Vollard 'had no shame and would now be able to undercut the painter's own hoped-for future prices.[14]

If a dealer was part of the vital support system for the artist, and indispensibly valuable in this role, he was nevertheless a salesman motivated as much by the desire to make a profit as by a love of art. The greater the difference between the sum paid to the artist and the sum paid by the purchaser, the greater his profit. This could work against the artist's interests and was only manipulable by the artist after a market for his work was established. That in turn usually required the agency of a dealer, so that the young aspiring painter was at a real disadvantage when first approaching dealers. He needed a good dealer to make adequate income. He needed a reputation to attract a good dealer. What could break this hopeless cycle overnight was critical acclaim in the press. Here is a reason why some critics became so powerful. By recommending an artist, they could not only increase the value of his works but suggest that they would retain that value, and, if the artist was a new name, buying early could comprise an interesting investment. The vicious circle could be broken and a growing reputation be established. As demand grew, prices could rise, further suggesting the importance of the work in question, further fuelling the rise in prices, and appearing in the process to fulfil the promise first noted by the critic.

\*     \*     \*

To sell one's painting to the state was an honour and a public sign of recognition. Although many purchases by the state were made through the Salon on behalf of provincial museums throughout France, the Third Republic had in Phillippe de Chennevières a Director of the Beaux-Arts who showed remarkable independence of the authority of the Institut. In 1881 he supported a plan to have Manet decorate the Trocadéro Museum in Paris with the assistance of Carolus-Duran, Cazin, Duez and Besnard. Although the project was not fulfilled, it was significant support for the ailing Manet and an unacademic assessment of what was best in contemporary art for the purpose.

Living artists were not displayed in the hallowed halls of the Louvre, but in the Luxembourg Museum or, in the case of weather-proof sculpture, in the surrounding Luxembourg Gardens between ornamental gardens and trees. Hanging cheek by jowl in the museum the large paintings represented an official assessment of the finest of contemporary art: to have a work hanging there was a major honour and a substantial recognition of an artist's significance. Baedecker's Guide to Paris expressed this assumption succinctly in 1894: 'The works of the most distinguished masters are generally transferred to the Louvre, or sent to provincial galleries, about ten years after their death; so that a more comprehensive survey of modern French art cannot be obtained in one place.'[15] Amongst the painters represented there in 1894 were Bashkirtseff, Baudry, Bonheur, Bonnat, Bouguereau, Breton, Cabanel, Carolus-Duran, Cazin, Benjamin-Constant, Cormon and Courbet, Dagnan-Bouveret, Elie Delaunay, Detaille and so on. Fantin-Latour's *Studio in the Batignolles Quarter*, his homage to Manet, was there as too were Gérôme's *Cock Fight*, Hébert's *Malaria*, Lhermitte's *The Reapers' Pay Day*, Meissonier's *Napoleon III at Solferino*, Gustave Moreau's *Orpheus* and Whistler's *Portrait of the Artist's Mother*. The list ranged from Robert-Fleury and Henner to Harpignies and Tissot. Sculptures included Rodin's bronze *St John the Baptist Preaching* and works by Barrias, Chapu, Dubois, Falguière, Frémiet, Puech and Barthélemy.

For all its splendours Degas despised the system and the honour which it bestowed. Declining to submit a work for the Luxembourg Museum when sounded out by Mallarmé who was acting on behalf of Roujon, the new Director of Beaux-Arts, Degas pointed to its function of conferring recognition for artists:

> I told him, most certainly not, of course. These people want to make me think that I have 'arrived'. 'Arrived', what does that mean?... It means hanging on a wall next to a lady by Bouguereau and the Slave Market by Toto Girod? I want none of it... They have the chessboard of the Fine Arts on their table and we, the artists, are the pawns... They move this pawn here, that pawn there... I am not a pawn, I do not want to be moved.[16]

State patronage conferred honour and recognition independently of dealers, but dealers and particularly critics were central to establishing a reputation which attracted the eye of the state as patron in the first place. It was just imaginable that this could occur unannounced through the Salon. But it was most unlikely.

An insight into the scale of purchases made by the City of Paris in the mid–1880s is provided by figures from 1885 when a total of 43,500 francs was expended on five paintings and five sculptures from the Salon.[17] The same year the Ministry of Fine Arts purchased *Les Foins* by Bastien-Lepage for 25,000 francs (see Plate 285). Glory was inevitably reflected into those dealers' rooms where such artists' works were to found.[18]

The *Art Journal* reported that the official valuation of works of art belonging to the City of Paris in 1885 was 12,256,860 francs. In addition to this the civic buildings and streets of Paris housed artworks to the value of a further 4,178,000 francs, and churches in Paris housed art valued at 8,078,551 francs. On the Boulevard Morland, a government sculpture store accounted for a further 390,000 francs and sculpture in the street 1,000,000 francs which the *Art Journal* considered 'a curiously low figure'.[19]

\*   \*   \*

Purchasers of artworks in Paris had to be numerous to sustain dealers, although the American market which had proved so important to Durand-Ruel, was burgeoning and a crucial factor. In France there were many significant collections of contemporary art although these were sometimes associated with collections of older work and occasionally of spectacular older collections. Sir Richard Wallace added works by Delacroix, Meissonier and Rosa Bonheur to an immense collection that included paintings by Rembrandt, Poussin and Boucher, worthy of the most important state museums. Wallace lived in the Bois de Boulogne and was devoted to Paris, donating to the city the celebrated, elegant and still functioning drinking fountains known as Wallace fountains.[20] The Wallace Collection is large, wide-ranging and splendid but it contained only safe contemporary works to hang alongside its old masters. Other collectors had quite different tastes. By the 1880s, paintings by the Barbizon school were increasingly sought by collectors, in particular J.F. Millet's work, but certain collectors maintained close contact with practising artists. For example, the famed singer Faure was one of the first buyers of Manet and Degas. He had acquired Manet's *Bon Bock* for 6,000 francs and Degas' *Carriage at the Races* for 1,500 francs. In 1874 he bought two works by Degas for 5,000 francs and 8,000 francs respectively.

One collector very closely involved with painters was Henri Stanislas Rouart (1833–1912), an important collector of contemporary art and a painter in his own right. After serving as an artillery officer, he turned to business. He became attracted to painting and exhibited at the Salon between 1868 and 1872. He became friendly with Degas and contributed to Impressionist group exhibitions between 1874 and 1886. Earlier he had known Corot and Millet who had encouraged him to paint out of doors, and he possessed works by both of these painters. The collection grew and ranged from old masters (El Greco, Breughel, Poussin, Claude, Chardin, Fragonard, Goya, Tiepolo) to Delacroix, Courbet, Daumier and Millet. His Impressionist interests led to the acquisition of works by Manet, Degas, Monet, Renoir, Morisot, Gauguin and Lautrec. After his death his collection was sold at the Galerie Manzi-Joyant in Paris from 9–11 December 1912.

In fact Rouart opened his collection to visitors on a regular basis. Not a celebrated or honoured painter himself he nevertheless associated with painters and through his own experience had a knowledge of technique and execution in painting that permitted an intimate appreciation of the processes and achievements of the artists he collected.

Amongst contemporary writers with significant collections were the Goncourt brothers. After the early death of Jules de Goncourt, Edmond continued to collect with discrimination just as he continued to associate with the artists of his day and comment upon their personalities in his Journal. Edmond de Goncourt's collection, like that of any discerning collector, revealed his individual taste and personality. His particular enthusiasms were for Gavarni, the lithographic artist and satirical observer of modern Paris, eighteenth-century French art (especially drawings and prints), and Japanese art. He wrote scholarly texts on each of these subjects. The Journal on the other hand reflects personalities and temperaments:

> Rodin, behaving just like a *faun*, asks to see my Japanese erotica, and there is admiration before these lowerings of women's heads, these angular necks, these nervous extensions of the arm, these contractions of the feet, all of the voluptuous and frenetic reality of intercourse, all of these sculptural positionings of bodies sunk and encased in the spasm of pleasure.[21]

The Goncourt house at Auteuil had been purchased for 83,000 francs in 1868. Jules de Goncourt had spent his last days there and a medallion of his was inserted into the wall. The house was devoted to the collection, a veritable 'temple of art'[22] 'This collection,' wrote Edmond, 'is at once my wealth and my friend. It shows what a poor devil may achieve by time, the exercise of determined will.' He sought in his collection of French, mostly eighteenth-century drawings, 'the most important executed by every master of whatever artistic rank'.[23]

For Edmond de Goncourt collecting appeared a creative act in itself. To bequeath his collection or establish a museum on his death, would, he felt, preserve the works but destroy the excitement of collecting: 'As for the objects that I possess, I do not want them in a museum, in a place where people pass by bored by what they see. I want every one of my objects to carry to a collector, to a unique being, the little joy that I had on buying them'.[24] The sale took place on 15–17 February 1897 at the Hôtel Drouot sale-rooms in Paris.

Just as Rouart the collector had also been a painter, albeit as a subsidiary activity rather than a full-time commitment, so artists themselves often acquired paintings, sculpture and prints incidentally during their careers, through friendship and exchanges of works as well as through purchases. Certain painters, however, deliberately built up collections out of professional enthusiasm. In the case of the highly honoured Léon Bonnat, the collection has been preserved at the Musée Bonnat in Bayonne. Bonnat, winner of the Prix de Rome, professor at the Ecole des Beaux-Arts, president of the Museums Commission, holder of the Legion of Honour, bequeathed his collection to the City of Bayonne. Amongst the most highly esteemed painters of his day, Bonnat was aware of his position: 'They say of Bonnat', wrote Thadée Natanson, 'that he removes his gloves only in bed. In reality he kept them on even for painting.'[25] The Natanson family were important patrons for Vuillard and Lautrec, with a taste in contemporary art very different from that of the glorious Institut-member Léon Bonnat who twice resisted the acquisition of a Lautrec portrait by the Luxembourg Museum. According to Natanson, the most sympathetic quality of Bonnat was his devotion to the objects of the past,[26] an enthusiasm reflected in his own painting and in his collection of works by contemporary artists of similar tastes.

If Bonnat's collection reflected the Institut and Salon system, that of Edgar Degas reflected a much more subtle taste, the result of his own experience of an academic training and the closest subsequent involvement with Impressionism and the painting of modern life. The sale of Degas' collection in March 1918 (he died in 1917) listed 247 works comprising 93 paintings and 154 pastels, drawings and watercolours. In addition, there were thousands of prints ranging from Japanese prints to those of Gavarni, Daumier, Manet and others.

Degas collected assiduously from the 1890s onwards, buying sometimes direct from painters, sometimes through dealers such as Vollard, and sometimes at auctions. He possessed several works by both Ingres and Delacroix. He considered Ingres' drawings 'marvels of the human mind'.[27] Not surprisingly he also had work by Manet and the Impressionists Pissarro, Sisley, Renoir, Morisot and the American Mary Cassatt, as well as Gauguin's *La Belle Angèle* and Van Gogh's still life of *Apples, Pears, Lemon and Grapes* of 1887.

Historically speaking the most significant collection of Impressionist paintings assembled by a painter was that owned by Gustave Caillebotte, for in bequeathing it to the nation, Caillebotte had insisted that its ultimate destination was to be the Louvre. The Caillebotte Bequest became a cause célèbre of the day, polarising opinion both for and against the recognition of Impressionist painting. Impressionists had, as we have seen, largely side-stepped the established structure of tuition to paint out of doors and they had for the most part chosen to organise group exhibitions (between 1874 and 1886) or exhibit through dealers, rather than the Salon which offered them little encouragement. In the growing acknowledgement of the Impressionists' importance, the affair of the Caillebotte Bequest was a critical event and ultimately decisive in its effect. The Collection itself was uncompromising. Apart from two Millet drawings, Caillebotte possessed many works by Cézanne (5), Degas (7), Manet (4), Monet (16), Pissarro (18), Renoir (8) and Sisley (9). Manet's *Le Balcon*, three Monets of *Gare St Lazare* and Renoir's *Moulin de la Galette* and *La Balançoire* were part of the Caillebotte's Bequest and were still highly problematic and unacceptable to members of the Institut. Eventually, in 1947, the Jeu de Paume, part of the Louvre Museum in Paris, made the Caillebotte Bequest its core to which Impressionist works from other collections were added.[28]

Renoir was the executor of Caillebotte's will and in 1894 he had written to Henri Roujon, Director of the Beaux-Arts, informing him of the bequest, which Caillebotte envisaged going to the Luxembourg Museum and subsequently to the Louvre. This took seventeen years to achieve, including three years negotiation with the Luxembourg Museum and even then not all of the collection was accepted. In 1897 a letter was sent by the Académie des Beaux-Arts from the Institut to the government condemning the gift and expressing 'the unanimous regret of the members of the Academy on seeing a collection of paintings, unworthy of such a hospitality in every respect, figuring for several days on the walls of the Luxembourg Museum.'[29] In fact they had voted 18 to 10 and not unanimously. The issue was discussed at the French Senate on 15 March 1897, where the collection was described as 'a defiance to the good taste of the public and the antithesis of French art.'[30] The reply of the Director of the Beaux-Arts was significant for what it suggests of the complexity of art in Paris at the time and of the reduced authority of the Institut and Salon in determining the nature of that art: 'it was considered very difficult, in the present state of divisions of opinion on questions of art, to take any attitude other than that of a liberal eclecticism.'[31]

*     *     *

The increasing complexity of art in Paris in the mid-1880s and into the 1890s was reflected in the emergence of the second major Salon and the plethora of alternative salons and exhibitions of every kind. Prices related directly to success and the selective promotional systems of the whole structure, which included commercial academies, the Ecole des Beaux-Arts, the Prix de Rome, the Salon and the activities of critics and dealers.

A very celebrated work could produce impressive sums of money. Rosa Bonheur whose *Horse Fair* was a major attraction at the 1853 Salon offered it at 12,000 francs for a French museum, adding that it would cost 40,000 francs if an English museum wished to buy it. Eventually the Metropolitan Museum, New York, paid over 250,000 francs for the painting in 1887. A quarter-size version at 25,000 francs was sent to England for engravings to be made by Thomas Landseer. 'The sale of engravings', wrote the dealer Ernest Gambart, 'had been very profitable, and the exhibition of the original established the artist's reputation on such a secure basis that her following pictures were able to command high prices and were bought up immediately when finished'.[32] A second small copy was made and sold for 25,000 francs and a watercolour version sold for a further 2,500 francs.

When Meissonier sold *La Rixe*, a historical genre scene of fighting swordsmen, to Napoleon III the price paid was an unprecedented 150,000 francs. Meissonier became the most expensive painter of later nineteenth-century France. Henri Chauchard, owner of the department store Magasins du Louvre and occupant of a mansion on the Rue Velasquez in Paris, was a collector with immense buying power who apparently needed extensive advice about what to buy. Works by Ziem and Bouguereau jostled alongside Millet's *Angelus* (Plate 104) in his collection. When he turned his attention to purchasing a painting by Meissonier, his celebrated *1812*, Chauchard excelled himself, and everyone else, by paying 840,000 francs. The painting is, furthermore, very small. In the later 1880s the unknown Van Gogh in assessing his own chances of selling paintings considered a price as low as 50 francs reasonable:

> Now the prices are 50 francs. Certainly not much — but as far as I can see one must sell cheap to rise and even at a costing price. And mind, my dear fellow, Paris is Paris. There is but one Paris, and however hard living may be here, and, if it becomes worse and harder even — the French air clears up the brain and does good — a world of good.[33]

Baedecker's Guide to Paris in 1889 suggested that 15 to 20 francs was reasonable daily pocket money for the tourist.

From 840,000 francs for a Meissonier to 50 francs for a Van Gogh — this was the range of prices from highest success to aspirant newcomer in the art world of Paris. The tables have since turned in the posthumous reputations of these two men, but Meissonier had his money to spend and Van Gogh did not.

# 14. Sculpture in the Making

'The crowd', observed Rodin 'goes into ecstasies over poses which are never seen in nature and which are considered artistic because they recall the posturings of the Italian models who offer themselves at the studio. That is what is generally called beautiful drawing. It is only sleight of hand, fit to astonish boobies.'[1]

Rodin only slowly gained recognition after repeatedly being turned down by the Ecole des Beaux-Arts and after working upon architectural sculpture. There were few dealers who would organise sculptural exhibitions, and consequently the Salon continued to provide a major exhibiting opportunity for sculptors. Furthermore, their costs for accommodation, materials, equipment and the transportation of works were high. The position of the sculptor was distinct from that of the painter. Beginning an apprenticeship, unless a student at the Beaux-Arts, led to decorative architectural work, as for Rodin and Dalou, and it was difficult to escape the status of an artisan executing the work of others. Even when the apprentice progressed to working under a master in his studio, this still involved assisting in his work. Much that was practical and technical could be learnt efficiently in this way, but it did not encourage the development of the individual's talent unless the master were quite extraordinary in his outlook and attitude.

The status of sculpture was frequently considered to be less elevated than that of painting. Despite the achievements of Barye and Carpeaux this remained largely the case until the eventual emergence of Rodin. His technical fluency and brilliance provided sculpture with the status of work of the imagination, highly charged with emotion and ideas, bearing literary and religious meanings that far outstripped the artisan's approach to commissioned work or the architectural sculptor's vocabulary of decorative motifs from triglyph to caryatid.

67. Auguste Rodin with the Duchesse de Choiseul at the Hôtel Biron, Paris. The walls are lined with hundreds of drawings slipped into frames.

Dalou's image of good tuition was far from that generally available: 'How do I understand teaching? An atelier of five or six students, at the most, with a master who knows how to teach the elements of his discipline and who leads you with confidence to the ends of art, who helps you understand nature through the museum, who makes you return to nature upon leaving the museum'.[2] More common, for the fortunate, was to assist with a master's own commissions, as Rodin did under the successful Carrier-Belleuse from whose oeuvre early works by Rodin are still being discovered and reattributed.

The realisation of a sculptural idea presupposed an interplay with the material and what it would permit, be it a block of stone or mass of clay, an interchange of will and material qualitively different from handling the pliant pigments of painting. Consequently the process of evolving a sculpture was different. The initial idea could of course begin with drawings and the sketchbook as with a painter, although the sculptural concept would be three-dimensional so that the disposition of figures, masses and spaces was essentially unlike that of a painter's drawing which envisaged the disposition of masses, rhythms and lines across a flat surface. For the sculptor the organisation of lines and forms presumed their three-dimensional realisation in which changing silhouette and a shifting viewpoint demanded an awareness of masses and planes in a more complex continuity of surface. In addition the practised sculptor would instinctively bear in mind the physical difficulties of supporting the weight of parts of his sculpture and the opportunities afforded by different materials, each of which demanded distinct disciplines and processes.

68. Ernest Barrias, *The Mother of Cain*, c. 1885, terracotta, Petit Palais, Paris.

Drawings could be used for a variety of purposes. As well as recording an initial idea, they could be used to build up a library of poses. Rodin covered whole walls with rapid drawings from the moving figure and this provided a changing sequence of images to edit and relate one to another in defining his sculptural compositions (Plate 67).

More explicit than drawings, were wax or clay studies rapidly modelled from life. At the maquette, or model stage, the main rhythms embodied in poses, hollows, solids, planes and edges or silhouettes could be established in three-dimensional space without resolving questions of detail and without any painstaking finish being applied. Ernest Barrias' terracotta maquette for a sculpture entitled *The Mother of Cain* is an example of this (Plate 68). This immediacy and directness is now increasingly appreciated and maquettes, which reveal so much of the sculptor's working process are now more frequently exhibited. In essence they were studio works, made as preliminary studies and not as exhibition pieces although Rodin was instrumental in blurring this distinction. Barrias' terracotta has all the drama and anguish of his theme expressed in the tension of the two figures stretching away from each other over the collapsed figure of the murdered son. The immediacy of the process of modelling and cutting into the pliable terracotta was not achieved by Barrias in his highly finished and prosaic large-scale sculptures for monumental sites or for the Salon.

Terracotta, cheap and responsive to manipulation, was ideal for capturing observations of the figure and compositional ideas in this way. Once fired and fixed in its configuration of forms, it provided a permanent record of this stage of the project in hand. Several variants could be evolved in this manner for future reference. Terracotta maquettes were intended to be useful and despite their usually small size often had a sense of inherent scale that was related to the envisaged final work. The problems of finish and detail were irrelevent in the maquette, permitting the sculptor to define his forms by modelling, by cutting into the clay or by building it up with small pellets of clay.

However, terracotta could also be used for finished works, and in the eighteenth century had been much employed in this way — particularly for small-scale intimate

69. Jules Dalou, *Foundry Worker*, c. 1895, terracotta, 19 cm. high, Petit Palais, Paris. A study for Dalou's *Monument to Labour*. The face is hidden by the industrial mask of the metal-worker.

70. (*facing page, top left*) Auguste Rodin in working clothes, photograph from 1880, albumen print, 21.8 × 16.8 cm., Musée Rodin, Paris.

71. (*facing page, top right*) August Rodin with the plaster version of *The Hand*.

72. (*facing page below*) Edouard Dantan, *A Corner of the Studio*, 1880, oil on canvas, Musée des Arts Decoratifs, Paris. The sculptor is working on a relief of the *Triumph of Silenus*.

subjects. Dalou admired such works, as did Carrier-Belleuse. In its material qualities and its firing in a kiln, terracotta retained associations with ceramic works, and ceramic sculpture continued to be produced at the Sèvres factories near Paris.

Dalou made extensive use of terracotta for his projected but unrealised *Monument to Labour*. Plaster was used for the architectural model of the tower, around the base of which were niches housing workers of various trades (Plate 69). Terracotta was used to define more clearly the forms of the individual figures. Whilst a polished surface is not presented in the terracottas, all of the dramatic basic forms are established and the compositional features are fully resolved.

For larger preparatory studies terracotta was awkward and firing large works was a difficult and sometimes disastrous undertaking which could completely destroy the original. The unique properties of plaster were much more useful. Whilst an armature would be required, demanding a degree of premeditated certainty over the pose of a figure plaster set hard without the need for firing. It could be used wet or it could be carved dry, permitting effects of fluidity or of a highly finished surface. Whilst the finished plaster was relatively fragile, it also allowed details of surface to be resolved with precision. A photograph of Rodin emphasises the messiness of the process (Plate 70) and the sculptor's close exploration of his physical materials, qualitively different from that of the painter, and an essential feature of the sculptor's daily practice. Quite apart from the capacity of plaster to define representational detail, it recorded with the same clarity the sculptor's process of work, and every shift of surface, form and outline (Plate 71).

The most important use of plaster was to bring a sculpture to its final form before casting in bronze. The revival of the accurate and ancient lost-wax method of bronze-casting allowed minutely precise reproduction of the plaster original. Works in plaster were often therefore proposals for works in bronze, associated for example, with competitions for monuments. For all its frailty and weight the large plaster sculpture gave a detailed impression of a potential bronze and was much used in this way at the Salon where the City of Paris would purchase plaster sculptures and simultaneously provide the major funding required for translation into bronze and subsequent erection in the street.

By contrast, the slow and irreversible process of stone-carving demanded physical stamina and completely different skills and techniques. Plaster could be carved and on a medium scale remained cheap; furthermore, the materials were relatively easily portable. The stone-carver, whether working in granite or marble, had to manipulate considerable weights both to and from the studio (Plate 72). Not surprisingly the sculptor's studio was almost always a factory-like assemblage on the ground floor with ready access to transport. Before attacking the stone, the sculptor needed a clear idea of his finished forms which at various stages could be drawn upon the block. He needed also a thorough knowledge, learnt from experience, of the ways in which particular kinds of stone, and even particular blocks of it would respond to carving. In the carving, the aims of the artist and the demands of his material were involved in a close interplay if the result were to be successful. Hence, the stone-carver engaged on figurative work often referred to drawings and maquettes, to anatomical models and to the life-model during the process of carving, when any slip of the chisel, hit too hard or in the wrong direction, in ignorance of the stone's grain or weaknesses, could be disastrous. The finished surface was necessarily approached slowly by a painstaking process. To carve a complex free-standing composition in marble, such as Barrias' *First Funeral* (Plate 73), again on the theme of Cain and Abel, required skill and control, not merely in the smoothly finished and academically explicit anatomy but in the irrevocable cutting away of large volumes of stone, and in the delicate care demanded when carving the scarcely supported legs which extend into the space outside the main mass of the work. A sculpture of this kind involved cutting all around the central core of the mass of stone,

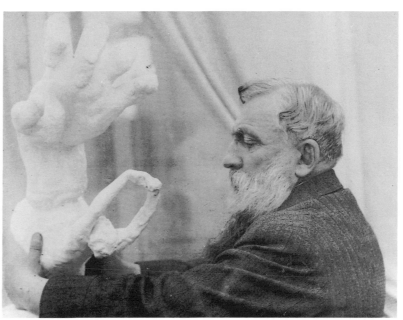

preserved here where the bodies join. To achieve this, mechanical processes of copying were frequently employed, in particular the use of the pointing machine which permitted drilling of the block to measured points as well as the enlargement or reduction of a sculpture.

The sheer physical labour of such an undertaking called for rationalisation of a sculptor's time and effort. Two distinct phases were discernible: cutting away the majority of surplus stone in order to rough in the sculpture, and finishing the sculpture. In practice, assistants normally executed the first phase, which nonetheless had its risks, and the sculptor concentrated his efforts on the latter stage. He had also, of course, defined the sculpture in his preliminary studies.

Such assistants were known as *practiciens*. The painter Gaudefroy exhibited a picture of one of Dalou's *practiciens*, in this case working on a final plaster for *La République* at the Salon of 1889 (Plate 74). 'We open the door', wrote Paul Mantz, 'of a studio where one of the modest collaborators of the master's works on the execution of Dalou's high relief, *The Republic*.'[3] The painting was bought by the State. Dalou had worked unsuccessfully as a *practicien* during his years in London. It was one source of income for a sculptor. For work in marble Dalou used *practiciens* extensively before completing the carving himself. Rodin, working with marble in mind, evolved works initially in clay and made plaster casts for execution in marble by *practiciens*. The same plaster casts could be used for bronze casting. The *practicien* was frequently an essential figure in the process of executing the final version of a major work. It was the artist's duty to organise his workshop and procedures in a way that overcame the difficulties of materials and assistants to produce the sculpture.

Materials, equipment, *practiciens*, models, maquettes, firing and casting made the sculptor's studio into a workshop (Plate 75). The expense involved demanded a particular kind of patronage, particularly if large bronzes were undertaken for this also entailed the services of specialist foundries and considerable costs. This meant that

73. (*facing page*) Ernest Barrias, *The First Funeral*, 1878–83, marble, Parc de l'Hôpital Ste-Anne, Paris.

74. Alphonse Gaudefroy, *The Practicien, c.* 1888, oil on canvas, bought by the State 1889. Whereabouts unknown. This line engraving of the painting was published in the *Catalogue Illustré* of the Salon des Champs-Elysées, 1889. The assistant is working on Dalou's relief *La Republique*.

75. The Studio of the sculptor A. Croisy. Work is in progress on a funeral monument with maquettes in evidence.

76. Edgar Degas, *The Tub*, *c.* 1886, bronze, 50 × 21.6 cm., Hébrard cast, The Art Institute of Chicago (Wirt D. Walker Fund, 1950).

77. Jules Dalou, *Tomb of Victor Noir*, 1890, bronze, Père Lachaise Cemetry, Paris.

major works, if envisaged in bronze, were usually unrealisable unless related to a specific and usually public project. Thus, the use of materials is related to patronage, and as a result of this the sculptor was more closely committed to both a public role, and often a political role, that was not so urgently felt by the painter. The intimacy of *The Tub* by Degas is emphasised by its loose handling (Plate 76), whilst a greater degree of finish is required for a public monumental work such as Dalou's *Tomb of Victor Noir* in Père Lachaise Cemetry (Plate 77). Here the outward signs of the modelling are expunged though it makes use of a similarly high viewpoint. Degas' sculpture is closer to a maquette in its handling. His only exhibited sculpture, the *Little Fourteen-year-old Dancer* was highly finished, but his bronzes of this kind were cast after his death. Dalou, on the other hand, was executing a public sculpture with a political aim in mind, representing the assassinated journalist Victor Noir with all the realism that he could muster.[4] Dalou's was a revolutionary work but any major public bronze required substantial funding from subscriptions or from patrons, often corporate and even governmental and for whom a monumental sculpture had a more or less political role. To execute a major bronze meant acknowledging the patron's aims. In this, the professionalism of the sculptor was subject to pressures closer, perhaps, to those felt by the architect than the painter. To reconcile the sculptor's private aims and individual abilities with the aims of a commissioning body and the public's response was difficult. The effects of such pressure could influence the scale, site and even the viewpoint of a work as well as its subject and medium. To be too independent or original was to court financial disaster, rejection or unsympathetic display of the sculpture. Rodin faced this several times. The figures of his *Burghers of Calais* were designed for a low base: 'The people of today, almost elbowing them, would have felt more deeply the tradition of solidarity which unites them to these heroes. It would have been, I believe, intensely impressive. But my proposal was rejected, and they insisted upon a pedestal which is as unsightly as it is unnecessary.'[5]

\*   \*   \*

78. Honoré Daumier, *The Sad Face of Sculpture placed amongst the Paintings*, 1857, lithograph, published in *Charivari* 22 July 1857. Daumier is open-mouthed in top hat at left.

With its traditions of a different kind of illusionism to that of painting, with colour integral to its material, with its distinct processes and attitudes to scale, viewpoint, space and site, sculpture was less prolific and less well appreciated than painting both at the Salon and in other exhibitions. Daumier, himself a sculptor as well as lithographer and painter, had recognised this in 1857, as a lithograph of that year illustrates: it depicts *The Sad Face of Sculpture Placed amidst Painting* (Plate 78). The people seated around the sculpture's plinth stare at the pictures: they ignore the sculpture.

Yet looking at sculpture required special techniques: greater familiarity with the flat images of painting militated against appreciation of a handling of surface, plane and contour, considerations of the utmost concern to the practising sculptor. This gulf was deepened by photographic reproductions reducing sculpture to a convenient flat surface devoid of scale, weight, variety of viewpoint and most other material qualities, stressing instead only the image and proportions seen from a fixed viewpoint. The sculptor himself, who had fashioned every aspect of the work, could look with different eyes. His subtle effects could be destroyed by overcrowding, bad placing against a wall, or by bad lighting. Yet the articulation of a surface could be seen as rich and revealing subtle control, as Rodin demonstrated to Paul Gsell whilst inspecting an antique marble in his own collection at Meudon: 'He lighted a lamp as he spoke, took it in his hand, and led me towards a marble statue which stood upon a pedestal in a corner of the atelier.' It was a small copy of the Venus de Medici. 'He slowly turned the moving stand which supported the Venus. As he turned, I...noticed in the general form of the body a

79. Heavy sculptures delivered by horse and cart to the Grand Palais for the Salon of the Société des Artistes Français of 1893.

multitude of almost imperceptible roughnesses, what at first seemed simple was really of astonishing complexity.'[6]

In the crush of the Salon there was little hope of such sympathetic and sensitive display. In the mass of exhibits, the demand for scale and drama necessary to attract the attention of visitors, critics and patrons, overrode such subtle questions. Even delivery of sculptures to the Salon was a struggle which required planning and forethought, carts, horses, hoists and ramps (Plate 79). As with paintings, prime sites were sought competitively. Rodin's rise to notoriety and ultimate glory is revealed in a photograph of the sculpture display at the 1898 Salon de la Société Nationale des Beaux-Arts where his *Balzac* occupied a prime site framed by semicircular collonades on the main axis of the great iron exhibition hall. Rodin was in fact on innovator in the display and siting of his works. Just as he had sought a minimal plinth for the *Burghers of Calais*, so at the Salon of 1899 he exhibited his bronze *Eve* with its integral bronze base buried in sand in order to increase its realism and minimise the loftiness (both figurative and physical) associated with the use of a plinth. Rodin was a celebrated figure by the 1890s, but it was 1906 before the first of his works was placed on a prominent public site in Paris.

\*     \*     \*

In 1886 Raffaëlli painted the bronze-caster Eugène Gonon at work in his foundry in Paris (Plate 81). He is depicted with four assistants piecing together the final and highest relief element of Dalou's enormous sculpture of *Mirabeau replying to Dreux-Brézé in the Meeting of 23rd June 1789* (Plate 82). Dalou's colossal relief illustrates the moment just after the French revolutionary has uttered the words 'we are here by the will of the people; only bayonets will remove us', a subject effectively stressing the continued viability and vigour of Republicanism in the Third Republic: the relief had a political purpose. Gonon was an essential contributor to its realisation. Dalou had received the commission for a plaster model on 15 October 1881. A year later, he was ready to cast his clay version in plaster which was in turn cast in bronze by Gonon in 1882. Dalou was extremely eager to produce a bronze which corresponded in the smallest details to his original and Gonon was a particularly significant choice of founder in this, for his father, Honoré Gonon, had been instrumental in the revival of the lost-wax (*cire perdue*) bronze-casting process which had tended to give way to the cheaper less precise modern industrial process of sand-casting. Sand-casting allowed the workmen to adjust the forms of the cast in a manner impossible in the lost-wax process. Gonon was continuing his father's revival of the old technique used in ancient times and in the Renaissance. It involved making a precise negative cast, or mould, from the original, executed in sections for later assembly. The moulds were coated with a layer of wax with tubes extending through the mould through which melting wax would escape as moulten liquid bronze was poured into the assembled mould replacing the wax which was therefore 'lost'. In this way the outer surface of the bronze corresponded accurately to the original. A highly specialised and dangerous process, bronze-casting was rarely undertaken by sculptors, who relied upon experts in the technique. Ironically, it was the very expertise of Gonon which permitted Dalou's work to be cast so precisely: the caster himself made no alteration to the form, and needed all his skill for his contribution to remain unnoticed. For all the danger and despite the expert technique needed by the bronze-caster, Dalou considered that 'a caster, as able as he might be, is only a collaborator of the same order as a *practicien* for execution in marble'.[7] Furthermore, the colour of a bronze patination could be adjusted with applied chemical treatments and Dalou was eager to avoid this too, in the belief that the patination produced by weather was preferable to that produced by founders. Only after his death did Dalou permit industrial casts of his work in order to provide income for a charity and for his daughter. In his lifetime he was scrupulous, insisting on the lost-wax process even for his enormous *Triumph of the Republic*. Casters' marks and signatures are normally to be found discreetly applied in bronze sculptures. The *Triumph of the Republic* was cast by Thiébaut Frères of Paris, one of the most prolific of contemporary foundries for bronze-casting, used also by Barrias, Bartholdi, Sarah Bernhardt, Chapu, Falguière and many other sculptors.

80. Jean-Alexandre Falguière, *Diana, c.* 1882, bronze, 43.5 × 40 × 26.1 cm., Smith College Art Museum, Northampton, Mass. (given by Mrs H. Ellis Straw in 1972 in loving memory of her sister Ruth W. Higgins)

The cast bronze would require finishing to remove the sticks of bronze which had filled the discharge tubes through which the wax escaped, and to remove ridges which indicated the edges of adjoining sections of the mould. In a complex sculpture these could be numerous. They appear on plaster casts too, and Rodin sometimes retained them on a finished piece. Rodin almost always worked with the bronze-caster Alexis Rudier in Paris. As Rodin preferred bronze as a medium, their working relationship was of critical importance in Rodin's career. Bronzes could also be reproduced so that a sculpture could appear in a limited edition, marked 1/7, for example, indicating the first cast of an edition of seven. Bronze-casters were also on occasions employed to reproduce works in bronze after an artist's death, as in the case of Degas. This makes it difficult to ascertain the originality of a bronze. In this respect, and in the production of an edition, the bronze has some of the advantages and ambiguous status of a print. By the use of the pointing-machine and other processes sculptures could also be reduced in scale by assistants, and in the case of a popularly successful work, could be sold in considerable numbers on a scale suitable for a domestic context. An example of this is Falguière's *Diana* (Plate 80), the original of which was executed in 1882, and which appeared in a larger marble version at the Salon of 1887 but which also sold well in popular reduced versions. Despite the high cost of bronze-casting, such practices could

81. Jean-François Raffaëlli, *At the Foundry* (Chez le fondeur), 1886, oil on canvas, 128 × 116 cm., Musée des Beaux-Arts, Lyon.

82. Jules Dalou, *Estates General, Meeting of 23 June 1789. Mirabeau responding to Dreux-Brézé*, 1883, bronze, 236 × 654 cm., Salle Casimir-Perier, Chambre des Députés, Paris.

83. Enlarging the hand of Bartholdi's *Liberty* at Gaget, Gauthier et Cie workshops, Paris, Photograph from 1876–81, Musée Bartholdi, Colmar.

be highly rewarding financially for the sculptor as long as he could reproduce the original. But this was rarely possible in the case of monumental commissions. The successful sculptor's studio had to be run with astute business acumen if bronzes were to emerge; *practiciens*, founders and assistants were all important contributors to the work which carried the artist's name and reputation to the public. Hence it's resemblance to a factory.

The workshops of the foundry, facilities for casting in plaster, kilns for firing terracotta, hoists, transport facilities, the services of models and *practiciens*, as well as accommodation, had to be paid for, and the costs were inevitably high compared with the painter's simpler requirements of light, space, canvas, paints and frames. Furthermore exhibiting opportunities were fewer. Colossal sculpture involved engineering as well as architectural scale. The ultimate example of this was Bartholdi's *Liberty Enlightening the World*, known popularly as the *Statue of Liberty* (see Plate 215). The engineer Eiffel, whose Tower of 1889 still dominates Paris, perfected the structural support of *Liberty*. The commission was highly political in nature. After its completion and temporary erection in Paris, the colossal sculpture was shipped to New York where it stands at the entrance to the harbour, a gift from the French Republic to the American Republic rich in political connotations.

The sculpture is now the focus of distinctly American associations, largely still political in their way; the fact that it is a French sculpture and even the name of its sculptor remains obscure. Its construction in Paris was an immense undertaking as photographs of the work in process reveal (Plates 83–4). It was executed in the workshops of Gaget, Gauthier and Company at 25 Rue Chazelles, a firm which had constructed the cupola of the Paris Opéra. The process was intricate and precise requiring several models, including a full-size plaster version in sections built over wooden armatures and also carved wooden templates onto which the copper sheets of the final work were hammered. These were eventually assembled together and attached by flexible rods to Eiffel's hidden and rigid inner framework. This combination made the sculpture as light as possible with each section flexibly and independently attached to

84. *Work on one of the fingers of Liberty*, Cabinet des Estampes, Bibliotèque Nationale, Paris.

85. Emmanuel Frémiet, *Gorilla Carrying off a Woman*,
version of 1887, bronze, 44.5 × 30.5 cm., Musée
d'Histoire Naturelle, Paris.

the core, permitting heat expansion in the metal, as well as transportation and erection in sections. Photographs of the workshops reveal a scene recalling Paranesi's engravings of fantastic architecture. The colossal arm is visible with a smaller version alongside, whilst in the foreground workmen construct the wooden templates. *Liberty* was the ultimate public sculptural commission of the period, involving enormous funding, innovative engineering, and a whole factory of workmen and machinery to realise the sculptor's and the government's aim. It was the antithesis of the informal, private studio work. It involved many studies over many years and numerous committees. In an extreme form, it illustrates the engagement of the sculptor with politics on projects of large-scale public sculpture.

At the opposite extreme was the reproduction of sculpture for the individual purchaser, and this no less than large works involved factory processes and intricate financial planning. F. Barbedienne, who worked with the founder Siot, had devised a mechanical reducing process which was in use before the mid-century to permit the multiple reductions of successful sculptures. Gérôme, Dubois, Mercié and other fashionable sculptors used the process. Some bronzes were marked Siot-Decauville after the foundry, others Barbedienne after the inventor of the reducing process. By such means the sculptor could respond to his public market, making maximum use of his sculptural idea, and his expenditure of effort, time and money, to realise income from a wide range of purchasers who were all able to buy a particular celebrated work. The *Boule-Player* by the painter-sculptor Gérôme exists in a plaster version and in a version carved in marble, covered in wax and tinted, but it was also cast in bronze in three sizes, sometimes gilded or silvered. The small version was highly popular and a large edition was published. Similarly, Frémiet's bizarre eye-catcher, the *Gorilla Carrying off a Woman*, originally rejected at the Salon of 1859, in a subsequent second version became a popular success in 1887 and was issued as a reduced-scale bronze to meet popular demand (Plate 85). Such success encouraged a sculptor to respond again to a proven market and in 1895 Frémiet followed this success with the equally bizarre *Orangoutang Strangling a Native of Borneo*.

Some sculptors considered that the particular qualities of scale and specific materials precluded the reproduction and reduction of sculptures. Dalou was against this procedure in principle: 'A work is made for one material and to change them is to denature the work.'[8] Rodin however used many variations of his sculptures on several scales and in several materials. It made financial sense, and in Rodin's case, it made creative sense too.

Large scale was crucial to public monuments set up in the street. Haussmann's construction of the great boulevards of Paris gave the city a structure in which long, wide avenues converged upon focal points each of which provided sites ideal for major monuments. The Arc de Triomphe at *L'Etoile* had established an important precedent with its colossal sculpture of the *Marseillaise* by François Rude. Such public sculpture had a clear political purpose in the wake of the French Revolution, inspiring patriotism and a sense of political identity. During the Third Republic this purpose continued. The embellishment of Paris proceeded vigorously and critics spoke of 'statuemania'. In the absence of royal patronage, the government commissioned monuments to the Republic and to national heroes in military, historical and cultural spheres. In addition, monuments were raised by public subscription, sometimes associated with exhibitions. Dalou's *Monument to Delacroix* evolved this way. There was a demand for grandiose monumental sculpture which altered the appearance of the city and became public property. Competitions and subscriptions became a standard means of commissioning public sculpture, complementing even government commissions. Hence, substantial numbers of people became involved in a communal process of commissioning sculptures that altered the appearance of the streets, squares and public gardens of Paris.

# 15. Sites

Insofar as sculpture in the street relied upon sites defined by street-plans and adjacent buildings, the sculptor was caught up in architecture and city-planning in a way not available to the painter. As monumental works became part of public consciousness, the sculptor reached a far wider audience. Conversely, he lost much of his independence in the process and his profession necessitated the blending of personal creative ambitions with civic ambitions, a task not always accomplished with success, as Rodin's highly individual, inventive and problematic responses to public commissions revealed. It was necessary for a sculptor to carry the committee with him.

A sculptor's career not unusually began with the architecture of the street. Rodin worked on the restoration of medieval sculpture in an architectural context and Dalou executed architectural decorations even in his successful years, as his work at 6 Rue de Clignancourt of 1894 exemplifies. In the architectural context, sculpture could emphasise the focal point of a building and might need to be intelligible from extraordinary and distant viewpoints. Frémiet's *St Michael*, for example, needed an emphatic and clear profile to be seen on the highest pinacle of Mont St Michel off the coast of Normandy, a consideration lost in the reduced bronze versions produced for purchase: the detailed modelling becomes discernible on these versions whilst on Mont St Michel fine work was completely invisible.

The work by Rodin most closely associated with a specific fixed site from the commissioning stage onwards was *The Gates of Hell*. The commissioners intended Rodin to decorate doors for the Musée des Arts Decoratifs. After decades of work, the doors were a practical impossibility and the commission was abandoned. Instead they became one of the most fecund of Rodin's sculptures, spawning a multitude of motifs which Rodin evolved as independent works, of which the *Thinker* is one of many examples. The personal and creative importance of the doors exceeded by far the requirements of the commission. Personal and public ambitions could not in this case be reconciled. The work is seen in plaster dominating photographs of Rodin's Meudon studio about 1900, in all its magnificence and complexity amidst a multitude of the busts and figurative works that Rodin produced with such prolific and inexhaustible profusion (Plate 86). Yet the commission itself was as problematic as were the *Burghers of Calais* and the *Monument to Balzac*.

86. Rodin's studio at Meudon, photograph from *c.* 1900. Rodin's *Gates of Hell* dominate the background.

The Société des Gens de Lettres had originally commissioned the fashionable sculptor Chapu in 1888 to produce a monument to Balzac to stand in the Place Palais Royal. On Chapu's death in 1891 advice was sought from Falguière, Dubois and Mercié, all celebrated sculptors, who recommended that Chapu's maquette be enlarged by *practiciens*. Zola, as the new president of the society, rejected this advice and commissioned Rodin whose monument was eventually found unsuitable in 1898. The commission passed to Falguière and was completed by Dubois in 1902. Such difficulties illustrate the need to persuade committees and integrate their aims, which may remain unclear, into the finished work if the commission and all the work and expense involved were to proceed successfully to the installation of the sculpture in the street.

A safer process was to buy already completed work at the Salon, a policy employed by the City of Paris. Work could also be acquired by the Luxembourg Museum as an honour for display in the Museum or the Luxembourg Gardens. Dalou in fact insisted that his *Triumph of Silenus* of 1885 be installed in the Gardens rather than the Museum itself (Plate 87).

87. Jules Dalou, *The Triumph of Silenus*, installed 1898, bronze (Thiébaut cast), Luxembourg Gardens, Paris.

The public gardens of Paris are rich in sculptures which stand out against the trees of the Tuileries Gardens, the Luxembourg Gardens, the Jardin des Plantes and elsewhere. Such sites permitted good visibility in changing light, intimate settings free of the overtly political rhetoric of the street or the severity of the gallery. Many sculptors of the period 1880–1900 provided works for these gardens. Often they were funded by special committees and subscriptions. When the *Monument to Delacroix*, sited near the Luxembourg Palace was paid for by public subscription (Plate 89), the committee formed in 1884 for this purpose contained many of the most celebrated artists of the day, amongst whom were Bonnat, Bouguereau, Breton, Cabanel, Fantin-Latour, Gérôme, Lord Leighton, Meissionier, Puvis de Chavannes, Alfred Stevens, with the sculptors

88. Paul-Albert Bartholomé, *Monument to the Dead*, 1895, stone, Père Lachaise Cemetry, Paris.

89. Jules Dalou, *Monument to Delacroix*, 1887. Inaugurated 1890, bronze and stone, Luxembourg Gardens, Paris.

Dalou, Dubois and Falguière as well as Durand-Ruel, Antonin Proust, Rochefort, Sir Richard Wallace and Albert Wolff. Dalou won the commission and the monument was inaugurated in the Luxembourg Gardens on 5 October 1890. Unfortunately, the foundry employed underestimated the cost of casting the sculpture (estimated cost 40,000 francs, actual cost 50,000 francs), and the shortfall had finally to be paid off secretly by Dalou's friends.[1]

After the square, the street and the garden, the cemetery provided a major source of income for sculptors in the provision of portrait busts, medallions and funerary monuments. The immense Parisian cemetery of Père Lachaise, which contains the tombs of many renowned French and foreign figures, remains one of the most important collections of French sculpture. At its core is the dramatic and pathetic *Monument to the Dead* by Bartholomé (Plate 88). It provides the vanishing point of the cemetery's central avenue; its descending lines of grieving figures flanking the dark and empty rectangle of the door of the tomb, succinctly point not to particular religious images but to a simple expression of absence and loss.

To Dalou's *Tomb of Victor Noir* in Père Lachaise Cemetery, and the large collection of works by David d'Angers and his generation, the 1880s and 1890s added those of Mercié, Chapu, Barrias and others. Here also are found the tombs of artists, of Ingres, Couture, Corot, Daubigny, Baudry and Delacroix who insisted upon a monument of the utmost plainness which contrasts sharply with the spectacular monument by Dalou in the Luxembourg Gardens (Plate 89).

Dalou's *Tomb of Victor Noir* (see Plate 77) was funded by a national subscription. Dalou charged no fee. The plaster was exhibited at the Salon of 1890 and the effigy was inaugurated on 15 July 1891. The figure, devoid of all stylistic flourishes, lies at knee-level in starkly realistic pose recalling rividly the assassination of the journalist by Prince Pierre Bonaparte in 1870. Dalou depicts the body as if seen after the shooting. His ruthless realism made a political point. The funeral had witnessed a near battle between gendarmes and mourners. Victor Noir, a committed republican journalist had visited Prince Bonaparte as the second in a duel and was shot dead at the door. The trial declared the Prince innocent and republican feeling was infuriated. Dalou, himself a republican, made of this restrained and potent tomb sculpture a permanent reminder of the shooting and its circumstances by dispensing entirely with religious motifs and by achieving striking realism.

*　　*　　*

Big monumental sculpture was placed at major focal points in the network of Parisian boulevards. The Arc de Triomphe has no less than twelve radiating roads spreading out from it. Such a massive monument was visible therefore over a large area of Paris. City-planning rendered the site a focal point of the city's activity. Later monuments which followed this procedure included the July Column at the Place de la Bastille. In this way the city-scape was punctuated in a dramatic fashion by a series of patriotic monuments frequently in view.

The Third Republic for political purposes sought to strengthen parallels with the period of the French Revolution. The Universal Exposition of 1889 was the supreme example of this, as it marked the hundredth anniversary of the French Revolution. The three largest monuments of the 1880s were all associated with celebrating the Republic. Two of them, Léopold and Charles Morice's *Monument to the Republic*, and Dalou's *Triumph of the Republic* were erected at the intersections of major thoroughfares in Paris, whilst the third, *Liberty Enlightening the World*, was transported to New York as we noted earlier. The first two are related by a single commission, established in 1879 to erect a monument to the Republic at the Place de la République. The sculptor Léopold Morice, collaborating with his architect brother won the commission with a design featuring a large figure, symbolising the Republic, mounted on a high cylindrical pedestal flanked by torch-bearing figures. On a broader pedestal beneath this were mounted twelve bronze reliefs illustrating significant events of the French Republics, ranging from the beginnings in the storming of the Bastille to the Revolution of 1848 and the Franco-Prussian War and 14 July 1880. In front of this plinth stood a large bronze lion. The panels stressed the links between the First Republic and the Third; they could be read in sequence by walking around the monument. The assemblage as a whole was otherwise static and vertical in its distribution of forms. Whilst the precise centre of the busy cross-roads was pinpointed by the figure visible at a distance, the intricate panels invited close inspection.

Dalou's role in the commission was curious and the outcome spectacular. He had played an active role in the Commune of 1870 in Paris. In the midst of the slaughter and destruction, he became involved with the Federation of Artists of Paris which planned an end to state intervention in art, except to propose that the state employ artists for public commissions. The Federation set up a body to protect the Louvre Museum and Dalou was stationed in the Louvre for this purpose. This did not prevent the destruction by fire of the Palais des Tuileries at the Louvre. On the collapse and bloody defeat of the Commune, Dalou fled into exile in London returning only in 1879 when an amnesty for communards was declared. This was the year of the competition for the monument to the Republic. Dalou submitted his project anonymously. Whilst he failed to gain the commission itself, his project was accepted for construction at Place de la Nation in Paris, another major intersection of thoroughfares.

In fact his project was not strictly a monument to the Republic but a *Triumph of the Republic* which called upon the ancient format and iconography of the triumphal procession (Plate 90). He exhibited his plaster model, painted to resemble bronze, at the

90. (*a* and *b*) Jules Dalou, *The Triumph of the Republic*, 1879–89, bronze (Thiébaut cast) 12m × 22m × 8m, Place de la Nation, Paris.

91. Jules Dalou, *Study for the Triumph of the Republic*, terracotta, National Gallery of Australia.

Universal Exposition of 1889. Ten years later it was in place and the inauguration attended, according to some sources, by 250,000 people. Dalou was awarded the Grand Ribbon of the Légion d'Honneur. For Dalou and for the Republic which erected it, this work had specific political significance.

The monument was a colossal undertaking requiring forty tons of bronze in the casting, the elaborate intricacy of which was achieved by the Thiébaut foundry. Harnessed lions, on one of which is seated the torch-bearing Genius of Liberty, draw the triumphal carriage. On the carriage and surmounting a globe stands a gigantic figure of the French Republic, robes streaming in the wind. Beside the great bronze wheels at either side stride figures of Justice (female) and Industry (male). A putto accompanies the industrial worker with a collection of tools amongst which are dividers and paint-brushes. Behind the chariot the naked figure of Plenty distributes fruit from a cornucopia.

Terracotta studies show Dalou abandoning the single vertical focus in favour of a dynamic complex of figures urging the chariot forward and full of suggested movement (Plate 91). The rhythm which unites all of the figures and forms emphasises this movement in every detail. As monumental sculpture this is both intricate and massive, making maximum use of chiaroscuro in deeply hollowed-out and intensely dark spaces beneath the chariot, which contrast dramatically with the figure of the Republic silhouetted against the sky. The gesturing baroque poses of the component figures present distinctly different profiles from alternative viewpoints, and presented substantial technical problems to the bronze caster. The monument also presents a series of rich silhouettes when seen from a distance, yet the closest inspection reveals elaborate detail and painstaking control of surfaces. From a distance, the image of the monument is flattened and the viewpoint is horizontal; close inspection reveals the masses spiralling against the sky. In this work the commission fulfilled its purpose in the sculptor's terms and also in terms of its public and political role.

# 16. Public Painting

'The very thing for me, the Hôtel de Ville Job...if I could get it!...It's always been my dream to paint the walls of Paris!' cried Zola's hero in *L'Oeuvre*.[1]

If sculpture could play a public role in the city street, painting within major public buildings could aspire to a comparable role. The Paris Opéra, built between 1861 and 1874, occupies a major site at the junction of great boulevards in the heart of the city. It was decorated with a mass of painting in addition to its wealth of sculptures. The reconstructed Hôtel de Ville was also the focus of commissions for decorative paintings and murals, as were the Panthéon and the New Sorbonne.

At the Opéra, sculpture and painting combined to create an atmosphere of lavish opulence. The main façade incorporates Carpeaux's *Dance*, whilst Barrias and Chapu provided reliefs. The crowning lyre was sculpted by Aimé Millet and the Pegasus groups at the very top were by Lequesne. The enormous ceiling over the auditorium was painted by Lenepveu,[2] and Paul Baudry spent years of exhaustive study preparing the many paintings which decorate the foyer. The Opéra was a focal point of Paris; public, elegant and enormous, its construction was intricate and innovative, with its vast chandelier, its foyers and halls, its great staircases and landings it allowed for relatively few seats in the auditorium. Within this context painting and sculpture played a vigorous, assertive and decorative role, drawing upon major recognised talents of the day, many of whom remained highly active and respected in the 1880s and after.

The civic pride and splendour of the Opéra were continued in the decorations of the Hôtel de Ville. Well over forty artists were commissioned to provide paintings and sculpture. Alongside the academicians of the Institut, Gervex, Benjamin-Constant, J.P. Laurens, Bonnat, Dagnan-Bouveret, Tony Robert-Fleury, Jules Lefèbvre, Cormon, Frémiet, Barrias, Mercié and others, there were the more individual talents of Eugène Carrière and Puvis de Chavannes. Carrière provided small works, Puvis provided magisterial murals depicting *Summer* and *Winter*. Puvis' reputation was at its height by the mid-1880s. His harmonious flattened compositions were authoritative decorative works, constructed in assiduously adjusted intervals of line and colour. They had a profound effect upon many younger artists as numerous painterly and literary tributes to Puvis' talents reveal. He, more than anyone else, had the ability to reconcile public imagery in civic buildings with an awareness of the demands of decorative painting. He was admired not only by Seurat, Gauguin, Denis and Rodin but by a wide band of contemporary artists and critics. His austere control of vast canvases contrasted strongly with the hectic illusionism of other mural painters and he became immensely successful, executing major decorative cycles for Lyons, Amiens and Boston.

Puvis dominated the decorations of the New Sorbonne and Panthéon. His hemicycle for the Sorbonne covers a surface of extraordinary proportions by means of intervals of trees and groups in near-symmetry, comprising a painterly frieze harmoniously divided along its length including nothing superfluous and strict control maintained to the furthest corners. The screen of trees closes-in the picture space, limiting the illusion of depth. The landscape visible through and beyond the trees provides a rhythmic arch which appears to encompass the viewer without suggesting deep recession. The figures are largely painted from in front and are placed one beside another in a rhythmic sequence and are not inserted into a perspective structure. Hence, there is little overlapping of figures, and their scale is fairly evenly maintained across the whole painting. All of these qualities and devices stressed the wall-surface and permitted Puvis

92. J.-L. Ernest Meissonier, *Study for the Triumph of France*, c. 1884, decoration for the Panthéon, Paris.

to reconcile decoration with the depiction of figures caught up in a symbolic theme.

The building was erected in 1885–9 by Nenot, and a didactic purpose was envisaged for the commissioned artworks. Its pediments depicted *Science* (by Mercié) and *Letters* (by Chapu). It housed busts by Delaplanche (*Homer*), Falguière (*Archimedes*), Barrias (*Pascal*) and Dalou (*Lavoisier*), as well as paintings by Puvis, Benjamin-Constant, Lerolle, Cazin, Roll and Lhermitte who abandoned his customary rustic themes to depict an anatomy lesson, at the request of the commissioners who set the themes.

Painting to order, in terms of theme, scale and purpose, was a sign of the artist's professionalism and was embedded in the teaching of the Ecole des Beaux-Arts where the Prix de Rome was pursued along strictly defined lines. Such a manner of selling work relied upon the artist's proven ability to fulfil the commission as the patron wished. Self-expression was necessarily disciplined by this process. It was the antithesis of the easier and flexible system of selling works at either the Salon or at a one-man or independent group exhibition, for the commission preceded the execution of the work. It is not surprising that patrons expending large sums of money deferred to reputation in these circumstances. That reputation relied upon precedent and recognition. The great civic decorative projects, the most prestigious and important commissions of the 1880s and 1890s, necessarily went to established, reputable and reliable artists. Such commissions were themselves a clear sign of recognition and repute before the brush touched the canvas.

If the Opéra stood for cultural celebration, and it is significant that the new building was sited at the core of Paris, the New Sorbonne stood for learning. By contrast the Panthéon stood for both religion and the heroes of France. The great dome of the building completed in 1790 by Soufflot, dominates the Latin Quarter near the Sorbonne. Built on the site of the tomb of St Geneviève as a church dedicated to the patron saint of Paris, it bacame a temple to great French heroes during the French Revolution and was named the Panthéon. It became a church again in 1806 only to revert to the Panthéon after the Revolution of 1830. Reconsecrated in 1851 it was secularised for the burial of Victor Hugo in 1885.

Decorations added in the 1880s indicate the major reputations of the day. Puvis de Chavannes dominated by the authoritative and distinct style of his mural paintings. Meissonier who worked on designs for a *Triumph of France* (Plate 92), oberved: 'Only Puvis de Chavannes holds his own; as for the others they only gild the monument'.[3] Puvis' themes depicted the life of St Geneviève of Paris for the south aisle of the nave and the north aisle of the choir, standing out in the strongest contrast amongst Bonnat's horrific *Martyrdom of St Denis* (see Plate 232), Elie Delaunay's *St Geneviève interceding with Attila* and J.P. Laurens' *Death of St Geneviève*. In addition there were paintings by Cabanel, Lenepveu and a mosaic vault designed by Hébert depicting *Christ showing the Angel of France her Destiny*. Amongst the distinguished figures re-interred at the Panthéon were Emile Zola and Victor Hugo. Rodin's characteristically problematic *Monument to Victor Hugo* was intended to be placed here. There was in addition sculpture commissioned from three of the celebrated sculptors of the time, Frémiet (*Statue of St Gregory of Tours*), Jouffroy (*St Bernard*) and Falguière (*St Vincent de Paul*).

For such an extraordinary synthesis of national pride and religion only the best, and that meant the most esteemed, would suffice. The decorations of the Panthéon sum up the contemporary view of who those artists were. It is significant that Rodin was considered in this context, and it is impressive that Puvis could dominate the commissions without membership of the Institut or a professorial post at the Ecole des Beaux-Arts. He achieved this by his earlier performances in mural decoration. He was in this respect an irresistable candidate.

\*      \*      \*

Decoration preoccupied many artists in the later 1880s and 1890s from Paul Gauguin to Albert Besnard. Without a commitment to public murals and civic pomp, certain patrons commissioned decorations for their homes. Vuillard's decorations for the house of Dr Vaquez are a lavish and extreme example of this. Such commissions were a response to an extraordinary patron, but individual patrons were growing in number and increasingly had the daring, imagination and money to employ experimental and relatively little-established artists. Such decorations as Vuillard's did more than reflect modern-life for they altered the interior dramatically too, making a profound impact upon its appearance: they could no longer be seen as objects merely punctuating the walls of a room.

This applied equally to Vuillard's decorative panels of the public gardens of Paris. They reflected modern life, but also in decorating it, they urged a new awareness of the contemporary city and progressed far beyond the purpose of Salon painting.

The Nabis group, with whom Vuillard was closely associated, seized other opportunities too, particularly in relation to the theatre, by designing sets, costumes and programmes for Lugne-Poë's Théâtre de l'Oeuvre. Such designs brought decoration and painting together and were overtly public without invoking connotations of civic dignity.

Many artists pursued comparable paths in public decorations that were also commercial. The Eden Theatre, for example, a building in an Indian style near the Opéra, had ceilings by Clairin, the close associate of Sarah Bernhardt. Her own theatre (formerly the Théâtre des Nations) was decorated with paintings; in the public foyer looking out onto the square of Le Châtelet hung a dozen tall mural paintings by her friends Clairin, Louise Abbéma and by Alphonse Mucha who also celebrated and promoted her talents in numerous posters. In projects such as these, artists alter the street and public space by developing an art that is commercial, promotional and decorative.

93. Henri de Toulouse-Lautrec, *Paintings decorating La Goulue's booth, erected at La Foire du Trône*, Paris, 1895.

Toulouse-Lautrec also pursued this path. His rough canvases of 1895, several metres high and attached to the *outside* of the booth of the dancer *La Goulue* were emphatically promoting her talents on a monumental scale (Plate 93). His caricature of Oscar Wilde is up to three times life-size. The gusto employed by Lautrec is preserved in all its raw and rapid application. This is a stylistic trait of the painter used for promotional ends, associating an image of dynamic exhuberance with La Goulue as she danced at the Moulin Rouge in order to attract custom to her latest performance after she had left there.

The dividing-line between an art that is promotional and an art that simply reflects modern life can be slender. The theatre and the print made it more so. Meissonier's painting was the ultimate in respectability and his prices were immensely high. Yet his painting of *Polichinelle* is on a popular theme, one that also inspired Manet to execute a comparable lithograph, just as Meissonier's images sold popularly in reproduction. Similarly, themes pursued by Seurat in easel paintings occurred also in posters by Chéret that reached an immense audience through street display and were primarily promotional lithographs. Scenes of the theatre, *café-concert* and circus were painted by Degas, Renoir, Tissot and Seurat, but in the work of Lautrec they may take the form of either easel paintings exhibited at the Moulin Rouge and elsewhere, or that of posters whose primary aim was to promote and advertise particular personalities and events. Here is a confluence of the easel painting, destined for limited exhibition in a salon or gallery with the mass-produced poster destined for a thousand advertisement hoardings. The hoarding provided a new, immense and nonspecialist audience for the artist; the artwork was both original and mass-produced in the poster and the client (who replaced the patron) had his name written large across it. In the process artists turning to posters abandoned the solitude of the studio for the decoration of the street.

They found demanding patrons who recognised that their pictorial talents could sell merchandise. By this process, the individual artwork became less precious for it was no longer unique but it found in return a vast public, and it continued to be collected as we

94

have discussed earlier. The relationship with that public spread a new image of Paris and changed the city in a way beyond the reach of the Beaux-Arts, the Salon and great civic commissions. Posters embodied a vitality, set a tempo and made an impact that had considerable effect upon the life of the theatre and nightclub in particular. They changed the Parisian's awareness not simply of what was available for purchase, but of the artistic richness of the capital of art.

Edmond de Goncourt noted in 1889 of a Chéret exhibition that 'This poster artist really has the laughter of colour and the laughter of physiognomy and the laughter of frisking bodies'.[4] Earlier the same year he had noted in his journal that in Paris 'one sees only posters and collectors of posters'[5]. Degas recounted that the artist Forain compared a painting by Tiepolo 'to a poster by Chéret. It is his way of admiring them. Perhaps it is no worse than any other.'[6]

Chéret, Mucha, Lautrec, Bonnard, Vuillard, Steinlen, Ibels and many others produced posters (Plate 94). Bonnard, Vuillard and Lautrec used the same lithographic studio of the printer Edouard Ancourt. Between 1891 and 1901 Lautrec produced 357 lithographs. As we have noted the lithographic process was effective and economic for posters with long print-runs and its techniques were vigorously explored by artists. Here was a medium that was monumental without being pompous, public without being civic, and decorative without being precious. It challenged the fine art printmaker as much as the painter in his studio. Circumventing the Salon system by a wide margin, it almost circumvented the dealers too. It promoted the artist by promoting a product. On occasions that product could even be an exhibition of paintings.

# 17. The Great Exhibitions

Returned on foot from Rue d'Amsterdam to Auteuil through the crowds. A mauve sky, which the illuminations filled with something like the glow of an enormous fire — the sound of countless footsteps creating the effect of the rushing of great waters — the crowds all in black, that reddish burnt-paper black of the present-day crowds — a sort of intoxication on the faces of the women, many of whom were queuing up outside the lavatories, their bladders bursting with excitement — the Place de la Concorde, an apotheosis of white light, in the middle of which the obelisk shone with the rosy colour of a champagne ice — the Eiffel Tower looking like a beacon left behind by a vanished generation, a generation of men ten cubits tall.[1]

This was Edmond de Goncourt's impression a few days after the opening of the Exposition Universelle of 1889, marking the centenary of the French Revolution, bolstering confidence in the Third Republic and gathering pavilions from many nations around the four massive legs of the Eiffel Tower which provided the newly constructed centre-piece of the Exhibition. In the summer Edmond de Goncourt dined with Zola and others on the platform of the Eiffel Tower:

up there we were afforded a realisation, beyond anything imaginable on ground level, of the greatness, the extent, the Babylonian immensity of Paris, with odd buildings glowing in the light of the setting sun with the colour of Roman stone, and among the calm sweeping lines of the horizon the steep jagged silhouette of Montmartre looking in the dusky sky like an illuminated ruin.[2]

The opinion of many had been outraged by the project to build the 300 metre tower. The proposal, reported the *Art Journal* in 1887, 'has very naturally, excited the

94. Alphonse Mucha, *Sarah Bernhardt as Medea*, 1898, lithographic poster, 208 × 77 cm., Musée des Arts Decoratifs, Paris.

indignation of everyone who has at heart the interest and beauty of Paris. How the abortion got itself accepted as possible and desirable is not yet known.'[3] Seurat was inspired to paint it during construction (Plate 97), but early in 1887 a manifesto had been sent to the Director of Works for the 1889 Exhibition deploring the proposal and claiming that it would dwarf Notre-Dame, the Ste Chapelle, the Tour St Jacques and the Louvre. Amongst the signatories were the highest authorities of the visual arts at the Institut including Meissonier, Bouguereau and Bonnat.

The Exhibition, including the Eiffel Tower, was a colossal success registering over 32,000,000 visitors who stretched the facilities of Paris to the full but brought money, commerce and wonder with them. The unveiling of Dalou's *Triumph of the Republic* in September 1889 further strengthened the image of the Third Republic. Eleven years later in 1900 a further Exposition Universelle was held in Paris and an enormous ferris wheel was constructed revolving slowly above the rooftops of Paris, a circular counterpoint to the 'obelisk' of Eiffel's Tower (Plate 95).

Such Exhibitions concentrated enormous crowds of people of many nationalities into the hotels, hostelries, galleries and museums of a Paris that was expanding. New building was encompassing Montmartre to the north, Montparnasse to the south, and

95. *The Champs de Mars with the Eiffel Tower at the Exposition Universelle of 1900 with the Big Wheel visible in the distance*, Cabinet des Estampes, Bibliothèque Nationale, Paris.

96. L. Fillol, *The Monumental Gate at the Exposition Universelle*, 1900. The portal is surmounted by Moreau-Vauthier's *City of Paris* (or *La Parisienne*)

new suburbs were rising at Auteuil, St Cloud and Neuilly. If the Exhibitions had a national purpose in re-establishing confidence in the Republic after the disaster of the Franco-Prussian war and the Commune, they also had a corresponding international purpose to increase trade and establish Paris as a busy and elegant capital in a productive France. The city was increasingly adorned with sculpture and the ruined buildings were repaired or re-erected. The ruins of the old Tuileries Palace were swept away and new monuments added to the Tuileries gardens and the Luxembourg Gardens. Paris had to appear the thriving heir of a great culture.

The art of Paris was itself a draw to visitors and the visual arts had a central place in these enormous Exhibitions. The effect upon artists was two-fold. There were many commissions arising from the staging of these Exhibitions and there were enormous displays of art organised as part of the events themselves.

At the 1900 Exhibition, for example, the elaborate and domed Monumental entrance was surmounted by an overlife-size figure of the *Parisienne* by the fashionable Moreau-

97. Georges Seurat, *The Eiffel Tower*, 1889, oil on panel, 24 × 15 cm., Fine Art Museum, San Francisco.

Vauthier (Plate 96). The figure appears crude, but Moreau-Vauthier's generalised embodiment of the modern Parisian woman was designed to be seen from a low viewpoint; 48 metres below her silhouette against the sky was more important than detail and she continues the upward curves of the exotic architectural ensemble of which she formed the summit. The strained pose and broad handling of forms show the sculptor fitting into the context of his commission. This sculpture over 6 metres high, was assembled in the studio in the midst of scaffolding and planks with a half-size maqette to one side for reference during enlargement and with a separate small study of the head high up on the scaffolding for detailed reference for the face which required deep eye sockets and a firmly projecting jaw in order to articulate the light and shade when seen from far below (Plate 98). Facial expression was less important at this distance.

The Monumental Entrance and the sculpture were temporary constructions — part of the mass of commissions and competitions directly caused by the Exhibition. The gateway was designed by René Binet to avoid the crush witnessed at the 1889 Exhibition and to deal with 60,000 people per hour approaching the ticket offices. In addition the monumental entrance was decorated with friezes by Guillot and Jouve, electric lamps and coloured and gilt surfaces.

This was only one of the multitude of commissions instigated by the great Exhibitions. They ranged from monumental sculptures and mural paintings for new buildings intended to remain as permanent features of Paris, down to designs for the diplomas and medals awarded. They demanded a large labour force of artists ranging from graphic designers to architects and they consequently provided a wealth of opportunities for artists of every rank from artisan to academician.

Amongst the themes of the Exhibitions, modernity and the achievements of science were an important theme. Despite the apparently ambiguous nature of its function, the Eiffel Tower represented an impressive and innovative feat of engineering technology. By contrast sculptors and painters found few precedents to help them in the depiction of scientific achievement and Barrias' *Electricity* of 1889 scarcely made its message clear with its hefty studio models accompanying a globe with zodiacal signs and plaster lightning flash. On the other hand, the spectacular Palace of Electricity surmounted cascading waterfalls with a mass of architectural sculpture crowned with a figure embedded in an angular star of glass and electric light bulbs. Paris was being transformed by the electric illumination of its streets, parks and skyline. Modernity was posing new problems for painters and sculptors along with new opportunities. Elaborate exhibition buildings demanded an army of stone-carvers and sculptors assembling and installing gigantic sculptures in a hectic race against deadlines. These public works were declamatory and decorative, and some of them were permanent. The Grand Palais, the Petit Palais and the Alexandre III Bridge in Paris were all designed for the Exhibition of 1900 and all still stand. Sculptural groups were a significant feature of them all. Amidst an industrious field of stone-cutters the sculptors climbed the scaffolding with their maquettes to chisel reliefs and figures, precariously mounting planks balanced upon blocks to reach the furthest corners of carvings barely visible from the ground (Plate 99). The iron structure of the Grand Palais, which resembles a giant greenhouse or engine-shed, was clad in intricately carved stone, and the Petit Palais which faces it followed suit.

Inside the Exhibition buildings temporary decorative sculptures in plaster were erected by the hundred in the burgeoning casting workshop. Rarely can plaster have been manipulated on such a scale or used so prolifically as by the professional casters or *mouleurs* at the Exhibitions of 1889 and 1900 in Paris. The large atelier factory for plaster-work set up in the Galerie des Machines in 1900, employed sixty workers at 12–25 francs per day. They enlarged artist's small maquettes in sections to fit shaped wooden replicas of architectural features before the sculptors and ornamentalists

98. Augustin-Jean Moreau-Vauthier, *Monumental figure of the City of Paris, under construction*, 1899–1900. At right is a full length maquette and a small maquette of the head is visible at the top.

99. F. Bell, *Sculptors at work on the Grand Palais*, 1899. The maquette is visible at right.

100. Georges Récipon, *Harmony overcoming Discord*, 1900, copper, Quadriga surmounting the Grand Palais, Paris.

101. *Installing sculpture at the Exposition Universelle*, 1900.

returned to work on them. Finally, moulds were constructed and the *staffeur* poured in the plaster. A contemporary noted that half a sculpture of a child might be seen three metres high leaning against a pier of the building: 'It is the most picturesque confusion where one is astonished that one day there will be born from it an ensemble like that of which the small maquette provides an initial idea'.[4] It then needed transporting and installing — difficult, exacting and prolific work (Plate 101).

For the painters there were competitions ranging from diploma designs to colossal murals. Each had its own committee and competition. Albert Besnard was amongst the candidates for the diplomas in 1900, but the competition was won by Camille Boignard, an unknown 22 year-old student from the Ecole des Beaux-Arts.

All of this was intended to be public, spectacular and optimistic. The surviving monuments from 1889 and 1900 confirm this — from the Eiffel Tower to the Alexander III bridge. Immense amounts of money were expended in constructing the Exhibitions and immense amounts earned. Decorative art played a central role and the artistic community was proffered unprecedented opportunities for recognition and advancement. On the Alexander III Bridge over the Seine 6,000,000 francs were expended, of which 1,000,000 francs were for decoration with bronze figures, stone figures and gilded Pegasus groups. Heavy sculptures were cast and assembled in great numbers for Parisian public gardens; usually over-life size and often naked academic figures emerged between the bushes where none had been before. The sites of Paris became the sights of Paris. The Great Exhibitions provided employment and opportunities for vast numbers of artists and the thousands of artists in Paris responded with alacrity.

\*   \*   \*

102. Joseph Pennell, *Early Evening Effect*, *Paris Exhibition*, 1900, lithograph in grey-blue, 26 × 18 cm., published in *The Studio*, 1901.

At the Exposition Universelle of 1889 two major retrospective exhibitions were held providing reassessments of artistic achievement, one encompassing the art of the previous ten years and the other stretching back to the Revolution of a hundred years earlier. If the Salons were prolific in their display of art in Paris, in 1889 these exhibitions extended the display of art even further. Included amongst the many artists shown at the *Exposition Centennale* were Bastien-Lepage, Béraud, Cazin, Cézanne, Fantin-Latour, Manet, Monet, Pissarro, Puvis de Chavannes, Raffaëlli, Roll and Tissot. The variety was immense and not surprisingly raised many questions by its overview of a hundred years of diverse and often antagonistic developments in art. In addition, the alternative Salons flourished. In the autumn, the Salon des Indépendants opened with works by Anquetin, Dubois-Pillet, Van Gogh, Luce, Lucien Pissarro, Rousseau, Seurat, Signac, Toulouse-Lautrec and others. Dealers exhibitions, group exhibitions and one-man shows all multiplied, filling Paris to capacity with the work of its artists. Critics and spokesmen were busier than ever and the crowd of visitors to Paris was immense. As a factory of art Paris was in full production. The painter Jules Breton was moved to lyricism, declaring 'Let the light which the great Exposition of 1889 has diffused, by bringing together so many masterpieces, long continue to shine'.[5] Breton even accepted the achievements of Manet and Impressionism, and the retrospective exhibitions of 1889 also began to recognise their historical importance. This gradual acceptance was not achieved without discord.

At the Galerie Georges Petit in 1889, Monet and Rodin exhibited together. Rodin resented Monet's placing of his 150 paintings which he felt was unsympathetic to his sculpture. According to Edmond de Goncourt 'The gentle Rodin, emerging suddenly as a Rodin unknown to his friends, declared "I am sick of Monet, I am sick of everyone, I shall think only of myself."'[6] In fact, Monet was still receiving an unsympathetic response from much of the press, yet he was represented by three paintings at the *Exposition Centennale*, and the tide was steadily turning towards recognition and celebrity. A significant indicator of the broad reassessment taking place is the changing response to Manet's achievements. Jules Breton, who saw some qualities in Manet's work, concluded ultimately that Manet 'is a rather mediocre pupil of Goya and Velasquez and later of the Japanese school'.[7] Albert Wolff was convinced that Manet's reputation would sink dramatically leaving only a slight but durable trace in the history of French painting. Wolff disapproved of Manet's disdain for his public and market. He had recounted to Manet with relish that Courbet had criticised the modelling of his *Olympia* (Plate 103), 'It is flat, it is not modelled. It is like a cardgame Queen of spades getting out of a bath'. But Wolff did have the grace to recount also Manet's reply that 'Courbet drives us mad with his modelled forms: *his* ideal is a billiard ball'.[8] Manet's acid wit, like that of Degas, was grudgingly admired by Wolff: 'The cruellest words which circulate in the studios are Manet's',[9] but he was dismayed to see so much of Manet's work filling the studio unsold with apparently little effort being made by Manet to sell it. He considered the looseness of Manet's handling of paint was a result of financial independence which permitted him to dwindle away his wealth whilst producing work that, in the eyes of Wolff, showed neglect of finish and therefore neglect of the market. 'The first sketch is almost always magnificent', noted Wolff, 'but he lacks the artistic education to take it further.'[10] He also recorded the last letter he received from Manet which echoed their long-standing disagreements: 'I thank you, my friend, for the pleasant things you have said about my exhibition, but I would not be dismayed to read at last...the *shocking* article that you will certainly consecrate to me after my death'.[11]

The brushwork of Manet and of the Impressionists appeared to Wolff to result from a wilful lack of finish. Monet, he considered, 'paints as if from an express train'.[12] Manet, he thought, could not or would not finish his paintings to respond to the market. To Wolff such attitudes appeared arrogant and disastrous to his followers. As we have seen the Caillebotte Bequest in 1894, revealed the sustained and bitter opposition displayed

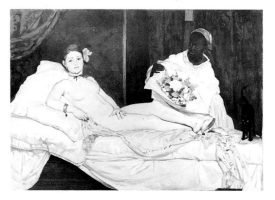

103. Edouard Manet, *Olympia*, 1863, oil on canvas, 130.5 × 190 cm., Musée d'Orsay, Paris.

by the Institut painters towards Impressionist art. The assessment of Manet's achievement was central to that dispute. There was a significant struggle over the inclusion of Manet's *Olympia* in the Centennale exhibition at the Exposition Universelle of 1889. Manet had, as Wolff indicated, spent much of his fortune by his death in 1883, leaving his widow in finanical difficulties. She had priced *Olympia* at 10,000 francs in the studio sale which followed in 1884.[13] In 1889 Monet took the initiative, which was to cost him much effort, of organising a subscription to buy *Olympia* for the Louvre at the price of 20,000 francs. He wrote personally to people he considered sympathetic to Manet, requesting money towards the purchase. 'It is the best hommage that we could render to the memory of Manet,' he wrote to Zola 'and at the same time it is a descreet means of coming of the aid of his widow'.[14] Zola refused to contribute asserting that Manet must find his own way to the Louvre. The collector Faure refused, as did the painter Mary Cassatt. Rouart sent 1,000 francs, as did the critic Duret whilst the dealer Durand-Ruel proferred only 200 francs. Rodin gave just 25 francs, Puvis de Chavannes 300 francs. By mid-October 1889 the fund had passed 15,000 francs. After the Salon split of 1889, further support was rallied from the members of the new Salon including Carolus-Duran, Bracquemond, Roll, Gervex, Cazin and Besnard. Such subscriptions provide an image of the growing and broad appreciation of Manet's painting across a wide range of artists. In January 1890 a fiasco occurred when the *Chronique des Arts* prematurely announced the success of the subscription, thereby making relations with the Louvre even more difficult. Eventually a committee under the Director of the National Museums examined the painting. They refused to commit the Louvre but agreed to admit the painting to the Luxembourg Museum for public display unless or until the Louvre accepted it. A payment was made to Mme Manet in 1890 and on Clemenceau's order *Olympia* entered the Louvre in 1907, twenty-four years after Manet's death.

The struggles attending the Caillebotte Bequest and Manet's *Olympia* reveal the substantial opposition to art that did not conform to the canons of practice formulated by the Institut and the Salon. To accept them was a revolutionary step which seriously challenged the authority of those bodies, admitting in the process the decay and dissolution of a whole structure of teaching, patronage and recognition. It also meant acknowledging the new structure of alternative salons and individual initiatives.

1889 witnessed a further reassessment of nineteenth-century French art with the sale of the Secretan Collection in Paris. Meissonier realised high prices but the sale of Millet's *Angelus* was particularly revealing (Plate 104). Sold for a small price by Millet in 1859, it was subsequently sold to a M. Van Pract for 5,000 francs, and then to a J.M. Wilson for 26,750 francs. At the Wolson Sale of 1881 it was bought by Secretan for 160,000 francs. Bidding began at 100,000 francs, proceeded to a 250,000 francs bid by the dealers Knoedler of New York for the Corcoran Art Gallery, and progressed remorselessly to 400,000 francs whereupon Antonin Proust announced the interest of the French Government. Bidding ceased at 502,000 francs whereupon disagreement over the bidding procedure caused uproar. Bidding reopened, finally concluding with Proust's bid of 553,000 francs to shouts of 'Vive La France!'[15]. The saleroom, the retrospectives of the Great Exhibitions and artists themselves, were reassessing the achievements of recent French art. In thirty years, albeit posthumously, Millet's reputation was transformed. At the same time, Manet (also posthumously) and the Impressionist painters had begun their journey to the Louvre Museum.

The Expositions Universelles of 1889 and 1900 occurred at a period of maximum exposure of painting and sculpture in Paris. They attracted an immense international audience to Paris and transformed its appearance both temporarily and, in parts, permanently. The art exhibitions were enormous requiring massive labour and the most intricate organization and assessment. The crowded sculpture display featured Barrias, Frémiet and Paul Dubois in 1900 but the reputation and following of Rodin and Dalou was in the ascendant and finally challenging their position (Plates 105–6). Amongst the

104. Jean-François Millet, *The Angelus*, 1855–7, oil on canvas, 55.5 × 66 cm., Musée d'Orsay, Paris.

105. Paul Renouard, *The Sculpture Gallery at the Grand Palais, Exposition Universelle*, 1900, lithograph, published in *The Studio*, 1900. Frémiet's *St Michel* is visible top left.

painters the wealth of new and experimental art from Impressionists, Post-Impressionists and Symbolists was shaking respected conventions and accepted reputations. As sculptures were manoeuvred onto miniature railway lines for installation, and as paintings were crated, selected and hung by the thousand, a profound reassessment and restructuring of art in Paris was underway. The Exposition Centennale of 1900, assembled by Roger Marx, stretched from David to the turn of the century. The overview was thorough. Meissonier, Detaille, Falguière, Tony Robert-Fleury, Benjamin-Constant, Bonnat and Henner all found their place, as did Puvis de Chavannes, Gustave Moreau, Roll and Besnard. But there was now recognition too for Manet, Renoir, Monet, Sisley, Pissarro, Degas, Caillebotte and Morisot. When a critic could comment that a work by J.P. Laurens was shown 'between two superb Monets'[16] an irresistable tide had turned.

106. *The Sculpture Store at the Grand Palais, Exposition Universelle,* 1900. Paul Dubois' *Joan of Arc* arrives by trolley on rails at right.

# 18. *How Are the Mighty Fallen?*

According to Jacques-Emile Blanche 'Bastien-Lepage and Gervex were the two painters best-known and most in demand during the 1880s. At the Salon des Champs-Elysées, Gervex had shown a painting of a masked nude woman. All Paris thought that it could identify her.'[1] Blanche points succinctly to the curious roots of popularity. Rodin would have nothing of such artifice:

> Whatever is false, whatever is artificial, whatever seeks to be pretty rather than expressive, whatever is capricious and affected, whatever smiles without motive, bends or struts without cause, is mannered without reason; all that is only a *parade* of beauty and grace; all, in short, that lies, is *ugliness* in art.[2]

Rodin held Puvis de Chavannes in the highest esteem: 'To think that he has lived among us...to think that this genius, worthy of the most radiant epochs of art, has spoken to us! That I have seen him, have pressed his hand! It seems as if I had pressed the hand of Nicolas Poussin!'[3]

As we have seen Puvis was widely esteemed amongst the greatest painters of his day,[4] holding a position of successful individuality neither belonging to the Institut nor exhibiting in small groups with adherents. Today Rodin far exceeds Puvis in recognition and reputation. Just as the Expositions Centennales reassessed the past, so each generation reassesses the past. As the structures of patronage, teaching and recognition dissolved and were transformed, new structures evolved relating the artist to his public in new ways, and the reassessment of the past continued in a new context. So Meissonier with all the glory of his reputation and despite the enormous sums commanded by his diminutive paintings is now relegated to obscurity, whilst at the opposite extreme Vincent Van Gogh is a name known to all with an interest in Western art despite the almost total lack of public knowledge of his life and work in the 1880s. A little before Van Gogh was planning to sell paintings for 50 francs, Meissonier was reserving works for the Louvre as the ultimate recognition of his efforts and, ironically, as the mark of his place in the history of French art: as Albert Wolff reported 'He has several times been offered 300,000 francs for two panels. But *The Etcher*, as much as *The Man at the Window*, will not leave the artist's studio except to go one day to the Louvre.'[5]

Whilst the glories of success were known in their lifetime by Meissonier, Puvis de Chavannes, Bonnat, Baudry, Carolus-Duran and others, for many now familiar names fame was posthumous and fortune was someone else's. For thousands of artists who were part of art in Paris there was no fame in their lifetime and no fame subsequently. Their talents, but perhaps also the structure of support in teaching, exhibitions, the activities of dealers and critics, had failed them. So many painters, sculptors and printmakers crowded Paris that patronage was inevitably inadequate to support more than a chosen few; the means to that selection and recognition were fiercely guarded and access to them was ruthlessly competitive. For some, success itself could be disastrous, and for others it was neither desired nor desirable. A critic in *The Studio* magazine, devoting an article to the painter Aman-Jean in 1896, commented

> I doubt if M.Aman-Jean will ever attain the great, but to my mind scarcely enviable, successes of some of our fashionable 'official' portrait painters, such as MM. Carolus-Duran, Boldini etc; and I like his art too well to wish him any such rewards as these, for no-one with any independence, any real taste, will let himself be infatuated in this way.[6]

When Meissonier, after the Exposition Universelle of 1889, was awarded the Grand Cross of the Légion d'Honneur it was the first time that it had been bestowed upon a painter, yet Manet, like Degas, declined official honours. In Wolff's words 'he considered it as a consecration of his art from the commercial point of view, like an official classification of his works in collections.'[7]

Honorable mentions, diplomas, medals and prizes together with the Légion d'Honneur were an integral part of the structure of recognition, conferring privileges, esteem and sales. Both Manet and Degas had the finanical means to assert their independence. Meissonier however came from a destitute family: he enjoyed the security of success and the recognition implied in the honours awarded him for the work he pursued. For an artist to live by his work was a formidable challenge and hardship was as familiar to Meissonier in his youth as it was to Monet in his.

The quest for recognition was, by its nature, competitive. Results were determined by talent and contacts, and recognition led to further competition. Jules Breton rose rapidly from the rank of *chevalier* of the Légion d'Honneur in 1861 to *officier* in 1867, but it took another twelve years for promotion to *commandeur* — thirty-eight years in all. Bonnat achieved this rank in fifteen years and went on to become *grand officier* in 1897 leaving behind him, not only Breton, but Bouguereau, Lefèbvre, Carolus-Duran, Henner and Detaille. All of these men were members of the Institut. Success promoted further success but it remained competitive to the top. Conversely, lack of success led to further lack of success, and the hardest competition was at the bottom. This made medals important just as it made the Prix de Rome and critical acclaim important. The Grand Cross, won by Meissonier in 1889, was also held by the sculptor Paul Dubois from 1896, Bonnat from 1900 and Hébert from 1903. This was the greatest official honour for a living artist. *Grand officier* status was held by Puvis de Chavannes in 1889, Hébert, Gérôme and Carolus-Duran in 1900, Henner and Bouguereau in 1903. The honours went inevitably to the successful and powerful in the world of art; the list is a concise summing up of the men of authority, and yet that authority was already undermined and was short-lived in the subsequent history of French art. Restrained critics admitted that

> We lack the means to establish with rigour the relative importance of militant personalities and we must be persuaded in advance that the future will overturn many of our conclusions. We know this and the conviction tortures us...We live too close, and our opinions, like all human opinions, are never more than the illumination of a moment.[8]

107. Antonin Mercié, *The Glory and the Sorrow: Tomb of Paul Baudry*, bronze and stone, Père Lachaise Cemetry, Paris.

The future, says Paul Mantz, will rewrite the past. The past has indeed been rewritten. All that remains of the glorious recognition of Paul Baudry, for example, is the angel that delivers laurels to his tomb in Père Lachaise cemetry (Plate 107). Below his portrait bust a figure mourns his passing beside a palette of bronze. The reputation has passed with the man. At the funeral of Dalou in 1902, Carolus-Duran, Carrière, Barrias, Bartholdi, Bartholomé and Rodin were present. The funeral was simple with no military honours and no graveside discourse whilst the funeral of Chapu in 1891 had been accomplished with pomp. With the death of Puvis de Chavannes it seemed to some that 'a great light had gone out; a mighty force has withdrawn into the gloom'.[9]

Reputations develop and change after the death of the artist. Reputations have been constantly reassessed by artists, critics, historians and by the sale room, and changing viewpoints reveal altered perspectives upon the past.

A studio in Paris, in the capital of art, was the ambition and achievement of thousands. The geography of art in Paris is full of such rooms, their gaunt windows sipping the steady north light. Within the studio, be he Bonnard or Bonnat the painter steps back from his canvas, and considers its colours and forms, intuition prompting the adjustment of a red or a green. The light illuminates canvas and painter and is captured in both. The looking and the making go hand in hand. A painter looks at a canvas. A model poses or waits. In the corner paintings are stacked against the wall. Outside is the bustle of the street, and the milling public boulevard. One is stillness, creativity and isolation; the other is activity, business and competition. Paris proffered both in abundance. From Montmartre to Montparnasse there were artists at work, painting, printing, carving and looking. As the commitment to painting contemporary experience grew and spread, Paris itself increasingly provided not only artist's dwellings and means of support but also their subject. There was much in all of this that survived transformed in the twentieth century and many of the studios still exist. In the simple act of looking lay inexhaustible potential for the artist in his studio. In the simple act of applying paint to canvas, or modelling clay with the fingers, lay a cultural process generating an elaborate structure of both patronage and the refusal of patronage, of tuition and its rejection, of success and of failure, of recognition and obscurity.

108. (*facing page*) Schematic map of Paris showing the areas in which studios were concentrated in the period 1880–1900.

# PART TWO

## 1. Studios of Paris

For a young and aspiring artist intent upon study at the Ecole des Beaux-Arts one of the first urgent priorities was to find a studio and a cheap one (Plate 109). Paris was, and still is, full of studios of every kind, from the splendid to the squalid. There were, and are, whole streets of them. The studio's location was significant and they predominated in particular areas: those around the Avenue de Villiers on the Plaine Monceau were the height of fashion, whilst to the south beyond the Ecole des Beaux-Arts and the Luxembourg gardens, in the furthest reaches of Montparnasse, studios were cheap

109. Edouard Cucuel, *Studio Hunting; Artist's Studio to Let*, 1899.

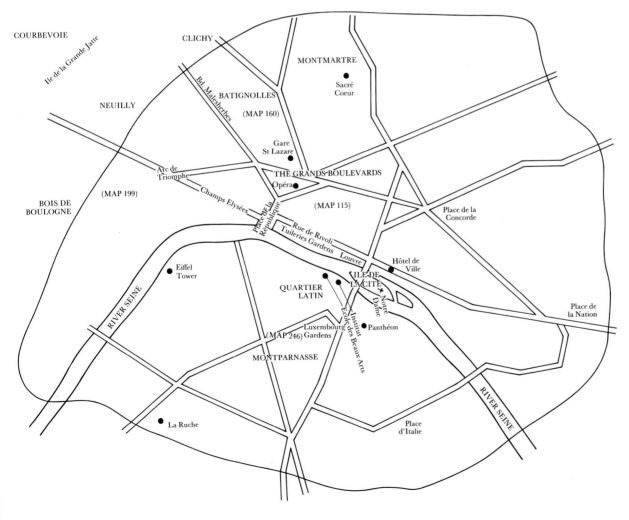

109

and mundane, hidden in courtyards with furniture workshops or lost behind the slaughterhouses that fed the city and supplied its great market Les Halles.

The other determinant of price was height. The ultimate token of success in terms of studio accommodation was the free-standing, purpose-built and usually lavish studio-house at ground level and these existed in all major areas that featured studios. At the opposite extreme was the garret, a converted attic studio with north-light constructed on the sixth, seventh or eighth floor without running water and without a lift. These proliferated from the smartest to the seediest areas, overlooking the street or a courtyard, sometimes with magnificent views of the rooflines of Paris. At worst their windows faced in the wrong direction, admitting broiling summer heat and direct light from the sun, a heat that scorched the leaded roof and a light whose shifting blaze made painting all but impossible by its constant movement and its brilliance. In, *L'Oeuvre*, Zola described the stiffling heat of such a cheap studio. His central character Claude Lantier, a *plein-air* painter, had chosen it from a mixture of financial necessity and a desire to tackle brilliant light in painting: 'It was a theory of his that the young 'open air' painters ought to take the studios the academic painters refused, the ones that were lighted by the full blaze of the sun.'[1]

In 1899 a roof-top studio overlooking the courtyard of the Rue St André-des-Arts, close to the Ecole des Beaux-Arts in the Latin Quarter cost a mere 800 francs for the year. This was on the sixth floor. An iron pump in the courtyard provided water which had to be carried up the six flights of stairs. The installation of equipment was equally arduous, and for an aspiring sculptor the effort involved in bringing clay or plaster, together with necessary water, up to such a studio was a real disincentive. Similarly the removal of completed sculpture was a formidable task. Sculptors did use such studios but were more likely to move out of central Paris to Montparnasse where workshop accommodation could be acquired at ground level in such areas as the Impasse du Maine at the heart of Montparnasse. But painters too had difficulties with roof-top studios, particularly in delivering large-scale works from the studio to the Salon around the steep tight bends of the stairs.

Rent in the Latin Quarter in 1899 ranged from 200 francs to 2,000 francs per year and the higher the studio, the cheaper its rent. Whilst in the Parisian apartment block the ground floor often housed the concierge or trade premises, above this at first floor were the best and dearest apartments, as the height increased accommodation was cheaper. This provided a unique and literal social stratification. The roof-top artist was on a level, for example, with sewing shops and servants quarters. The concierge was more likely to receive substantial tips from the most wealthy occupants of the lower floors; the occupant of a top floor discovered that 'the nearer the roof the less the respect he commands.'[2] To rent a studio three months rent in advance plus various taxes were paid, the occupant being required to give six months notice to leave. But such a studio could be made habitable for 150 francs and decorated cheaply with fine posters: 'My room was filled with brilliant posters by Chéret and Mucha and Steinlen.'[3]

Artists did not congregate all over Paris: their studios were focused in particular and distinctive areas. On the right (north) bank they stretched up the centre of Paris from the *grands boulevards* and the major dealers up to the *petits boulevards* of Montmartre, and on up to the highest reaches of the Montmartre hill around the new basilica of Sacré Coeur, an area still partly rural and partly under development by the 1880s. From here they also spread west (but not east). The streets around the Parc Monceau were especially luxurious and reserved for the wealthiest and most successful artists.

South of the Seine, on the left bank, studios proliferated in the Latin Quarter in close proximity to the Ecole des Beaux-Arts and were strung along the great southward-running Boulevard St Michel, flanking the Luxembourg Gardens, with its museum of living artists' work, to Montparnasse, which, for all that it lacked the splendour or the night life of northern areas, was nevertheless an area densely populated by artists in studio blocks, in impressive single studios and in cul-de-sacs and courtyards of cheaper studios, which comprised in effect villages for artists in the midst of, but separate from, the bustling street of the city.

What follows examines these areas, where whole streets remain dominated by studios, and the artists that inhabited them. Each has its distinct character. Together they provide a glimpse of Paris as a centre for artists, with its conflicts and competition, its successes and failures, a city in which artists were a considerable element of the population, striving for recognition and success against formidable odds. Where they lived and worked as much as when they lived and worked is revealing for it provides a glimpse of a time when the artists now celebrated after a hundred years assume a humbler place than those now neglected but glorious and honoured in their day. This in turn reflects the structure of oportunity and authority within which the successful and the unsuccessful alike were producing their paintings, sculpture, drawings and prints. It is a view of the art of Paris with less of the benefit of hindsight than is customary. As all these artists were at work simultaneously, within the range of a few years, this view provides a cross-section of the art-life of Paris in the late nineteenth century. Whilst it cannot be comprehensive, it provides an overview, the broad outlines of which are as clearly distinguishable as is the structure of Paris seen from the heights of Montmartre:

> Far below us lay the great shining city, spreading away into distance; and although it was night, the full moon and untold thousands of lamps in the streets and buildings below enabled us easily to pick out the great thoroughfares and the more familiar structures. There was the Opéra, there the Panthéon, there Notre-Dame, there St Sulpice; there the Invalides, and, uplifted to emulate the eminence on which we stood, the Tour Eiffel, its revolving searchlight at the apex shining like an immense meteor or comet with its misty tail stretching out over the city.[4]

# 2.  *The Grands Boulevards*

The river Seine with its two islands, the Ile de la Cité and the Ile St Louis, forms at once the main axis of Paris and its historical and geographic centre. Notre-Dame dominates the Ile de la Cité. During the Revolution many of its sculptures were destroyed or damaged and an opera singer had been enthroned there as the Goddess of Reason. By the 1880s its renewed splendour owed much to Viollet-le-Duc's restoration. He rebuilt the flèche in 1859–60 and added the grotesque chimeras that gaze over Paris. Downstream the first bridge is the Pont des Arts, a footbridge leading to the immense palace of the Louvre on the Right Bank. Up-stream on the Left Bank stand the Institut and the Ecole des Beaux-Arts. There are a few studios on the Ile de la Cité, their gaunt roof-top windows catching the north light and shaded on the brightest day, gazing across the river towards the hill of Montmartre which overlooks Paris from the north, a view emblazoned with light, reflected through tall windows.

'When they reached the Pont des Arts,' wrote du Maurier in his novel *Trilby*,

> they would cross it, stopping in the middle to look up the river towards the old Cité and Notre-Dame, eastward, and dream unutterable things, and try to utter them. Then, turning westward, they would gaze at the glowing sky and all it glowed upon — the corner of the Tuileries and the Louvre, the many bridges, the Chamber of Deputies, the golden river, narrowing its perspective and broadening its bed as it

went flowing and winding on its way between Passy and Grenelle to St Cloud, to Rouen, to the Havre...[1]

The view fascinated Zola's fictive artist Claude Lantier in *L'Oeuvre* to the point of obsession, providing Zola with an opportunity for astutely visual writing:

> The middle distance was marked by the Pont des Arts, with the thin line of its roadway, raised aloft on its network of girders, fine as black lace, alive with endless foot passengers streaming to and fro like so many ants. Beneath it, the Seine flowed away into the distance to the ancient, rusty stone arches of the Pont Neuf, away to the left as far as the Ile St Louis in one straight vista, bright and dazzling as a stretch of mirror.[2]

On the Right Bank alongside the Louvre, the Rue de Rivoli follows the central axis of Paris, from the narrow old streets behind the Hôtel de Ville in a fast straight line to the Place de la Concorde. The Louvre Museum on the one side and the Ecole des Beaux-Arts on the other, embracing the Seine, epitomise the achievements of the past and, for many in the 1880s and 1890s, the aspirations and hopes for the future. In one, the masters Poussin, David, Delacroix, in the other, the now-anonymous aspirants to both material and aesthetic success. As has been noted, the Louvre had suffered devastation in the Commune of 1871 losing a whole wing to the incendiaries. The Palais des Tuileries had stood gaunt and blackened for years before the demolition which itself was a formidable act of destruction. 'Internally', wrote Augustus Hare in his Guide to Paris in 1900, 'it was completely destroyed, but the walls, roofless and gutted, remained nearly entire, and the beautiful central pavilion of Philibert Delorme was almost entirely uninjured.'[3] With its removal, the vista which opened up from the Louvre to the distant Arc de Triomphe was straight and uninterrupted, fleeing the Louvre's embracing arms, through the Tuileries Gardens, to the Place de la Concorde and on along the Champs-Elysées to the gigantic triumphal arch at l'Etoile. If Manet, in his devotion to the painting of modern life and the life of the crowd, had revealed the vitality of Parisian life in the Tuileries Gardens in his *Musique aux Tuileries* of 1862, he was probably influenced by the ideas of his friend the poet Baudelaire, in his observation and recording of the shifting spectacle of the living city. The relationship between artists and the modern city was to flourish over the next fifty years, both providing and recording its image as a vigorous social organism: artists reflected increasingly and with enthusiasm the city which sustained them. Beyond the portrait of the individual person, artists portrayed the crowd in motion, the city about its business, the parks through which it breathed and where it played, the city at night, a mass of moving lights, the city in snow and the city in brilliant sun. The city viewed not topographically as a catalogue of static buildings but as a vital communal being. Zola described the swarming Champs-Elysées in comparable terms, the development of his narrative halting before the visual spectacle:

> The Avenue itself was filled with a double stream of traffic, rolling on like twin rivers, with eddies and waves of moving carriages tipped like foam with the sparkle of a lamp-glass or the glint of a polished panel down to the Place de la Concorde with its enormous pavements and roadways like big, broad lakes, crossed in every direction by the flash of wheels, peopled by black specks which were really human beings, and its two splashing fountains breathing coolness over all its feverish activity.[4]

For Degas, the Place de la Concorde was similarly the scene of human action in which the dislocated criss-crossing of paths suggested a lack of psychological communication between the busy city-dwellers of his *Portrait of Viscount Lepic and his Daughters* (Plate 110), the haphazard relationships of the city square demanding a composition as incoherent, in its calculated way, as a snapshot. For Seurat, in the winter, the great square exuded melancholy shadows and the minimum of movement, the cab in the right shuffling

110. Edgar Degas, *Viscount Lepic and his Daughters, Place de la Concorde*, 1875, oil on canvas, 79 × 118 cm. Not extant.

111. Georges Seurat, *La Place de la Concorde, Winter*, c. 1882–3, conté crayon, 23.2 × 30.7 cm., Solomon R. Guggenheim Museum, New York.

slowly from the scene, the fountain's mass still and silent at the left, the lamp-post bereft of figures passing by and isolated in the darkness (Plate 111).

For artists of the 1880s and 1890s in Paris the dichotomy of the Louvre and the art of the past, and the changing city brutally and dynamically remodelled by Baron Haussmann's new boulevards was much in evidence — to continue the great traditions or to accept the alternative challenge of the modern city, an unprecedented subject of which they were a part, employing unprecedented means to depict its flicker, its action, its light, buildings and people. The dichotomy was not easily resolved, but the centre of Paris was equally the centre of the dichotomy. Paul Baudry painted canvases for the Opéra but Pissarro and Degas painted canvases of the Opéra. In the streets and in the parks 'statuemania' reigned; from the Tuileries Gardens to the Luxembourg Gardens, from the Place Nation to the Rue de Rivoli sculpture proliferated, changing the focus of a street or square, embellishing lawns and fountains, presenting to the city a new self-image. Whilst Frémiet's statue of Joan of Arc graced the Place des Pyramides on the Rue de Rivoli with its gilded bronze forms invoking national pride and patriotism, the painter De Nittis was evoking the city itself. Edmond de Goncourt wrote in his *Journal* in 1883,

> De Nittis is the varied and talented painter of the Parisian Street. This evening in his studio I was looking at *The Place des Pyramides* [Plate 112] which he has retrieved from Goupil in order to give it to the Luxembourg, the sky of Paris with its washed out blues, the stone of the houses with their grey colour, the colouring of the poster catching the eye in the general cameo, is marvellous.[5]

As Paris affected its artists, so they responded in many works by changing and developing the image of the city and its inhabitants in a cultural relationship as rich for the visual arts as it was in music and in literature. The Opéra built by Garnier between 1861 and 1875 was lavish in the extreme, encrusted with carving and sculpture, its grand staircase over 10 metres wide with a balustrade of onyx, with rosso and verde antico, at once an assertion of the capital's cultural pride, an opportunity for painters (especially Paul Baudry and Lenepveu) or sculptors (including Carpeaux's magnificent *Dance*) and a subject in itself for artists.

The Opéra stands at a focal point of the *grands boulevards*, the great wide avenues with which Haussmann had transformed the city, sweeping away narrow and meandering medieval streets. The boulevards are wide and straight. In paintings by Gustave Caillebotte these arteries of traffic recede like rectilinear ravines to vanishing points located far across the city, in a different area of Paris and in all probability the focal point of an architectural or public monument, the brilliant summer light of Paris splintering the individuality of people and buildings into an image of urban vitality (Plate 113). Caillebotte frequently included the observer in his canvases of the boulevards, a figure scrutinising the life of the street from the high viewpoint of sixth and seventh floor apartment balconies. The new boulevards radically altered the appearance of Paris and not only in the layout of its streets: the view from high balconies replaced the busy courtyard and its closed-in domestic intimacy with a dynamic vista uniting thousands of dwellings, actions and beings in a single sweep of the eye (Plate 116). What the observer sees is the mass of activity, not its intimate detail as in the courtyard but a new urban complexity and speed. Caillebotte used Impressionist means to effect this generalisation, contrasting the individual viewpoint and space with the blaze of light and the bustle of activity of the vast communal thoroughfare. In this way the observer, with residual hints of an apartment depicted by balcony or window frame, represents an analogy of the process of looking outward, observing the city as an dynamic organism, an experience common to the dwellers of all the apartments that lined the boulevard. Monet's paintings of the Boulevard des Capucines retain at the far right minimal indications of the mouldings of the building from which he observed the city street in

112. (*facing page*) Giuseppe de Nittis, *La Place des Pyramides*, 1895, oil on canvas, 92 × 74 cm., Musée d'Orsay, Paris. Frémiet's *Joan of Arc* is in the middle distance and the Louvre beyond.

113. Gustave Caillebotte, *Man on Balcony, 1880* oil on canvas, 116 × 90 cm., private collection, Switzerland.

115

action. Both his subject and his viewpoint were significant. The great boulevard leading to the Opéra is a wriggling mass of human business, its carriages and people losing all individuality in the light and movement. Impressionist technique with its plethora of rhythmic brushmarks was ill-suited to individual detail, but it was a brilliant means for the depiction of the generality of activity within which particular cabs and figures all but lose their form completely. This high viewpoint was significant too for the street was observed from No. 35, the studio of the photographer Nadar,[6] who himself made use of aerial views — even using a balloon to capture Paris upon his photographic plate. It was in this studio that the first Impressionist group exhibition was assembled and displayed in 1874. Twenty-one years later, at 14 Boulevard des Capucines, Louis and Auguste Lumière made their first public displays of cinematic photography. The boulevard and photography both provided views of the city which the painter could scarcely ignore.

The Boulevard des Capucines becomes the Boulevard des Italiens where Rodin had a studio, after passing behind the Opéra and running eastwards to join the great boulevard which forms the northern perimeter of Paris' central core. This boulevard runs straight through several areas, adjusting its name as it does so, from the Boulevard Haussmann, after its designer, briefly becoming the Boulevard Montmartre, and then the Boulevards Poissonnière, Bonne-Nouvelle and St Denis. In Zola's novel *Nana* the 'heroine' had a flat on the Boulevard Haussmann, in a new building behind the construction site of the Opéra. Caillebotte, the painter lived at No. 31 (1879–82). Camille Pissarro painted thirteen views of the Boulevard Montmartre from a window of the Grand Hôtel de Russie at 1 Rue Drouot. In 1897 he painted street parades and immense crowds filling the boulevard and replacing its customary traffic. Whilst the viewpoint and format of the buildings remained constant, the city changed with the light and with the activities of the inhabitants who created and comprised the living entity of the city (Plate 114).

114. Camille Pissarro, *Boulevard Montmartre, Mardi Gras Parade*, 1897, oil on canvas, 63.5 × 77.5 cm. The Armond Hammer Collection, Los Angeles.

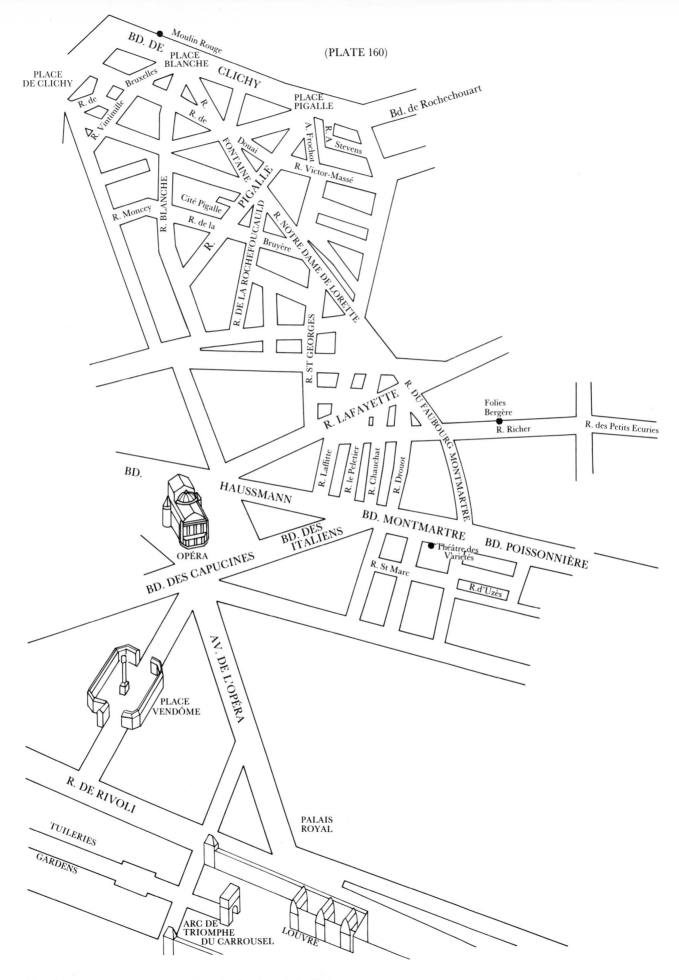

(PLATE 160)

115. Map: from the Louvre north to the Boulevard de Clichy.

116. Gustave Caillebotte, *Boulevard seen from above*, 1880, oil on canvas, 63.7 × 53.5 cm., private collection, London.

To the north of the Boulevard Montmartre the steep ascent begins up to Montmartre itself and the streets become far less grand, austere and formal. In the Rue du Faubourg Montmartre

117. Jean Béraud, *Evening in front of the Théâtre des Variétés, Boulevard Montmartre*, oil on canvas, Musée Carnavalet, Paris.

> there till two o'clock in the morning, restaurants, brasseries and butchers' shops blazed with light, while crowds of women clustered around the doors of cafés in this last living, lighted part of Paris, this last market open to nocturnal bargaining, where deals were being struck quite openly, group after group, from one end of the street to the other, as in the main corridor of a brothel.[7]

On the boulevard itself the blazing light of the foyer of the Théâtre des Variétés poured into the street. Jean Béraud observed it at street level amidst the throng with all its grotesque enthusiasm, elegance and intrigue, building tiny portraits, as Degas might have done, into his view of the active crowd observed at close range (Plate 117). Few artists lived between this great thoroughfare and the river, although Desvallière's family home at 14 Rue St Marc was an exception. On the other hand, many artists frequented this area. Around the corner from Desvallière's studio were two of the premises of the Académie Julian, in the Passage des Panoramas where George Moore lived as an art student and at the Rue d'Uzès where Tony Robert-Fleury and Bouguereau were tutors. Most of the studios close-by were further north, up the steepening slope of Montmartre. The great boulevards divided them from the central splendours of Paris.

119

118. Henri de Toulouse-Lautrec, Loie Fuller at the Folies Bergère, 1893, oil on canvas, 63 × 45 cm., Musée Toulouse-Lautrec, Albi.

# 3. North to the Boulevard de Clichy

North of the great boulevards the night life increased and became less salubrious and the presence of artists studios increased. One of the main routes north which ascends steeply to the Place Blanche is the Rue Notre Dame de Lorette where Delacroix had had a large studio at No. 54.[1] The lithographer Gavarni who lived on the first floor of 1 Rue Fontaine closeby, had scrupulously observed the road's inhabitants with a frankness which so fascinated the Goncourt brothers that Edmond de Goncourt avidly collected his prints and devoted a monograph to Gavarni. Zola left no doubt about the sexual nature of much of the nocturnal trade here:

> The Rue Notre Dame de Lorette stretched out dark and deserted in front of them, with shadowy women's figures discernible here and there. The district was straggling home, and poor whores exasperated at a night of fruitless soliciting, unwilling to admit defeat, went on arguing in hoarse voices with any stray drunkard they could catch at the corner of the Rue Bréda or the Rue Fontaine.[2]

North of the Boulevard Montmartre the Folies-Bergère opened its doors at 32 Rue Richer — 'a very popular resort,' noted Baedecker in his guide of 1894, 'half-theatre and half *café-chantant*. Visitors either take seats or promenade in the gallery'.[3] The Folies-Bergère opened in 1869 combining theatrical spectacle, ballet, pantomime and especially acrobatic troupes with *café-concert*. Its large balconied hall attracted every aspect of Parisian society. Manet, in one of his most perversely enigmatic works, the *Bar at the Folies-Bergère*, painted it in 1881 (Plate 119). The barmaid is symmetrically placed and well-dressed. She appears to stand before a mirror, the gilded edge of which is

119. Edouard Manet, *The Bar at the Folies-Bergère*, 1881, Salon of 1882 , oil on canvas, 96 × 127.4 cm., Courtauld Institute Galleries, London.

visible behind her parallel to the lower edge of the painting. A reflection fills the background of the painting with ambiguous space showing chandeliers and one of the extensive balconies of the Folies-Bergère. In the top right of the picture the green-booted ankles of a trapeze artiste hover in the air poised for swinging descent. Below her the seething crowd watches and converses. Yet the central figure is an image of stillness amongst her bottles, fruit and flowers. Here two startling ambiguities occur. The barmaid stares from the canvas, and it is impossible to ascertain whether she stares at the scene in the main hall of which the reflexion is a reversed synopsis, or at the viewer of the painting who is thereby encouraged to assume the identity of customer or client. At the right of the canvas there is further ambiguity over the back view of a girl whose pose is identical to the barmaid's as she consults with a customer. The mirror's edge makes clear that she is a reflexion, yet the angle at which we see her denies this possibility for her position indicates that she cannot reflect the central figure. Closer scrutiny reveals that the bottles of wine and Bass beer, visible at the bottom left, do not correspond convincingly with what appear to be their reflections. As a seat on the balcony is empty and a man appears on the right, a narrative may be implied although this is scarcely precedented in Manet's work. There is, furthermore, no way of imagining the position of the floor which supports the barmaid, her table and customer for no balcony edge is indicated between the table and the distant balcony's reflection.

Far less enigmatic, though in terms of detail less explicit was Toulouse-Lautrec's depiction of the dancer Loïe Fuller at the Folies-Bergère twelve years later (Plate 118). The establishment continued to thrive and Loïe Fuller's spectacular dancing with swirling and flowing robes was characteristic of the Folies-Bergère's entertainment. Loïe Fuller impressed many artists and was admired by Rodin as well as Lautrec. Further north along the Boulevard de Clichy, cafés and evening entertainments proliferated. Degas and Lautrec depicted them. They also lived close together in this area. The geographical concentration of studios and café life was a significant factor in the art of both men.

Camille Pissarro lived at 42 Rue des Petits-Ecuries in this vicinity, as did the Symbolist Charles Maurin. Closer to the Rue Notre Dame de Lorette, in the Rue St Georges the tragedienne and sculptor Sarah Bernhardt lived whilst her studio was uphill on the Boulevard de Clichy at No. 11. For a time the Goncourt brothers lived in the same street, transforming their apartment into a treasure house for their collections.

Renoir also had a studio in the Rue St Georges at No. 35 and the poet Stéphane Mallarmé wrote to him here, incorporating the address into a cryptic verse on the envelope:

À celui qui de couleur vit,
Au 35 de la rue du vainqueur
Du dragon, porte ce pli, facteur[4]

According to one account:

The rectangular room had one of its large sides entirely of glass and exposed to the West. During the summer, the sun would fill the room with light, in spite of the curtains of thick material designed to control it. The walls were covered in light grey paper and a few unframed canvases were hung against them. Against the walls grew, in piles, canvases painted or white, of which the visitor only ever saw the backs. There was no other furniture except for two easels, a few cane chairs of the most ordinary kind, two collapsed old armchairs covered with a very faded flowered material, a tired divan recovered with a material of indeterminate colour and a white wooden table upon which tubes of colours were piled together with brushes, bottles of oil or turpentine and spattered paint rags.[5]

Renoir began work at 8 am. pausing periodically to smoke whilst his model rested. He would lunch at mid-day in the small Crèmerie de Camille opposite before returning to work unitl 5 pm., after which visits from friends were welcomed.

The sunlit studio recalls Zola's description of the *plein-airiste's* studio in *L'Oeuvre* and could only have been hot in summer and flooded with light. In winter any immense studio window made a studio stove a vital possession. For Renoir the brilliant light was an asset in the studio where its fleeting and changing illumination preserved the effects of light out of doors. Yet the studio also permitted Renoir to work from the naked model, observing directly the effects of full light on flesh in a manner difficult to arrange outside. In the studio Renoir could reconcile his dedication to depicting daylight with his admiration for the posed and rich exoticism of Ingres and Delacroix odalisques, or the feminine delicacy of eighteenth-century painters.

Later, in 1897, Renoir was at 64 Rue de La Rochefoucauld, a street of gaunt, shuttered, pale-yellow buildings rising up towards Montmartre, reserve and decorum reflected in its architecture. The sculptor Franceschi lived at No. 17 in 1886. At No. 14, lower down the hill, stands the restrained elegance of the studio of Gustave Moreau, (now the Gustave Moreau Museum) (Plate 120). It provides a model of the wealthy painter's studio, but its site is problematic as the street runs north-south, so that the northern wall is obstructed by adjacent buildings. The north lights of the two colossal studios in fact overlook the garden behind the adjacent building and barely affect the street facade. The top studio is scarcely visible from the street, its double height being boxed in behind the almost vertical roof. Discreetly decorated with classical forms, the street façade gives little indication of the practical magnificence of the studios within which rise through a space capable of accommodating four floors of an apartment building. The large, steel, girder-framed studios are entirely glass-walled to the north to provide, unlike Renoir's studio in the Rue St Georges, the maximum of even illumination. They are connected by a spiral stair of rococo elegance despite its simplicity of detail (Plate 121). Below the great studios which house the large canvasses the rooms are small and wood-panelled for warmth and comfort, but even here whole walls open out to reveal deep cupboards equipped with hinged panels for the storage of paintings and drawings. Despite youthful celebrity and later popularity amongst Symbolist artists and writers in the 1880s and 1890s, Moreau exhibited and sold little. His means did not necessitate a close attention to exhibitions or the Salon from which he abstained for many years. Storage was more important and a great proportion of Moreau's work remains in his studio. It would in fact be impossible to remove the many large canvases without either unstretching them or dismantling the windows, for the studio lacks a slot in its fenestration for the removal of major canvases. The studio in this case reflects the man, for although he was a friend of Degas, his art was not at all concerned with the depiction of modern life. On the contrary, he depicted subjects of suggestive obscurity with their roots in a scholarly study of classical literature and religion.

Moreau entered the Ecole des Beaux-Arts in 1846 as a student of Picot. Two years later he became friendly with the painter Chassériau. His debut at the Salon followed in 1852. Travelling to Italy allowed Moreau to study Carpaccio, Gozzoli and Mantegna but he also met contemporary French artists there including Degas, Puvis and Elie Delaunay. There followed a period of Salon success with *Oedipus and the Sphinx* (1864), *Jason* (1865) and *Orpheus* (1866) although disillusionment at the response of critics subsequently persuaded him to withdraw from exhibiting at the Salon between 1869 and 1876. In the 1880s he again withdrew from the Salon (except for 1886). From the mid-1880s his painting was of increasing interest to Symbolist artists and writers. Official recognition made him *chevalier* of the Légion d'Honneur in 1875, *officier* in 1883 and a member of the Institut in 1889. He had been well represented at the 1878 Exposition Universelle and exhibited watercolours at the Goupil Gallery in 1886. His teaching was influential after his appointment as professor at the Ecole des Beaux-Arts in 1892 with Matisse and Rouault amongst his students. In this post and at the Institut

120. Exterior of Gustave Moreau's studio, 14 Rue de La Rochefoucauld. Now the Musée Gustave Moreau. The north-lights of the studios are just visible at the side.

121. The staircase linking the lower and upper studios in Gustave Moreau's house at 14 Rue de La Rochefoucauld.

he succeeded Elie Delaunay. He left his studio to the state together with its contents which included 18,000 drawings and the majority of his canvases.

The small entrance hall leads up a short flight of steps to the sequence of small and warm rooms which are lined with folding racks of drawings, many of which are studies after Renaissance artists, amongst them copies after drawings by Michelangelo and Leonardo. They frequently concentrate upon composition rather than the touch or finish of the originals. In addition, the wealth of drawings for Moreau's own works record every stage of his development of major compositions, from initial compositional studies up to large drawings that are essentially cartoons for large canvases. Some of these are squared up ready for transfer to the canvas, employing a grid of approximately 2½ centimetres squares on a drawing measuring 2 by 1.3 metres and this sometimes involved assembling large cartoons from up to six sheets of paper. These complement the *ébauches*, studies defining in oil paint the tone, composition and main colour areas of the painting. In fact Moreau's procedure, though thoroughly academic up to this point, becomes extraordinary once work begins on the final canvas, for he was evidently reluctant upon many occasions to resolve or finish his paintings in a technically consistent manner: frequently he employed several techniques simultaneously. Contrasting with the broad and painterly handling, aspiring step by step from brown underpainting towards stronger colour and Ingresque finish, Moreau also applied a linear technique over the broader handling, which took on an etched appearance in even and clear lines outlining exotic details to be filled-in sometimes with jewel-like, precise and small areas of colour. The majority of his later canvases were unresolved in this way, for he allowed the smudges of broader handling to suggest motifs in the evolution of the final canvas. This preoccupation with suggestion was the antithesis of the highly resolved finish of such contemporaries at the Academy as Bonnat or Hébert, and it was equally distinct from the handling employed by Impressionist painters. It may, in itself, partly explain Moreau's aversion to exhibiting at the Salon insofar as his own aims were distinct from those appropriate to success in that context. Moreau's experimental use of paint, ranging from wriggling impasto to incised filigree lines, clearly reveals his working technique which owes a debt to established procedure but which extends it to personally expressive ends. It contrasts sharply with the degree of control embodied in Degas' *Portrait of Gustave Moreau* now also exhibited in the studio (Plate 122). Degas' small, full-length portrait is a model of tonal and colouristic control, evolving from indications of drawing in black paint to areas of soft half-transparent browns which are gently but decisively distinguished from the thin painting of the blue-black background. Colour is lightly applied within the warm browns, sketchily indicating structure and tone, whilst the face, which in fact occupies a small area, is resolved to a much greater degree: it is precise, decisively modelled and little paint has been applied with a very small brush. Nonetheless Degas has indicated the precise planes of cheek, upper lip, temple and eyebrow and has modelled they eye with precision. Degas' painting reveals his working process. In this his approach to finish is at odds with that, for example, of Ingres in whose portraits all signs of the process of painting are obscured by an even smoothness of surface. Yet Degas is using an established procedure; the difference is that he reveals its stages in the final canvas portrait study of Moreau, capitalising upon the different degrees of finish to concentrate attention upon the psychologically potent and most individual elements of the person before him, Moreau. Subsidiary elements are handled more loosely although their tone and colour-strength is precisely kept in place. This can be seen in the richer creamy tones of the brown used for the chair, the firm dark grey of the hat and loosely painted gloves which succinctly establish the floor surface at the lower right — as do the feet at the lower left. Degas presents the elegant Moreau through a whole hierarchy of degrees of finish in his handling of paint, its material qualities, its strength of colour and tone, to focus attention upon a portrait head that is scarcely 4 centimetres high. This process of working emphasised control in a manner

125

122. Edgar Degas, *Portrait of Gustav Moreau*, 1867, oil on canvas, 40 × 27 cm., Musée Gustave Moreau, Paris.

123. Jules Lefèbvre in his studio with portrait and sitter.

124. Studios in the Rue de La Bruyère.

that reveals Degas' formal training, but it is in strong contrast to Moreau's own mature technique which remained open to suggestive readings of unresolved marks, divergent techniques, and, potentially, the loss of such severe and accomplished control. Whilst Degas' technique was adaptable to the recording of modern life, Moreau's provided a rich source of inspiration for the poetic and fantastic imagery of his major compositions which denied the possibility of finish as understood by either Ingres or Degas.

Uphill from the Moreau studio, the Rue de la Bruyère crosses from the Rue Blanche and Rue Pigalle to the Rue Notre Dame de Lorette. At 5 Rue de la Bruyère, Jules Lefèbvre (1836–1912), one of the most popular tutors of the period was based (Plates 123–4). A pupil of Cogniet at the Ecole des Beaux-Arts from 1852, he had won the Prix de Rome in 1861 and had made his Salon debut three years later. After his return to France in 1867, he was increasingly successful, receiving the first award of the Légion d'Honneur in 1870, becoming a member of the Institut in 1891 and rising to *commandeur* of the Légion d'Honneur in 1898. He was awarded the medal of honour at the 1886 Salon and a *grand prix* at the 1889 Exposition Universelle. At the Alexandre Dumas Sale of 8–13 May 1892, Lefèbvre's *Femme nue* realised 25,000 francs. It was his teaching activities, particularly at the Académie Julian, which made him a figure of renown and respect amongst Salon applicants. Lefèbvre himself was a stalwart Salon exhibitor.

Closeby, at 3 bis Rue de la Bruyère, was a Symbolist painter of originality and decorative skill, Lucien Lévy-Dhurmer (1865–1953). Gabriel Mourey described him in *The Studio* magazine in 1897:

So I called upon him at his studio, and found myself in the presence of a young man rather below the middle size, with close-cropped hair and fair, curly beard, a keen and piercing glance, and the simplest and most unostentatious manners, quick and witty in conversation, evidently by nature meditative and strong willed.[6]

Born in Algeria, Lévy-Dhurmer became an accomplished and innovative symbolist artist, whose work was both suggestive and decorative, ranging from the delicately

127

sinister *Portrait of George Rodenbach* and *Eve* (both pastels) to the forceful and iconic Breton painting *Our Lady of Penmarc'h* (Plate 125). He derived inspiration from musical and literary sources and also executed ceramics. He obtained an honourable mention at the Salon of 1896 and a bronze medal at the 1900 Exposition Universelle, but he was closely associated with the exhibitions of Symbolist groups including Sâr Péladan's mystical Rosicrucian Salons.

Halfway along the Rue de la Bruyère, the Rue Pigalle heads north to Montmartre. Benjamin-Constant once occupied No. 27 'a fine hotel approached through large doors opening onto the street across a good-sized gravel courtyard' Living accommodation was in sumptuous large rooms, but the small studio had only a top light which Benjamin-Constant considered unbecoming to sitters.[7] A few yards up the Rue Pigalle

125. Lucien Lévy-Dhurmer, *Our Lady of Penmarc'h*, 1896, oil on canvas, 41 × 33 cm., Collection M. Robert Walker, Paris.

from this point a short private cul-de-sac, the Cité Pigalle, contains an elegant studio at No. 5 with north lights on first and second floors, and a panel between them containing casts of horsemen from the Parthenon frieze (Plate 126). The two windows are framed by a single moulding placed centrally within a restrained classical façade flanked by crisp but shallow pilasters to form a studio house of distinction, with its own reception courtyard and hidden away from the noise and traffic of the Rue Pigalle. The big north lights are simply glazed with opening windows set within them. This provides a haven of peace within the bustling city and is a model example of the successful or substantial studio of an independent artist.

Studios often inhabited courtyards or traffic-free and almost invisible private streets with discreet entries through gates controlled by a lodge and concierge or through archways into cul-de-sacs behind the main street façade. The area south of the Boulevard de Clichy abounds in them, close to the activity and convenience of the city yet lost amongst gardens and courtyards they form groups of artists' dwellings like hamlets within the city.

The painter Gustave Colin lived at 14 Rue Fontaine, which continues the line of the Rue Notre Dame de Lorette north-west to the Place Blanche on the Boulevard de Clichy, and Degas also lived there between 1879 and 1886 at No. 19 bis 'the most beautiful apartment on the third floor to be found in the whole Quartier'.[8] Degas was an urban artist par excellence and the area he inhabited was always in a lively part of Paris. As we have seen, his art was a unique blend of a commitment to depicting modern life and a respect for academic expertise reflecting the art of the past. According to the writer George Moore, Degas resolved this antithesis in his depiction of the nude which rejected the established formulae of the Salon: 'The naked woman has become impossible in modern art; it required Degas' genius to infuse new life into the worn-out theme. Cynicism was the greatest means of eloquence in the Middle Ages, and with cynicism Degas has rendered the nude again an artistic possibility.'[9]

126. Studio at 5 Cité Pigalle.

Degas had studied under Louis Lamothe, a pupil of Ingres at the Ecole des Beaux-Arts from 1855. He travelled extensively in Italy, and in 1862 he met Manet. An increasing dedication to depicting modern life led to close involvement with Impressionism and he contributed ten works to their first group exhibition at Nadar's studio on the Boulevard des Capucines in 1874. He did not embrace their spontaneity, however, and nothing unplanned affects his compositions. He was a brilliant and dedicated draughtsman of the human figure. His art is an intricate and masterly balancing of the opposing forces of tradition and modernity. Both the Louvre and the street were vital sources for his painting. He lived in Montmartre for twenty years frequenting the literary and artistic circles of the Café Guerbois and the Nouvelles Athènes, avoiding the struggle for recognition associated with the Salon and preferring instead to exhibit independently through dealers and the Impressionist group exhibitions (all eight except 1882). He encouraged younger artists to join this exhibition procedure. He also, particularly in his later years, accumulated a remarkable and individual collection of artworks that incorporated both Ingres and Delacroix as well as Corot, Manet, Cézanne and Gauguin.

'However much I did my drawings in town I should be working in my studio for two or three hours a day. And then I lunch every day, with only rare exceptions, at the Café de La Rochefoucauld in front of the little market, at the corner of the Rue Notre Dame de Lorette and of the Rue de La Rochefoucauld.'[10] The studio and the street were both, characteristically, crucial to Degas method of work. Spontaneity of vision occurred in the observation of the city and its people, but it was inevitably in the studio that the final work was painstakingly evolved: 'I have never done with finishing off my pictures and pastels' wrote Degas to Henri Rouart in 1873.[11] Owners of works by Degas were reluctant on occasions to lend them to the artist, for fear that he might continue to work upon them. He acknowledged the importance of the quick sketch but reserved his real

127. The entrance to the Avenue Frochot from the Rue Victor-Massé.

128. Jean-Louis Forain in his studio with Jean-Loup, his son, 1898, photograph Mme, I. Chagnaud-Forain.

respect for thoroughly controlled drawing: 'By these means, one can obtain very interesting results, a telling sketch, for example; but the hardest thing in the world is to execute a well modelled head: that is great art.'[12] Degas despised official honours however and commented cynically upon the eager impatience with which they were sought my many of his contemporaries.

Degas had studios in one of the dense little hamlets of studios which lie north of the Rue Victor-Massé (formerly the Rue Laval) but south of the Boulevard de Clichy. They are almost invisible from either thoroughfare but ascend through secluded private lanes with gates and gardens. The area of the Cité Malesherbes, the Avenue Frochot and the Rue Alfred-Stevens, named after the Belgian painter who owned the land, are peppered with studios. Degas had studios at 37 Rue Victor-Massé which overlooks this complex and in the Avenue Frochot (Plate 127). The fashionable painter Toulmouche, who was responsible for setting up a complex of studios south of the Seine at Montparnasse was at 37 Rue Victor-Massé. Later in 1897, Lautrec was in the adjacent Avenue Frochot at No. 5, a stroll away from the Moulin Rouge.[13] A frenetic and prolific depictor of the night-life of Montmartre, he produced over a thousand paintings, 5,000 drawings and more than 300 prints and posters without reference to the Salon, its demands and its opportunities. On the contrary his frame of reference was the area in which he lived and worked, as well as, in part, the proximity and attitudes of Degas.

Before approaching the wide boulevards that skirt the base of Montmartre itself, the studios slightly to the west in the Rue de Douai, Rue Blanche and Rue Vintimille are significant, for J.L. Forain, whose cynicism and urbane modernity owe much to both Degas and Lautrec, occupied 56 Rue Blanche (Plate 128),[14] whilst Eugène Boudin was at 11 Place Vintimille (now Place Adolphe-Max). Boudin, the son of a sailor, excelled in views of beaches along the Channel coast of France and had been a formative influence upon Monet was a plein-air painter of light, water and the crowd. He exhibited regularly at the Salon between 1859 and 1897 by which time his reputation was well-established. Boudin obtained a gold medal at the Exposition Universelle of 1889 and ten years later, the year following his death, he was the subject of a posthumous retrospective exhibition. This was held at the Ecole des Beaux-Arts and comprised 304 paintings, 73 pastels and 20 watercolours. It can only have delighted Durand-Ruel who had bought most of Boudin's works in 1881 and had promoted them vigorously with exhibitions in 1883, 1889 and 1891 in Paris and in 1898 in New York. Monet, who had respected Boudin so highly in his early years was also based in this area, at 20 Rue Vintimille, in 1879, having occupied nearby 17 Rue de Moncey the previous year. Later Edouard Vuillard had a studio in the Place Vintimille.[15]

Crossing both the Rue Vintimille and the Rue Blanche, the Rue de Douai runs east into the Rue Victor-Massé. The acutest contrasts of artistic outlook and practice could be found in the Rue de Douai, for at No. 69 was Tony Robert-Fleury (Plate 129), active tutor at Julians's Academy and celebrated Salon painter, whilst along the road at No. 65, by 1905 the young Pierre Bonnard (Plate 130) was to experiment to spectacular decorative effect with ways of painting derived equally from the lessons of Impressionism, Japanese prints and Gauguin. Bonnard had studied at the Académie Julian in the mid-1880s alongside Vuillard, Sérusier, Ranson, Vallotton and Maurice Denis, the core of what became the Nabis circle of painters. Bonnard's revolutionary France-Champagne poster appeared in 1889. It was highly decorative and not in the least academic. In 1890 he was sharing a studio with Vuillard and Denis. Avoiding the official Salons, Bonnard exhibited with the Barc de Bouteville's Gallery and Durand-Ruel after his debut at the Salon des Indépendants in 1891. As well as paintings, he executed major theatre designs, for the Théâtre de l'Oeuvre, decorative commissions and book illustrations. His loose drawing style of the 1890s was efficiently suited to recording impressions of unposed subjects in streets, gardens and interiors, but provided the source material for paintings which, though filled with light and ravishing colour, were nevertheless studio works of calculation and poise. His synthesis of looking and making, of observation and composition, has at times, like that of Lautrec, qualities exploited in a manner which refers to Degas. But Bonnard, like Lautrec, was essentially an original individual, creative in his own right. He depicted Paris in its yards, gardens and streets: the city itself, in its light, movement and people was a crucial theme of his early years. The studio in Rue de Douai around 1905 was filled with paintings hung across its walls, assembled into screens and stacked against the walls, its striped wallpaper overlaid with irregularly placed and unstretched studies and works in progress. His vision of the city was irrepressibly optimistic, a spectacular celebration of its light, movement and inhabitants.

Paris allows for every aspect of its complex living continuity to be displayed, from the degredation and visciousness depicted by Lautrec or Forain to the rapturous enjoyment reflected by Bonnard. For many of its artists it was far more than the physical context within which they worked, for it was also frequently their subject. As we have already suggested, they in turn moulded the way in which it was seen, adjusting its self-awareness in the process. In such painters of light as Monet or Bonnard there is an assertion of a Paris that is luminous and splendid in its ordinary aspects and daily life, embodying an optimism less evident in the cool assessment of Degas or the vigorous and grotesque life depicted by Lautrec. Novelists, particularly Zola, frequently described Paris as a curious enigma, the spectacular city providing a backdrop for abjectly miserable personal struggle or failure. Paris has that visage also. George Moore saw it upon arriving in Paris and he retained the memory of it: 'We all know the great grey and melancholy Gare du Nord at half past six in the morning; and the miserable carriages, and the tall, haggard city. Pale, sloppy, yellow houses; an oppressive absence of colour; a peculiar bleakness in the streets.'[16]

129. Tony Robert-Fleury in his studio.

130. Pierre Bonnard in his studio at 65 Rue de Douai, c. 1905, photograph courtesy of M. Antoine Terrasse.

# 4. The Boulevard de Clichy

'Montmartre is a dead town that lives on memories', or so it appeared to Andre Warnod in 1923.[1] Montmartre retains the aspect of a distinct area to this day but few signs of its village atmosphere remain unless the explorer seeks carefully. High above the centre of Paris overlooking its heart, Montmartre has at numerous times asserted its independence, most notably during the Commune of 1871. In the mid-nineteenth century the large new thoroughfare of the Boulevard de Clichy running from the Place de Clichy to the Place Pigalle and continuing along the Boulevard de Rochechouart, cut through the northern slums of Paris isolating Montmartre by its physical boundary but, conversely, making it more conveniently accessible (Plate 131). Poorer artists began to move there. As Paris filled with visitors for the Expositions Universelles, particularly those of 1889 and 1900, artists increasingly migrated north to Montmartre. The extraordinary cupolas of the basilica of Sacré Coeur rose white upon the summit of the hill in the later 1880s — the first service was held there in 1891 — and Montmartre could be seen from all over Paris, attracting the eye northwards even from south of the Seine. The relationship of Montmartre to central Paris was changing although in the 1880s and 1890s its own character with windmills, quarries and steep gardens remained in evidence. Along the 'petits boulevards' at the base of the steep slopes customs posts had once existed; they imposed tolls and, especially important, taxes upon wines entering the city. This sense of a boundary remains discernible, not least in the proliferation of bars and dubious entertainments where once the wine flowed cheaper than in central Paris.

The Boulevard de Clichy has many studios along its southern flank. Emerging from the rising streets of the Rue Notre Dame de Lorette, the Rue Pigalle and the complex

131. Pierre Bonnard, *Place de Clichy*, *c.* 1895. The painters Roussel, Vuillard and Bonnard at left by the Monument to Moncey. At right Toulouse-Lautrec, his cousin and Maurice Denis. Private Collection, Paris.

A. Renoir

132. Pierre-Auguste Renoir, *Place de Clichy*, c. 1880, oil on canvas, 65 × 54 cm., Fitzwilliam Museum, Cambridge.

north of the Rue Victor-Massé, they spread out along the boulevard, facing north to Montmartre itself, some of them crowning seven storey apartment blocks sloping back along the line of mansard roofs, whilst others form substantial purpose-built dwellings of architectural pretensions. Today a thoroughfare of roaring traffic, the Boulevard de Clichy was already busy in the 1880s but still spacious with its central avenue of trees between the carriages, and with occasional two-storey buildings of a provincial appearance.

In the 1880s and 1890s the area was fast being developed to accommodate the expanding populace of the city. It was not a smart or elegant area. It presented an aspect of the city that was frequently menacing and sordid, the air of the rural village rapidly succumbing to the arrival of towering apartment blocks standing gaunt against the skyline of windmills and streets so steep that they had steps up them. Renoir depicted the Place de Clichy, vibrant with light and movement about 1880 (Plate 132).

133

133. Norbert Goeneutte, *The Boulevard de Clichy under Snow*. 1876, oil on canvas, 60 × 73.5 cm., The Tate Gallery, London.

Goeneutte, just a few years earlier, silhouetted his figures against an avenue silenced by snow, with not enough carriages to disturb its stillness, a gaunt perspective of young trees seen against buildings of contrasting heights, the tall one on the left with regular stone projections ready to link onto an adjacent building as and when it replaced the low two-storey house depicted beside it (Plate 133). This same discontinuity attracted Van Gogh and he portrayed it more than once in 1887 (Plate 134). As in Goeneutte's image the wide central sanded area shows straggling winter trees and few people. The skyline of the boulevard is an irregular confusion of seven-storey apartment blocks between two-storey buildings, bleak gable ends anticipating the high modern Parisian street façade still to come, in emulation of the great boulevards further south. The Boulevard de Clichy was in a transitional state and the distinct identity of Montmartre was experiencing an encroachment from central Paris. Paul Signac, at the time of the early

years of the Salon des Indépendants, was living in this area too. His pointillist rendering of the Place de Clichy in snow (Plate 135) indicates his close association with Seurat, but he also exemplifies the drift of artists north to the quieter thoroughfares of Montmartre. The view is close to that of Goeneutte a decade earlier including some of the same buildings and trees. Little appears to have changed, but Montmartre was fast being transformed. By the 1890s it was a hive of studios and the population was changing.

134. (*left*) Vincent Van Gogh, *The Boulevard de Clichy*, 1887, coloured crayons and ink on paper, 38 × 52.5 cm., Rijksmuseum Vincent Van Gogh, Amsterdam.

135. (*right*) Paul Signac, *The Boulevard de Clichy under Snow*, 1886, oil on canvas, 46.5 × 65.6 cm., Minneapolis Museum of Fine Arts (Bequest of Putnam Dana McMillan).

136. Vincent Van Gogh, *Street Scene-The Boulevard de Clichy*, 1887, oil on canvas, 46.5 × 55 cm., Rijksmuseum Vincent Van Gogh, Amsterdam.

137. Georges Seurat, *An Artist in his studio*, c. 1884, conté crayon on paper, 31.7 × 22.8 cm., Philadelphia Museum of Art (A.E. Gallatin Collection).

Signac occupied a studio at No. 130 on the Boulevard de Clichy from 1886–8. Sailor, painter, political activist, and theorist of Neo-Impressionism, Signac was a prime mover in the establishment of the juryless Salon des Indépendants, founded in 1884. He remained close to Seurat in this, in his technique and in his study of the theoretical writings of Chevreul, Helmholtz, Sutter, Rood and Charles Henry with reference to whom Signac and Seurat together transformed Impressionist technique into a systematic and less pragmatic analysis of light. Signac was literally close to Seurat in one other respect for Seurat occupied No. 128 bis Boulevard de Clichy from 1887.

Signac and Seurat exhibited at the eighth and last Impressionist group exhibition in 1886 with Pissarro and Forain, but their independence from established exhibiting opportunities was already evident. In 1889 Signac was visiting Van Gogh in Montmartre just a little further up the steep hill of Rue Lepic. His most celebrated theoretical text *D'Eugène Delacroix au Néo-Impressionisme* was published in 1899 by which time this area of Paris had witnessed much of the development of what was subsequently called Post-Impressionism through the activities of Seurat, Van Gogh, Lautrec and many others.

One drawing by Seurat shows a painter working on steps on a large composition (Plate 137). Work approaching mural-scale and involving an intricately controlled technique sustained across complex and carefully worked out compositions was an important feature of Seurat's major canvases. Like Degas he united direct observation of Parisian life, which in Seurat's case was recorded in *pochades*, small easily portable oil studies executed in the open air, with the evolution of major compositions in the studio, reconciling in this way traditional procedures with the innovations and lessons of Impressionism. Thus, the studio played an essential role, its wan but steady light permitting a meticulous and painstaking study impossible in a street, park or on a river bank. Seurat's painting *Les Poseuses* deliberately points to the contrast in subtle ways, by including a glimpse of part of his large painting *Sunday Afternoon on the Island of the Grande Jatte*, a scene of Parisians relaxing on an island in the Seine. The *Grande Jatte* depicts sunlight and shadow recorded directly in *pochades* which were subsequently used to develop the large, minutely organised composition glimpsed here. By contrast the models pose in the opalescent light of the studio, all stillness and poise. Seurat counterposes the public world with the privacy of the studio, the *plein-air* artist with the academy nude, one kind of light against another, fashionable dress against the changeless, styleless nude. He appears to depict his model in three poses as if to catalogue her forms more fully by providing three views and a timelessness is evoked thereby which contrasts with the fleeting activity of the riverbank. The echoing perspective of *La Grande Jatte* is truncated by its position on the studio wall, emphasising its physical flatness and the shallow, restricted recession permitted by this corner of the studio. *Les Poseuses* indicates that Seurat's independence arises from a balance of conflicting contemporary tendencies: it is a rich new synthesis of the methods of the Impressionist painting of modern life on the one hand and the time-honoured procedures of the Beaux-Arts studios on the other. He had studied at the Beaux-Arts under Lehmann from 1878 and was a meticulous student of the Louvre collections. He made copies after Raphael, Holbein, Poussin and Ingres. His sense of tradition and his respect for the lessons of the past were strong. His discovery of Impressionism was reconciled to these lessons via the theories of colour, line and composition derived from the same writers that impressed Signac, he turned his back upon the official Salon after his rejection there in 1884. His painting is a sign of the increasing interaction of approaches to painting that enriched Parisian art from the mid-1880s. His involvement with the Indépendants shows how such complexity was made increasingly feasible through the organisation of independent groups and their independent exhibiting facilities. Despite his early death in 1891 at the age of thirty-two, Seurat reflected much of this diversity in his work, resolving conflicting tendencies meticulously in major studio compositions.

The *Seine at Courbevoie* was sold for a mere 630 francs at the Arsène Alexandre Sale in 1903. By contrast, a drawing of the *Bridge at Courbeovie* (see Plate 241) realised 68,000 francs at the A. Natanson Sale in 1929. His small output of works was to rise rapidly in value in the twentieth century.[2]

A little further east along the Boulevard de Clichy on the north side at No. 104 was the *atelier libre* teaching studio of Fernand Cormon (1854–1924). Cormon gained notoriety and success from prehistoric scenes for the Salon although he executed highly coloured mural decorations of Paris too (an example being his ceiling paintings at the Petit Palais which clearly reveal a response to post-Impressionist colour comparable with that of Paul Besnard). Lautrec, Van Gogh, Emile Bernard and Anquetin were amongst his students. A gaunt, thin figure he was a popular and an active participant of Salon juries. His neolithic *Cain* was bought by the state at the Salon of 1880, and he became a member of the Institut. His was amongst the many private teaching studios in Paris run by successful artists on a commercial basis. It was highly convenient for Lautrec and Van Gogh although it left little evident trace upon their work. Cormon's professionalism was geared towards the Salon and official commissions. The area around the Boulevard de Clichy was home to a number of teaching ateliers organised as commercial concerns comparable to Cormon's and headed by respected and officially honoured artists whose reputations attracted many students both French and foreign. The theatricality and size of Cormon's major compositions ensured that they attracted attention at the crowded market of the Salon. This was one kind of professionalism. It was in sharp contrast to the authenticity of experience which artists depicting modern life in this area brought to their handling of new techniques.

Just a few doors away at 90 Boulevard de Clichy were the slowly turning sails of an extraordinary windmill with stars strung on wires and a crescent moon silhouetted against the sky. Here the Moulin Rouge founded by Joseph Oller opened its doors on 1 May 1889 to capture trade from the milling crowds in Paris for the Exposition Universelle of that year (Plates 138–9). It was an enormous success advertising a 'Ball every evening, Wednesday and Saturday night festivity. Diverse attractions. High-life rendezvous'. The Prince of Wales, the future King Edward VII was amongst its visitors. It combined upon air *café-chantant* with spectacular dancing. It also displayed paintings by Alfred Stevens, Gervex and Cormon, although it was Toulouse-Lautrec who became most intimately involved with its life, of which he became a part as well as an observer, a brilliantly dynamic and original advertiser of its atmosphere and facilities in both paintings and posters.

138. The Moulin Rouge, Place Blanche, *c*. 1900, photograph.

139. The Gardens of the Moulin Rouge with elephant, stage and ladies of the town, 1888, photograph, Cabinet des Estampes, Bibliothèque Nationale, Paris.

140. Toulouse-Lautrec at the Moulin Rouge with Tremalada the Manager, photograph, 1889, Musée Toulouse-Lautrec, Albi.

141. La Goulue, Grille d'Egout, Valentin le Desossé and friend dancing at the Moulin Rouge, photograph of *c*. 1890. Cabinet des Estampes, Bibliothèque Nationale, Paris.

142. (*facing page, above*) Toulouse-Lautrec working in his studio on *The Dance at the Moulin Rouge*, 1890, photograph, Musée Toulouse-Lautrec, Albi.

143. (*facing page, below*) Edouard Cucuel, *The Moulin Rouge on the night of the Bal des Quat 'z' Arts*, 1898. The banner of the Atélier Gérôme is appropriately classical with its Roman insignia SPQR.

The Moulin Rouge faces the Place Blanche opposite the Rue Blanche, a brief interruption in the flow of the Boulevard de Clichy. Both the physical vitality of the dancers and the aggressively urban night-life of its clientèle were painted remorselessly by Lautrec whose achievement it was to revel in their grotesqueness under the glaring lights without a trace of moralising disapproval, verging upon caricature in a worldly mockery that revealed an overwhelming enthusiasm for its artificiality and energy, looking without disapproval upon its sordidness and vigour. For the painter of modern life this was an achievement comparable with the cynical objectivity of Zola's novel of the courtesan Nana, an analysis of the behaviour of the city which owed much to the cool reportage of Manet and Degas but which moved beyond them in the enthusiastic involvement in the life he depicted. Lautrec was instrumental in the fame of dancers at the Moulin Rouge (Plate 141). His response ranged from rough dynamic canvases to still paintings of unexpected tenderness in his depiction of prostitutes. Beyond that he promoted the Moulin Rouge and its star performers in posters of dramatically edited simplicity, a direct involvement in the business affairs of his subject matter never approached in comparable themes by Manet or Degas. In this way Lautrec produced a popular art that was the antithesis of Salon respectability, transgressing the bounds of painting, with all its connotations of preciousness, for a cheap and popular but no less brilliant decoration of street hoardings. Here was a new kind of professional activity for the practising artist, independent of the official structures of opportunity, display and recognition.

In Lautrec's studio the noisy dancing, drinking, singing and talking of the Moulin Rouge were transferred to canvas in silence and solitude, colossal canvases and small ones echoing in their asymmetrical compositions the hectic rhythms of the previous night. The diminutive and aristocratic painter perches upon a simple stool with his box of paints, palette in hand and hat upon his head, watching the painting evolve. He

recalled the movements, the lurid lighting and grotesque profiles of his subject without any of the trappings of respectability of the successful artist's studio and needed only the practical and minimal requirements of his profession not even using an easel, preferring to rest his painting against the enormous steps used for larger works (Plate 142). Lautrec did not share the pretentions of the Salon, and his art decisively broached its implication that painting was precious, hallowed and respectable, by means of a committed depiction of an unrespectable life-style of which he was himself an integral part.

The Moulin Rouge responded to art in Paris in one other way — it provided the setting for the Four Arts Ball, the Bal Quat'z' Arts, to which students and professors of the studios of painting, sculpture, engraving and architecture, flocked from all over Paris each spring after the submissions to the Salon were completed. The ball was a riotous assembly of nudity and fancy-dress to which the public were not admitted. At the door the *massiers* of the teaching studios checked the credentials of models, students and artists whose studios had been issued with carefully authorised tickets (Plate 144). Each studio prepared a float, a mobile *tableau-vivant* which processed to the Moulin Rouge and for which a first prize of fifty bottles of champagne was awarded at the climax of the ball. Within the Moulin Rouge lodges were assembled evoking the preoccupations of particular studios and the artists who directed them. The Atelier Gérôme constructed a float

139

144. Charles Léandre, *Ticket for the Bal des Quat 'z' Arts*, 1898. Made out to Edouard Cucuel, Atelier Gérôme.

145. Edouard Cucuel, *Parade of the Atelier Gérôme at the Bal des Quat 'z' Arts*, 1898, Gérôme's *Tanagra* is posed by a model before a gigantic palette (see plate 149).

146. The studio of Anders Zorn, 71 Boulevard de Clichy.

upon which, within the walls of the Moulin Rouge, a naked model posed as Gérôme's sculpture *Tanagra* before an immense palette (Plate 145). Banners swung emblazened with the name Gérôme and the Gérôme atelier's lodge represented a Greek temple. By contrast, the Atelier Cormon created 'a huge caravan of the prehistoric big-muscled men that appeal so strongly to Cormon; large skeletons of extinct mammals, giant ferns, skins, and stone implements were scattered about, while the students of Cormon's atelier, almost naked, with bushy hair and clothed in skins, completed the picture.'[3]

Gérôme himself was 'gaudily gowned in the rich green costume of a Chinese mandarin, his white moustache dyed black, and his white locks hidden beneath a black skull-cap topped with a bobbing appendage'.[4] J.P. Laurens, another respected Institut member, appeared in Norman costume, the sculptor Denys Puech as a courtier of Marie Antoinette's time and the painter Willette as a Roman Emperor. According to the art-student W.C. Morrow one member of Bonnat's studio 'went simply as a stink, nothing more, nothing less, but it was potent'.[5] Two hundred waiters served the meal and 'Steinlen, Grasset, Forain, Rodin — in fact, nearly all the renowned painters, sculptors and illustrators of Paris were there.'[6] Morrow asserted unconvincingly that 'It is well understood that such a spectacle would not be suitable for any but artists and students' who 'see in these annual spectacles only grace, beauty and majesty'.[7]

Cabaret life played an important part in the night-time activities of the Boulevard de Clichy. Few places can have been more curious than the Cabaret d'Enfer (Hell Cabaret) opposite the Moulin Rouge in the Place Blanche, its façade encrusted with imitation stalactites and falling figures of the damned and its entrance portal shaped as a terrifying open jaw beneath giant teeth and baleful staring eyes. Its sequels were established nearby at the Cabaret of Death and the Cabaret of Heaven.

Further along on the south side of the Boulevard de Clichy worked the printmaker and painter Charles Jacques (1813–94) who had risen from apprenticeship to a map engraver at the age of 17 to become one of the celebrated printmakers of his day, receiving numerous Salon medals including a gold medal at the 1889 Exposition Universelle. Another active printmaker-painter occupied 71 Boulevard de Clichy in a four-storey building surmounted by a large north light in the façade and roof, an elegant stone-fronted purpose-built construction (Plate 146). This was Anders Zorn (1860–1920), a vigorous Swedish artist whose modelling of form was complemented by a loose and dynamic handling of the media both in painting and etching, a highly original and talented artist who responded enthusiastically to developments in painting and the well established rebirth of printmaking in Paris. Having trained as a sculptor at the Stockholm Academy, in 1881 he visited London and Paris. He lived in Paris between 1886 and 1896 and became a founder member of the Société Nationale des Beaux-Arts. He considered the Boulevard de Clichy 'a less noble but more artistic neighbourhood' than his former dwelling in the Rue Daubigny and remained here for approximately eight years.[8] In 1896 he returned to Sweden. 65 on the Boulevard de Clichy was occupied by Jean-Léon Gérôme until his death in 1904 (Plate 147). Like Zorn's studio this is a four-storey purpose-built construction, the studio occupying the double-height fourth floor. The north light has a curved arch set in a slightly broken-forward projection of the façade and is surmounted by a cornice which recalls a pediment. Amongst the most feared and respected of the Ecole des Beaux-Arts tutors, Gérôme was dismayed by the rising popularity of Manet and the Impressionists, although he remained a life-long friend of Degas. He received the highest honours after the early success of his *Cockfight* in 1845. Made a *chevalier* of the Légion d'Honneur in 1855, he was promoted to *officier* in 1867, *commandeur* in 1878 and *grand officier* in 1900. In 1863, at the time of Manet's *succès de scandale* at the Salon des Refusés, Gérôme was appointed professor at the Ecole des Beaux-Arts where he taught with firm discipline for many years. Elected to the Institut in 1865 he continued to exert as much influence as his position allowed over the official artistic organisation of Paris, mounting a campaign against the acceptance, for example, of the Caillebotte Bequest of Impressionist painting in the period 1895–7. He was not averse however to entertainment. In his early years in Montparnasse, south of the Seine, he had been an active participator in a communal group of studios decorated on the outside with a painting of Chinamen and he had kept a celebrated pet-monkey who wore evening dress at his dinner table. As has been noted he attended the Four Arts Ball dressed as a Chinaman and evidently enjoyed the proceedings: 'At one corner was Gérôme's private studio high up in the top of the house, and standing on the balcony was Gérôme himself, enjoying the scene below'.[9] A student visiting this studio 'was politely ushered in by a manservant, and conducted to the door of the master's studio through a hall and gallery fitted with wonderful marble groups'.[10] Overwhelmed by such magnificence the student 'stood dazed in the middle of the splendid room, with its great sculptures and paintings, some still unfinished, and a famous collection of barbaric arms and costumes. A beautiful model was posing upon a rug. But most impressive of all was the white-bearded master.'[11] He had become fascinated by sculpture in the late 1870s, using tinted marble to heighten the life-like effect of his figures. His *Bellona* had been a considerable success and formed a focus of his teaching atelier's display at one of the Bal Quat'z' Arts. He had first exhibited sculpture in 1878 when his *Gladiators*, derived from a recent painting, were displayed at the Exposition Universelle of that year. *Tanagra* and *Bellona* followed. His figures were published as statuettes in bronze by the Siot-Decauville foundry and were a considerable success. Frémiet, with whom Gérôme has studied animals at the Jardin des Plantes, gave him lessons in sculpture. His procedure was to work in plaster and have this copied by professional marble-carvers under his supervision, or cast in bronze at the foundry. The Barbedienne process was used to reduce his figures for the more popular market.[12] He died whilst sleeping in his sculpture studio in 1904. According to Edmond de Goncourt, Gérôme was 'a very great spirit with the voice of a peasant'.[13] He had travelled widely, especially in the Near-East, Turkey and Egypt. He had married the daughter of the publisher and dealer Goupil and was dedicated to a strictly traditional academic approach to painting and sculpture. He forbade his students to make quick oil sketches in the open air (*pochades*) and considered the Impressionists a dishonour to French art. A preoccupation with the handling of paint textures appeared to Gérôme superficial 'but a question of the skin. Construction, to construct well, that is the only consideration.'[14] *Working on the Marble* of 1895 by Gérôme is an elaborate self-portrait showing Gérôme sculpting *Tanagra* (Plate 148–9). Exotic objects litter the studio. The white-haired Gérôme has mounted the low turn-table which precariously supports also his life-size sculpture and the model close beside it. He is meticulously finishing the thigh and the painting stresses the strict resemblance of sculpture to model. Amongst the significant trappings of the studio can been seen his *Hoop-dancer* at right, a reduced version of which the outstretched hand of Tanagra was subsequently to hold. In the background a small painting of Pygmalion and Galatea shows a sculpture in the same pose coming to life. Gérôme in tinting his sculpture sought a kind of verisimilitude but only in reference to the antique precedent of tanagra sculptures in the Louvre museum.[15]

Equally derivative in inspiration but from a very different source was the work of Henri Rivière who occupied 29 Boulevard de Clichy. His inspiration was Japanese and his printmaking techniques closely emulated Japanese examples. He also worked on shadow puppet theatre designs for the Chat Noir cabaret as did the graphic artist Steinlen.

In this boulevard crowded with artists, an unusual figure was the tragedienne turned sculptress Sarah Bernhardt. Fitting in some fifteen lessons in the midst of her tumultuous and erratic but always spectacular public career in the theatre, she became a passionately enthusiastic sculptor and was closely involved with the visual arts. The painters Georges Clairin and Louise Abbéma were amongst her most intimate friends. She provided them with studios in her castle on the remote fastness of the island Belle-

147. The studio of Jean-Leon Gérôme, 65 Boulevard de Clichy.

148. Jean-Leon Gérôme, *Working on the Marble*, 1895, oil on canvas, 50 × 36.8 cm., Pioneer Museum and Haggin Galleries, Haggin Collection, Stockton, California.

149. Jean-Léon Gérôme, *Tanagra*, tinted marble, Musée d'Orsay, Paris. Plate 148 shows the model posing for this sculpture.

Ile-sur-mer on the craggy Atlantic sea coast of Brittany. In Paris she found her apartment in the Rue de Rome too small for the making of sculpture and hired a big studio at 11 Boulevard de Clichy. From 1873 she would arrive there daily at 10 am. and if she was not rehearsing she would remain there all day, modelling in clay until tea-time when visitors were permitted. The painter Alfred Stevens was a frequent visitor amongst the actors and actresses there. Bernhardt first exhibited in 1875 and had success the following year with a sculpture called *After the Tempest*. Later she left the Boulevard de Clichy and her Rue de Rome apartment for a studio she designed herself on the corner of the Avenue de Villiers and Rue Fortuny where she remained for twenty-one years in the great hotel decorated by Clairin and a few of his friends. It cost her 500,000 francs and launched her into a life of credit.[16]

In 1888 the *Art Journal* periodical commented that 'Madame Bernhardt has been the cause of more Art in others than she has produced by her own hand'[17], listing Georges Clairin's stylishly seductive portrait of 1876 and a full length profile by Louise Abbéma of 1877, but noting also that 'chief among all these was the little profile, delicately rendered by Bastien-Lepage, which she has not prized sufficiently to keep'.[18] Bastien-Lepage delineated the actress-sculptor's profile with precision and sensitivity, her eyes lowered and mouth slightly open beneath the arch of her nose (Plate 150), features so closely followed in Bernhardt's sculpted self-portrait, surmounting an ink-stand, as to suggest that she was working with an eye as much to Bastien-Lepage's painting as to any assemblage of mirrors. She sculpted herself however as a sphinx crouched behind the inkwell, an ostrich feather plume inserted in her bronze hair (Plate 151). Later she fascinated the poster artist and painter Alphonse Mucha who promoted her most famous theatrical productions in the 1890s. She was also the subject of a portrait bust by Gérôme in 1895 (Plate 152). Worked in plaster for execution by craftsmen in marble, Gérôme's sculpture incorporated attached small figures, including a standing statuette of Tragedy, from which emerges the head of the actress in a high collar. Gérôme gave the original painted plaster to Bernhardt.

Moving along the Boulevard de Clichy eastwards, further functional studios remain visible beyond Nos. 13 and 11 with an imposing and purposebuilt block of studios on three floors at No. 9 (Plate 153). These three studios surmount an archway inscribed with the date 1882 revealing the development of the area for the specific use of artists in

150. Jules Bastien-Lepage, *Portrait of Sarah Bernhardt*, 1879, line engraving after the painting in oil on canvas, 43.2 × 32.3 cm., whereabouts unknown.

151. Sarah Bernhardt, *Fantastic Inkwell. Self Portrait as a Sphinx* (Encrier fantastique), 1880, bronze (with replacement ostrich feather). Thiébaut cast, 31.8 × 19 × 22.9 cm., Museum of Fine Arts, Boston (Helen and Alice Colburn Fund).

152. Jean-Leon Gérôme, *Portrait Bust of Sarah Bernhardt*, 1895, polychromed plaster, 68.6 cm. high, Musée d'Orsay, Paris.

153. Studios at 7 and 9 Boulevard de Clichy.

the period a few years before Van Gogh moved to Montmartre in 1886. The archway leads through to the Rue Alfred-Stevens which connects with the studio cluster just south of the boulevard abutting the Avenue Frochot and extending to the Rue Victor-Massé. The pointillist painter Edmond Petitjean occupied 3 Rue Alfred-Stevens. He was a close associate of Seurat and Signac who both lived further west along the boulevard.

Continuing east, a double bay of studio lights on three floors at 5 Boulevard de Clichy reasserts the importance of this thoroughfare for the artists who populated it so densely. Across the road No. 6 was used by the American painter Mary Cassatt, a close friend and protegée of Degas. The academician Jean-Jacques Henner, who had a studio just a little to the east along this thoroughfare, was an admirer of her work and maintained that he was instrumental in encouraging the Salon jury to accept her paintings. He recalled that in 1881 'in a discussion about Degas, in which all of the other Impressionists were criticised, I demanded support for Mademoiselle Cassatt'.[19] After studying at the Pennsylvania Academy, Mary Cassatt toured Europe in 1866 and settled in Paris in 1874, the year of the first Impressionist group exhibition on the Boulevard des Capucines. She exhibited with the Impressionists in 1877, 1879, 1880, 1881 and 1886. Durand-Ruel staged an exhibition of her work in 1891 and she was admitted to the Légion d'Honneur in 1904. Degas was attracted by her submission to the Salon of 1874 and they became close friends. In 1890 they visited a major exhibition of Japanese art together; she began to collect prints by Utamaro and to make prints inspired by Japanese work using flat colour and a definitive line.

There is a corner studio at 1 Boulevard de Clichy above what is now a café named the Rendez-vous des Artistes; it occupies the top two floors of a four storey building and is a simple, practical north light studio. It overlooks the Place Pigalle, which like the Place Blanche further east, is little more than a brief interruption of the boulevard. It was however a significant point for the artistic life of the area. In this square was the Café de la Nouvelle Athènes, a central focus for writers and painters of Manet's circle

154. Edouard Manet, *George Moore at the Nouvelles-Athènes*, 1878, oil on canvas, 64.5 × 81.5 cm., Metropolitan Museum of Art, New York.

155. Puvis de Chavannes in his studio *c.* 1896

(Plate 154). George Moore was an habitué there: 'I did not go to either Oxford or Cambridge,' he wrote in 1886,

> but I went to the Nouvelle Athènes. What is the Nouvelle Athènes? He who would know anything of my life must know something of the academy of the fine arts. Not the official stupidity you read of in the daily papers, but the real French academy, the *cafè*. The Nouvelle Athènes is a café on the Place Pigalle.[20]

The Place Pigalle and its café appeared in his memory as hallowed ground:

> With what strange, almost unnatural clearness do I see and hear — see the white face of that café, the white nose of the block of houses, stretching up to the Place, between two streets. I can see now the incline of those two streets, and I know what shops are there; I can hear the glass door of the café grate on the sand as I open it.[21]

It was important to him most of all for the presence of Manet and Degas, for their acid conversation, their ideas and their achievements as artists. Manet 'sits next to Degas, that round-shouldered man in a suit of pepper and salt. There is nothing very trenchantly French about him either, except the large necktie; his eyes are small, and his words are sharp, ironical, cynical.'[22]

Several studios survive in the Place Pigalle and behind it towards the Rue Alfred-Stevens. Highly influential artists worked in studios in this little square. In surprisingly close proximity to the scene of Manet's and Degas' discussions at the café Nouvelle Athènes was the studio at 11 Place Pigalle occupied for more than thirty years by the most celebrated Parisian mural painter of the later nineteenth century, Pierre Puvis de Chavannes (Plate 155). There was a large studio, two apartments, a bedroom and a dressing room. Puvis installed himself in this studio in 1852 and organised a teaching atelier there for study from the life-model. Later in his life it was here that Puvis worked on his thousands of drawings from the model comprising the archive of images and

156. Félix Vallotton, *Puvis de Chavannes*, 1899, woodcut, 18 × 13 cm., published in *The Studio*, 1899, vol. 15.

157. Edgar Degas, *Miss La-La at the Cirque Fernando*, 1879, oil on canvas, 125 × 79.5 cm., National Gallery, London.

poses incorporated into his vast murals which were executed in a separate hangar-like studio out of central Paris at Neuilly. In the Place Pigalle studio the walls were covered in 'drawings and sketches and photographs of his works, and for furniture, simply a big table, a few armchairs and a sofa'.[23] This sparseness also characterised the Neuilly studio and is evident equally in the measured, harmonious restraint of his canvases. In the Place Pigalle they filled his walls and were even hung on the wooden dado; a sculptor's turntable was used for small drawing studies, and a simple tressel table sufficed for paraphernalia. The interior was a blend of restraint and profusion, for Puvis was both a prolific artist and preoccupied with a severe editing of his work down to its essential features. His austerity was remarkable. He would receive friends before nine o'clock in the morning, amongst them the painter engraver Marcellin Desboutin, the associate of Manet and Degas, and later of the Rosicrucians.[24]

Puvis had studied under Scheffer, briefly with Delacroix and with Thomas Couture. His success began in 1861 when his paintings *Bellum* and *Concordia* were purchased by the state for the museum at Amiens. Honours followed: he was made *chevalier* of the Légion d'Honneur in 1864, *officier* in 1877, and *commandeur* in 1889 by which time his influence and fame were formidable. He executed enormous decorative commissions for public buildings at Amiens, Lyons, the Panthéon in Paris (1874–8), the Sorbonne (1887) which were discussed Part 1, and in 1894–8 for the Boston Public Library. He was never, however, a member of the Institut and in 1889 he became a co-founder of the Société Nationale des Beaux-Arts with Meissonier, whom he succeeded as president in 1891. His work was widely admired outside of official channels and is referred to in paintings by artists as diverse as Toulouse-Lautrec, Seurat, Gauguin and Matisse. His timeless evocations of an alternative and allegorical world were much admired by Symbolist artists and writers. Rodin sculpted his portrait, Félix Vallotton paid homage in a print (Plate 156) and Gaston La Touche depicted him as a visionary hero (Plate 237). He was uniquely able to retain his personal identity upon canvases of epic scale bringing meticulous control to public commissions. His commitment to reducing his images to their bare essentials stressed the flatness of his picture-surface and sustained rhythmic coherence across immense canvases. They were as unobtrusive as they were harmonious, qualities which were to be widely emulated by younger artists, through their instillation of emotional expression into flat areas of colour tuned one against another across the picture plane. This mural technique did not impress Gérôme who conceded that 'they are not bad from a distance...from a great distance, but they do not bear analysis. It is a series of mannequins ill-placed upon the ground.'[26] Also at 11 Place Pigalle for a while was the academician Jean-Jacques Henner whose nudes appealed to a very different clientèle, and whose figures emerging half resolved from deep brown underpainting occasionally recalled Puvis' idyllic compositions without any of the grandeur, austere palette or sheer scale.

Beyond the Place Pigalle the thoroughfare continues eastwards under a change of name as the Boulevard Rochechouart. At No. 84 was the Chat Noir bar and cabaret where Aristide Bruant insulted and assailed his audiences, and which was much frequented by the artists Toulouse-Lautrec and Louis Anquetin. The printmaker Steinlen designed its posters and Henri Rivière began its shadow puppet theatre.[27] The Musée de Montmartre preserves the original black cut-out figures for the production of Louis Morin's *Pierrot Pornographe*. Further nightlife was available at the Elysées Montmartre at 80 Boulevard Rochechouart which provided dancing and the spectacular entertainments characteristic of the area.

Further east was the Cirque Fernando, a small circus which had attracted Degas in 1879 and where Toulouse-Lautrec was painting nine years later. Degas' *Miss La-La at the Cirque Fernando* is a highly original and efficient application of an ancient device to a modern theme (Plate 157). The professional performer, the acrobat Miss La-La hangs by her teeth ready to spin on the end of a wire; she is seen from the auditorium below,

158. Henri de Toulouse-Lautrec, *In the Cirque Fernando: The Ringmaster*, 1888, oil on canvas, 100.3 × 161.3, Art Institute of Chicago (Joseph Winterbotham Collection, 1925).

159. Studios through three storeys at 35 Boulevard Rochechouart.

her body depicted from an angle scarcely envisaged in the art of recent years and now adopted in a scene of modern life with dramatic and artificial lighting from below. Degas stressed her muscular strength. She is a physical performer engaged in her profession and has no wider significance, yet to indicate her movement Degas employed the technique perfected by the antique sculptor of the discus-thrower: she is caught at the very moment before her spinning movement begins, its revolving flourish still potential and not actual, with every muscle ready, expressed in the outstretched arms as they begin to twist the body into a spiral which the circling bays of the circus building already mark out around the background of the painting.

By contrast Lautrec, in the same circular arena, uses the curving banks of seats to provide an arching rhythm that carries the image of his horse and rider forward (Plate 158). This too is dynamic and Lautrec's draughtsmanship stresses the physical to the point of caricature. His supple rhythms express movement in action in contrast to Degas' taut moment of poise. The relationship to Degas is as close however as their dwellings and the setting itself suggest.

Two bays of studios on three floors look north across the Boulevard de Rochechouart at No. 57, as they do at No. 47 where the Rue Bochart-de-Saron ascends to the boulevard. In the Rue Bochard-de-Saron an elegant purpose-built studio light faces east at No. 9 marking a studio-complex much in use at the turn of the century. A little further, at the Place d'Anvers, studio windows can be seen where the square falls back to the Avenue Trudaine running parallel to the boulevard. Enormous and splendid studio windows dominate No. 35 framed within the façade through a height of three stories, the top studio double height with large roof-light (Plate 159). Fernand Cormon lived off the boulevard at No. 38 Rue Rochechouart. To the south lies the Rue Alfred-Stevens and the Avenue Frochot where, as we have noted, Lautrec painted in the splendid seclusion of a private street of two-storey houses with gardens running up from the end of the Rue Victor-Massé. To the north, the steep hill of Montmartre itself is visible with its windmills and its stepped streets crowned by the basilica of Sacré-Coeur. Uphill, the atmosphere of the rural village survived in pockets of gardens and silent streets away from the traffic of the boulevard. But it could be splendid and sordid: its view was spectacular yet in the hours of darkness, its half-built streets could be menacing.

# 5. The Heights of Montmartre

A photograph of Mimi Pinson's house in the Rue de Mont-Cenis, which sheltered many artists, shows a girl at a waterpump, buildings with crumbling stucco and the cobbled street falling away sharply downhill (Plate 161). This image of Montmartre, probably in the quiet of the morning, evokes an air of gentle decrepitude and the near silence of a provincial backstreet. Jean Béraud's painting *Montmartre* presents a contrasting view of the district as the centre of high-spirited revelry up above the roof-tops of the city centre, his pleasure-seekers dancing, kicking and kissing in the street (Plate 162). The two faces of Montmartre go together. Briefly independent of Paris during the Commune, Montmartre had long enjoyed a precarious but distinct identity beyond the city proper. But we have seen how the great boulevards were encroaching along its base and tall tenements rising amidst its semi-rural, semi-urban streets. Revellers from other parts of Paris and from other countries slummed it in Montmartre, bringing their wealth to its

160. Map of the Boulevard de Clichy with Montmartre to the north and Les Batignolles to the west.

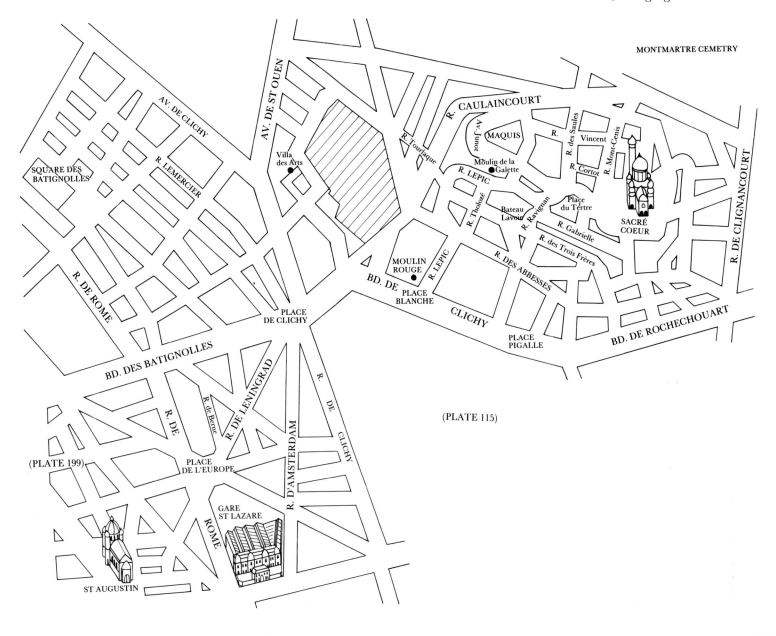

often sinister, libertine but persistently attractive backstreets (Plate 163), prey to the clever, enterprising and sometimes criminal proprietors of its establishments for entertainment. At the same time Montmartre provided cheap accommodation for artists moving north from the cosmopolitan and hectic city which Montmartre overlooks from a height.

North of the Place de Clichy in a cluster of small streets which back onto the Montmartre Cemetry, the fashionable and successful portrait artist and painter of exotic Near-

163. Clive Holland, *A Bye-Street, Montmartre*, photograph from *c.* 1902.

162. Jean Béraud, *Montmartre*, 1897, whereabouts unknown.

164. The Villa des Arts, 15 Rue Hégésippe-Moreau: entrance to the courtyard studios.

165. The Villa des Arts, view of the studios at the rear in Rue Ganneron.

166. *J. J. Benjamin-Constant in his studio, c.* 1895, photograph by André and Sleigh Ltd.

Eastern scenes, Benjamin-Constant, headed a teaching studio at 15 Rue Hégésippe Moreau (Impasse Hélène) in a studio complex known as the Villa des Arts (Plate 164–5).[1] Its evolution was a typical example of private enterprise operating within the world of artists and students. At the height of his success he was able to abandon the Impasse Hélène to move downhill to 'more fashionable quarters in the Rue Pigalle'.[2] Benjamin-Constant held open house on Sunday mornings. Within the double height of his studio a large balcony across a substantial portion of the room was hung with rich oriental rugs which also covered areas of the parquet-floor downstairs and the curtained divan in an alcove beneath the balcony. Immense rugs also hung on the walls and the interior must have presented a richly exotic atmosphere, punctuated as it was with curious objects, Moorish lamps, a stuffed cheetah, and, hanging from the balcony, a dessicated crocodile. In the midst of all this were paintings, large heavily framed society portraits, compositions for the Salon and the artist himself (Plate 166):

> he possessed a choice collection of Moorish rugs and curtains and ornaments of all sorts, and, with the aid of these, had transformed the place into quite a suggestion of a portion of the Alhambra itself. The block of buildings in which his place was situated consisted entirely of studios, some with and some without rooms belonging to them. It was in fact a veritable artists' colony, and was inhabited by quite a number of well-known men, as well as others less advanced in their profession.[3]

Benjamin-Constant had worked with Cabanel in 1867 and was much affected by a visit to Morocco in 1871. He was admitted to the Légion d'Honneur in 1893 and the same year was elected to the Institut. The Arabic exoticism of his studio interior and his paintings echoes that of the 'studio' of the writer Pierre Loti at Rochefort which had a room decorated as a mosque. In England the painter Lord Leighton transformed his house in Holland Park along similar lines.

167. Eugene Carrière working on *The Kiss of Evening* (Le Baiser du Soir) at the Villa des Arts, 15 Rue Hégésieppe-Moreau, 1901.

168. Maximilien Luce, *View of Montmartre*, 1887, oil on canvas, 46 × 81 cm., Rijksmuseum Kroller-Muller, Otterlo. Formerly in the collection of Camille Pissarro.

The painter Eugène Carrière also occupied No. 15–16 Impasse Hélène around 1889. Friend of Rodin and much admired by the Symbolists his ethereal and mysterious paintings were the work, as the critic Paul Mantz put it, of a 'friend of the fog, a dreamer enraptured by the incomplete; beings and objects fraternise in a confusion of smoke' (Plate 167).[4] Carrière, who had studied under Cabanel, was a friend of the writers Verlaine, Daudet, Mallarmé, Anatole France and Edmond de Goncourt. He executed decorations for the Sorbonne and the Hôtel de Ville, and opened an academy in the Rue de Rennes.

In the Impasse Hélène studio complex, perhaps the most successful figure of his day also had a teaching studio. This was Léon Bonnat who in time was to receive almost every available official accolade. Lautrec was briefly amongst his students at the Impasse Hélène, finding in him a difficult, demanding and unsympathetic tutor. Lautrec moved on to study under Cormon. Léon Bonnat's teaching studio closed in 1883 with his appointment as professor at the Ecole des Beaux-Arts.

169. Vincent Van Gogh, *View from the Artist's Window at 54 Rue Lepic*, 1886–7, oil on canvas, 46 × 38 cm., Rijksmuseum Vincent Van Gogh, Amsterdam.

Beyond this complex and beyond the cemetry to the east, approachable uphill from the Boulevard de Clichy via the Rue Caulaincourt or the Rue Lepic, access is gained to the high heart of Montmartre and its summit upon which Sacré-Coeur was slowly rising. Here fruit and vegetable shops still fill the pavements with their produce as they had when Van Gogh and the pointilliste painter Maximilien Luce were painting the abundant allotments of Montmartre (Plate 168).

A little higher and spectacular panoramic views of Paris open out to the south. Vincent Van Gogh, who in 1886 was living at 54 Rue Lepic with his brother Theo, was amongst the surprisingly few painters who accepted the pictorial challenge proffered by this immense space which encompassed the entire organism of central Paris as far as Montparnasse in the south. A painting from Van Gogh's window in Rue Lepic reveals the gable-end of a building marking the immediate foreground. At the left a facade already establishes a considerable distance before the panorama opens out into a haze of roofs, Van Gogh's broken dashes and marks efficiently summing up the eye's inability to concentrate upon such spreading wealth of detail as the city presents (Plate 169). Another drawing faces due south adopting different tactics to isolate the major archi-

170. Vincent Van Gogh, *View from Montmartre*, 1886, pencil with brown and white crayon on paper, 22.5 × 30 cm., Rijksmuseum Vincent Van Gogh, Amsterdam. The towers of Notre-Dame visible at left, the dome of the Panthéon right of centre.

tectural monuments of Notre-Dame's square towers (far left) and the dominant drum and dome of the Panthéon (right of centre) (Plate 170). The panoramic vista of Paris painted by Van Gogh from Montmartre adds aerial perspective through light, colour and brushwork as the detailed huddle of nearby roof-tops and a profusion of chimneys give way suddenly to an immense distance[4]. To the left rises the Tour St Jacques on the Rue de Rivoli with the bulk of Notre-Dame close beside it, a railway shed raises its triangular pediment as the eye scans the view, the Panthéon breaks the horizon projecting its dome into the sky and the roofs of the Louvre catch the light towards the right edge of the painting (Plate 171).

In Paris Vincent Van Gogh remained a figure of considerable obscurity. His success was utterly minimal despite his intense, authentic commitment, his knowledge of art and his brother's contacts in the world of dealing. He studied at Cormon's atelier with Lautrec and Bernard, and he exhibited in restaurants along the boulevard including the Café-Brasserie du Tambourin run by Agostina Segatin, a model, at 62 Boulevard de Clichy,[5] but very few auspicious opportunities arose and his prices were as low as could be imagined. His appetite for art was voracious however and his friendships with Bernard, Lautrec and Anquetin were important sources of learning for him. Montmartre, with its quarries, windmills and gardens, was Van Gogh's home in Paris and he painted the city centre well beyond arm's reach in the glittering distance.

Closeby at 87 Rue Lepic was the studio of the printmaker Eugène Delâtre. Living between the windmills of the Moulin Rouge and the Moulin de la Galette further uphill, he devoted several series of prints to Montmartre and its inhabitants. His 'Imprimerie Artistique' executed etchings by many famous figures, and Delâtre himself was an innovative technician in his own prints, experimenting, for example, with multicoloured etching techniques. He was amongst the first members of the Société des Graveurs en Couleurs and exhibited regularly at the Salon National des Beaux-Arts. From 1876 he had collaborated with his father Auguste Delâtre whose studio in the Rue

171. (*facing page*) Vincent Van Gogh, *The Roofs of Paris*, 1886, oil on canvas, 54 × 72 cm., Rijksmuseum Vincent Van Gogh, Amsterdam.

St Jacques had attracted Daubigny, Millet, Bracquemond, Meryon, Rops, Whistler, Charles Jacques and many other artists centrally involved in the rebirth of printmaking as an artist's medium in Paris. After the destruction of his presses in the Franco-Prussian war Auguste Delâtre spent time in England with Tissot and Dalou. He began to collaborate with his son Eugène upon his return to France.

Almost touching the Rue Lepic at its half-way point, the Rue Caulaincourt skirts the Montmartre Cemetry. By the 1890s it was beginning to undergo redevelopment, new blocks rising at odd points amongst its upresumptious dwellings, creating an air of half-built desolation. This is how Steinlen depicted Montmartre in a colour lithograph of 1899 (Plate 172); the blank gable-ends familiar to Van Gogh reappear to Steinlen's eye without the stimulating celebration of light with which Van Gogh bathed their forms. Steinlen's taste for the sinister was evident in his posters for the Chat Noir cabaret. Here it pervades the tedious half-formed street. At night such areas could be dangerous and their sinister ill-lit back streets the haunt of the vicious and the poor. Steinlen 'lives behind the Sacré-Coeur,' noted an anonymous writer in the *Studio* magazine in 1899, 'in the Rue Caulaincourt which a couple of years ago was nothing more

172. Théophile-Alexandre Steinlen, *Montmartre, c.* 1899, 15 × 20 cm., coloured lithograph published in *The Studio*, 1899, vol. 16.

173. Shop in the Maquis, Rue Caulaincourt, Montmartre, photograph before 1900, Cabinet des Estampes, Bibliothèque Nationale, Paris.

than a path across a sort of waste, with tea-gardens and shooting galleries and various queer haunts on the Paris side, with the vast plains of Clichy, and St Ouen and Clignancourt stretching out in the other direction like an ocean.' Steinlen's visitor also noted the desperate aspect of Montmartre, which had 'the melancholy that attaches to these desolate, unfinished districts, with their rubbish-heaps and their hoardings, their half-built houses, and their high, bare walls, whose monotony is but ill-concealed by the many coloured posters stuck upon them.'[6] Steinlen occupied a studio at 21 Rue Caulaincourt where Lautrec kept a studio for ten years up to 1897.[7] Steinlen's dwelling was extraordinarily ramshackle even in this area, for he inhabited Le Maquis a vast space covered in sheds constructed from 'demolition material, lengths of wood, old planks,

174. The Maquis at Montmartre, photograph from before 1900, Cabinet des Estampes, Bibliothèque Nationale, Paris.

619. MONTMARTRE. — Le Maquis en 1904

175. Théophile-Alexandre Steinlen, *Rue Caulaincourt, Montmartre*, 1896, lithograph, Cabinet des Estampes, Bibliothèque Nationale, Paris.

grills and iron...lost in flourishing green vegetation, (Plate 173–5).[8] Here lived 'rag-pickers, plaster moulders, bric-à-brac merchants, and a few artists'.[9] Steinlen lived amongst them in a construction known as the Cats' Cottage. Demolished after 1900, the Maquis stretched from the Moulin de la Galette to the Rue Caulaincourt. Steinlen's dwelling was named after the profuse population of cats which shared his accomodation and which frequently formed the subjects of his drawings. Having settled in Montmartre in 1880, he became involved with the Chat Noir cabaret, illustrated many magazines and books including Aristide Bruant's *Sur la route*, as well as *Les Soliloques du pauvre* and *Le Coeur populaire* by Jehan Rictus, and *Les Contes du Chat Noir* by Rodolphe Salis. He was a celebrated poster designer and much of his work reflected the street life of the poor in Montmartre. He exhibited at the Salon des Indépendants from 1893. This was a dangerous area, as Renoir's son recalled, 'At the point where the Clichy and St Ouen Avenues now branch off there was formerly a long area filled with shacks inhabited chiefly by rag-pickers, and also less desirable characters.'[10] The present Avenue Junot dates from 1910–12 and finally obliterated the Maquis which was riddled with private lanes such as that from 73 Rue Lepic. According to Jean Renoir 'the shacks of the people who lived there were hedged in by rank vegetation. The Maquis area... extended down as far as the Rue Caulaincourt. What is now the Avenue Junot was a confused jumble of rose bushes. These shanties, which had been built up by the occupants themselves without regard to the first rules of safety or sanitation, were free of all taxes or other legal controls...'[11] Amongst its inhabitants were the starving poet Bibi la Purée and numerous artists. On the south side of the Allée des Brouillards in the Maquis stood the Château des Brouillards, which in 1846 had housed the poet Gerard de Nerval and later the sculptor Walsey. Renoir lived opposite before 1895 in a building from which he observed the catastrophic fire which largely destroyed the wooden buildings of the Maquis. 'The next day,' wrote his son, 'the Maquis and its flowers were nothing but cinders'[12] For the Renoir family 'the difficulty of getting there

176. Studio on the corner of 21 Rue Caulaincourt and 5 Rue Tourlaque.

177. Studios at 20 Rue Tourlaque.

178. The Maquis, Montmartre, photograph from before 1900.

179. The Moulin de la Galette, Montmartre, photograph from c. 1900.

was largely compensated for by the low rents, the fresh air, the cows, the lilacs and the roses'.[13] This was at the end of the Rue Girardon in the last house of rectangular block (No. 6 in the row at 13 Rue Girardon) down a narrow lane amidst an orchard and rose-bushes. There were two upper floors and an attic studio as well as a garden 25 metres by 16 metres. For larger canvases Renoir had a studio on the Rue Tourlaque off the Rue Caulaincourt which Zandomeneghi recommended to him (Plate 177–8). Zando-meneghi occupied the ground floor of studios at 27 Rue Caulaincourt on the corner of the Rue Tourlaque and in 1886 Lautrec had a studio there also full of dust, frames, Japanese objects and on the wall his parody of the *Bois Sacré* of Puvis de Chavannes.[14] In the Rue Caulaincourt itself Renoir about 1910 had a studio at No. 73 and Steinlen, who used the basement, died there in 1923. 87 Rue Caulaincourt was the studio of the cari-caturist Charles Léandre.

Behind the Maquis at the crest of the hill stood the windmills that must, for Van Gogh, have recalled his native Holland. Small lanes and gardens abutted quarries that produced stone for the city and plaster of Paris. Van Gogh painted them with an Impressionist sensitivity to light that rapidly began to respond in technique to the innovations of Seurat and Signac. One of the windmills was particularly important for artists, for the Moulin de la Galette opened its gardens and buildings as a café-bar and dance hall (Plate 179). It was the haunt of painters from Renior to Picasso and the dancer La Goulue began her career here. Its clientèle however long remained inde-pendent of that frequenting the Moulin Rouge, for it retained something of its local and even semi-rural air, the rendez-vous of workmen with a day off, housemaids, artists and models: Renoir's effervescent and light-hearted image of dancing in the gardens here is in startling contrast to Lautrec's lurid depiction of its nightlife. As the American art student W.C. Morrow discovered 'invasions by foreigners were very rare at the Moulin de la Galette';[15] he also discovered why when pursued through the steep streets by local ruffians intent upon causing him physical injury. Bonnard in a painting of about 1905 depicted the Moulin de Galette from a high window looking up the Rue Tholozé, its distinctive arched gateway and the sails of its windmill terminating the perspective of his luminously painted street in which a few people pursue their path across the middle distance. According to Jean Renoir 'Toulouse-Lautrec was often to

180. Pierre-Auguste Renoir, *Dance at the Moulin de la Galette*, 1876, 131 × 175 cm., Musée d'Orsay, Paris.

181. Lucien Pissarro, *The Rue St Vincent, Winter Sun*, 1890, oil on canvas, 65.4 × 81.3 cm., whereabouts unknown.

182. The Lapin Agile at 4 Rue des Saules, photograph from *c.* 1900

be seen sitting enthroned in the window of a café on the corner of the Rue Tholozé and the Rue Lepic.'[16]

One home for the *atelier libre* teaching studio of Fernand Cormon, 'the ugliest and thinnest man in Paris'[17] according to Lautrec who became a *massier* under Cormon, was situated just off the Rue Lepic in this area at 10 Rue Constance. Crossing both the Rue Lepic and the Rue Caulaincourt at their closest point is the Rue Tourlaque running west to the cemetry.

Back along the Rue Caulaincourt by the small St Vincent cemetry the Rue St Vincent cuts eastwards across the steep and stepped Rue Mont-Cenis behind Sacré Coeur. Painted by Camille Pissarro's son Lucien in winter sunlight in 1889–90, its air of a small provincial town is visibly intact (Plate 181). Seurat also painted this quiet leafy street as a blaze of light (Plate 186). His pointilliste technique was used here by Lucien Pissarro and by Maximilien Luce whose studio was nearby in the parallel Rue Cortot. The two streets are joined by the Rue des Saules where Montmartre to this day has a silent and rural aspect as gardens descend vertiginously northwards away from Paris. Here, over the crest of the hill in the Rue des Saules stands the unpresumptious building of the Lapin Agile (Plate 182) a bar and restaurant which perhaps most effectively sums up in its history Montmartre's split identity, separate from Paris yet part of it; its habitués not only escaped the city's pressures at this northern point, they also relied upon the city that sprawled at the foot of the Montmartre hill. The Lapin Agile took its name from a rebus or visual-verbal pun. A certain André Gill commissioned a sign for the restaurant depicting a rabbit leaping from a cooking pot. Gill's rabbit (lapin à Gill) became an agile rabbit (lapin agile) and the Lapin Agile was given its name. Not as such a literary or artistic café, the Lapin Agile enjoyed very mixed company: 'the Lapin Agile, with the light of its glazed door blinking in the night, in the Rue des Saules, was for many, the inn of the last resort, the laboratory where Faust sold his soul, the door where more than one young man embarked upon an adventure of deception.'[18] The old

158

building had been a coaching inn in the eighteenth century, and was later called the Cabaret des Assassins after its murals of assassinations. In its days as the Lapin Agile entertainment was provided by the bearded Frédé (Fréderic Gerard) singing to a guitar (Plate 183). It was here that a magnificent ruse to mock the art-establishment was devised. Frédé's donkey, Lolo, was induced to paint a canvas with a brush tied to her tail and the canvas was submitted to the juryless Salon des Indépendants in 1910. After the work was accepted as a *Sunset on the Adriatic* by Boronali a manifesto was sent to the press, and in due course the work was apparently sold. By 1905 the walls of the Lapin Agile included amongst their decorations a painting by Picasso, a buddhist plaster relief employing a pose apparently used by Gauguin, a plaster cast of Apollo and a crucifixion by the sculptor Walsey.[19]

Returning south towards the crest of the hill the Rue des Saules meets the Rue Cortot where the composer Erik Satie lived at No. 6 from 1890 to 1898, a period during which his writing of music included fanfares for the mystifying opening ceremonies of the Rosicrucian Salons. Along the street at No. 12 stands a seventeenth-century house of importance for artists for many years (Plate 184). Once through its gate a silent enclosed garden leads past a studio to the main building. Behind this building the garden descends steeply at the back. This was Renoir's first dwelling in Montmartre. It was sparsely furnished and 'falling to pieces but Renoir did not mind. It provided the advantage of a large garden with magnificent views of countryside as far as St Denis'[20] and it was here that Renoir worked on his painting of the Moulin de la Galette, carrying it daily from his studio with the help of a friend. The rent was 1,000 francs per year. Renoir painted the garden here in 1875–6 as a mass of flowers and foliage, a lavishly colourful and fresh retreat from the city (Plate 187). Later Emile Bernard was to entertain Van Gogh and Gauguin here. The same garden was later painted by Suzanne Valadon viewed from an upper window of the house which she too was to inhabit in due course (from 1906–9) along with her son the painter Maurice Utrillo (Plate 185). It was

183. Frédé (Fréderic Gerard) playing the guitar at the Lapin Agile, Montmartre, photograph 1905, Cabinet des Estampes, Bibliothèque Nationale, Paris. A painting by Picasso is visible in the background.

184. 12 Rue Cortot in 1904. Now the Musée de Montmartre

185. Suzanne Valadon, *The Studio at 12 Rue Cortot*, 1919, oil on canvas, 73 × 92 cm., Provenance Galérie Pétridès, photograph *Atelier 53*, Paris.

186. Georges Seurat, *The Rue St Vincent, Montmartre, in Spring*, oil on board, 25 × 16 cm., Fitzwilliam Museum, Cambridge.

187. Pierre-Auguste Renoir, *The Garden at 12 Rue Cortot, Montmartre*, 1876, oil on canvas, 151.8 × 97.5 cm. the Carnegie Museum of Art, Pittsburgh (acquired through the generosity of Mrs Alan M. Scaife, 1965)

much frequented by artists, and since 1959 it has housed the Musée de Montmartre. Valadon had been an acrobat at the Cirque Molier. A fall ended her circus work and she posed as a model for numerous artists including Puvis de Chavannes, Renoir and Degas. She met many painters in Montmartre in this way, including Lautrec, and her own drawing was much encouraged by Degas. In 1892 she painted Erik Satie and later she was drawn into Apollinaire's circle of literary and artistic friends.[21]

At 16 Rue Cortot was Maximilien Luce, who exhibited at the Salon des Indépendants from 1887, a convert to Neo-Impressionism, and ultimately president of the Société des Indépendants in 1935 after Signac's death. Trained as a printmaker, he had illustrated periodicals in the late 1870s before studying under Carolous-Duran. He was a friend of Camille Pissarro and a contributor to anarchist literature including the periodical *Le Père peinard*. He also contributed illustrations to the periodical *L'Assiette au Beurre*. Much of his painting was executed in a sophisticated pointilliste technique.

The Lapin Agile and nearby 12 Rue Cortot continued to function vigorously during the spectacular experimental period of art in Paris from the turn of the century up to the First World War, Montmartre playing a vital part in the development of Cubism in particular. In these streets above Paris, creative activity flourished for many years, forming a polarity with Montparnasse to the south of Paris, its studios being handed down from generation to generation of artists. Particularly significant in this respect was the so-called Bateau Lavoir or 'floating laundry' (Plate 188) which clings to a steep incline of the Montmartre hill descending from the Place Emile-Goudeau off the southern end of the Rue des Saules, west of Sacré-Coeur and the Place du Tertre (now the focus of tourists' awareness of Montmartre's artistic history). This studio block at 13 Place Emile-Goudeau was structurally extraordinary. It appears at its entrance to be a low single-storey building, but inside it descends down wooden staircases to corridors and studios. The slope is so steep that the entrance is on the top floor and its studios are obscured from view by the hill itself and surrounding buildings. In the early years of the twentieth century the Bateau Lavoir was a hive of creative talent and its literary and

188. The Bateau-Lavoir at 13 Place Emile-Goudeau, Rue Ravignan.

artistic inhabitants played a crucial part in the origins of Cubism. Amongst them were Picasso in 1912, whose first Parisian studio had been nearby at 49 Rue Gabrielle, Kees Van Dongen, Derain, Modigliani, Juan Gris and the writers André Salmon, Pierre Mac-Orlan and Max Jacob. It was here that Picasso and his friends entertained Le Douanier Rousseau to a banquet. Four north lights are visible where the Rue Gabrielle meets the Rue Ravignan just off the square itself.[22]

In this little square with its steps, trees and small hotels the seclusion of Montmartre survives. The steep slope twists the descending streets southwards towards the distant Seine and the city centre of grandiose boulevards and magnificent public buildings with their museums, salons, dealers and opportunities. The magnificence of Motmartre lies in its seclusion and its view. The dense urban centre can be surveyed in a single glance from the heights of Montmartre, geographically close but nonetheless separate, spreading in the light to the furthest horizon as Van Gogh had painted it. Montmartre itself, by contrast, was steep, small and furrowed with narrow streets beyond the reach of the boulevards. It depended upon the city centre but from here the city centre appeared remote despite its proximity. Historically Montmartre had maintained this relationship for centuries as a result of its quarries and the taxes levied upon goods entering Paris. As the city grew and spread Montmartre became steadily incorporated into the city's own organism, and new high apartment blocks rose above its allotments and gardens. The artists of Montmartre reflected this ambivalent relationship; working aloof from the city centre, they neverthless needed its opportunities, its wealth, and its cosmopolitan public.

# 6. *Gare St Lazare and Les Batignolles*

Immediately behind the great railway terminus of the Gare St Lazare is one of the most extraordinary 'squares' of Paris. Inelegant and functional, the Place de l'Europe, which Gustave Caillebotte painted wet with rain in 1877, is the crossing point of three major thoroughfares (Plate 189). The six arms radiate in all directions and the Place is further complicated by the Rue de Rome which crosses it just off-centre, cutting the apartment buildings into acute-angled perspectives, two of which provide the underlying compositional motif of Caillebotte's painting, with the openings of other streets visible at the right. This diversity of directions is stressed by Caillebotte in his city dwellers who move purposefully in every direction without communicating one with another, each to a different destination, a light rain wetting their umbrellas, the cobbled roads and the buildings indiscriminately. Caillebotte presents the separateness of the inhabitants of the city, focussing upon the paradoxical effect of thoroughfares which in coverging upon these few metres of cobbles, unmarked by any monument, simultaneously diverge to distant and increasingly separate points. Whilst the nexus of roads implies an area of importance this is an enigmatically vacant point of the city.

The Place de l'Europe is extraordinary in another respect, for its whole conjunction of streets occurs literally above the railway line (Plate 190). The Place de l'Europe is largely formed by a huge iron bridge above the railway tracks that emerge in profusion from the Gare St Lazare. As a focal point of the urban city it is devoid of all magnificence except the rapidly receding perspectives of no less than ten means of arrival and departure. To the north-west the Rue de Rome abuts the railway like a cliff before the sunken open space of the tracks; south-east, past the Place de l'Europe, the engine sheds and façade of

189. Gustave Caillebotte, *The Place de l'Europe, Rainy Day*, 1877, oil on canvas, 20.9 × 30 cm., the Art Institute of Chicago.

the station suddenly terminate this intricate, dynamic city space. Its urbanity was not that of fashionable Paris, but that of a vital nerve centre of travel and communications.

Monet, painting inside the station, shows the Rue de Rome glittering in sunlight beyond the steam and iron of the station sheds (Plate 191). The multiplicity of his views of this station depict it as both changing and enduring, a scene of urban action in shifting light beneath a static structure, a palace of departures and arrivals, whose function is movement and exchange but which itself remains immobile. The paintings were not well-received initially. Even George Moore, who was later to admire Impressionism enthusiastically, was moved to hilarity by his first sight of Monet's views of Gare St Lazare: 'When we came to those piercingly personal visions of railway stations — those rapid sensations of steel and vapour — our laughter knew no bounds.'[1]

As big as a palace the Gare St Lazare was in reality the very antithesis of this for it was as public, accessible and as efficiently concerned with a population in transit as it could be. The station exemplified exchange and communication, linking the capital with

164

190. Gustave Caillebotte, *On the Pont de l'Europe*, 1876–7, oil on canvas, 105.3 × 129.9 cm., Kimbell Art Museum, Fort Worth. The engine shed of the Gare St Lazare is visible at right.

191. Claude Monet, *Gare St Lazare*, 1877, oil on canvas, 75 × 100 cm., Musée d'Orsay, Paris.

192. Victor Baltard, *The Church of St Augustin, Paris*, 1860–7. In the foreground is Paul Dubois' sculpture of *Joan of Arc*, See plate 106.

193. Edgar Degas, Stephane Mallarmé and Auguste Renoir, photograph from 1895, Cabinet des Estampes, Bibliothèque Nationale, Paris.

the rest of the country and beyond across Europe. It also linked Monet and his contemporaries to the suburbs and nearby towns whose names on the departures notice-board read like a catalogue of Impressionist paintings, its trains leaving Paris for Argenteuil, Médan, Verneuil, Bougival, Louveciennes, Eragny, Pointoise, Gisors, Rouen, and Le Havre.

Comparison of the Gare St Lazare with the nearby church of St Augustin elucidates something of the achievements of Impressionist painting in depicting the modern city. St Augustin, built in 1860–71 by Baltard, has an iron framework visible inside which is obscured on the exterior by stone (Plate 192). Iron arches rising to a considerable height mark out the bays of the nave, further arches crossing the nave to form an almost flat ceiling. This culminates in a vast iron dome above the altar. Outside, the west façade is decorated with sculptures by the academician Jouffroy, whilst the interior has paintings by Bouguereau. Essentially the plan of St Augustin is that of a basilica with a long nave leading up to the altar.

Gare St Lazare has features in common with nearby St Augustin for it too is essentially an iron construction clad in stone where it meets the street. Its shed resembles a basilica in the high apex of its central section with lower roofs to either side supported on iron columns. Whilst the church of St Augustin co-ordinates the movement of people to the high altar which forms a static focus, the Gare St Lazare is literally open to the world, its travellers arriving and departing from its many platforms. It has of course no religious content whatsoever: its reason for existing is the wholly secular activity of travel in and out of Paris. Both buildings illustrate aspects of modern Paris, but the church is ancient and rail-travel still new. Comparing Bouguereau's *St Lazarus* with Monet's paintings of the station reveals a comparable shift in art. Bouguereau in responding to the ancient patronage of the Church mustered time-honoured means to depict the saint. Monet, by contrast, employed newly evolved means to depict the activity of the city and of its inhabitants. There are almost no Impressionist paintings of religious themes. Churches appear solely as buildings which characterise the city street. Monet's patrons were not acting as the guardians of an ancient spiritual inheritance: they were simply the purchasers that the dealers could find. Monet's subject was not an evocation of a timeless scene, but the city portrayed going about its mundane business. Bouguereau was crucial to the system of opportunities represented by Institut and Salon. Monet had no such power, and despite occasional submissions to the Salon he did not rely upon it, but was part and parcel of the growing move towards independent initiatives effected through group exhibitions and the activities of dealers.

Paul Dubois whose sculpture of Joan of Arc stands in front of St Augustin was close to Bouguereau's position.[2] Having achieved success with his *Florentine Singer* at the Salon of 1865, he subsequently received many honours. Appointed to the Légion d'Honneur, he was promoted to *officier* in 1874, *commandeur* in 1886 and finally held the Grand Cross of the Légion d'Honneur in 1896. He was elected to the Institut in 1876, having served as curator of the Luxembourg Museum from 1873, and in 1878 he became Director of the Ecole des Beaux-Arts. He was amongst the most successful and celebrated sculptors of his day.

Off the Place de l'Europe is the junction of the Rue de Berne and the Rue de St Petersbourg (now Rue Leningrad) where Manet had his studio. In front of the Gare St Lazare is the Place du Havre which Pissarro painted several times in 1893 and 1897 from an upper window of the nearby Hotel Garnier, capturing the communal movement of carriages and figures filling the busy city street in front of the station.

Either side of the bulk of the station the Rue de Rome and the Rue d'Amsterdam splay out north towards the Boulevard des Batignolles which flows west from the Boulevard de Clichy and Montmartre. On the Boulevard des Batignolles itself the successful sculptor Aimé Millet occupied No. 21 where he died in 1891. He had studied at the Ecoles des Beaux-Arts from 1836 and was a pupil of David d'Angers and Viollet-le-Duc. By the 1880s he was a venerable figure in French art, having executed many major monuments including *Mercury* for the Louvre, *Justice* for the Mairie of the first arrondissement, *Apollo between the Muses of Dance and Music* for the façade of the Opera, *Phidias* for the Luxembourg Gardens (a state commission for 7,000 francs) and *Cassandre* for the Tuileries Gardens. The painter Charles Angrand, friend of Seurat and Signac, was at 45 Boulevard des Batignolles in 1893.

North of the Boulevard des Batignolles lies the Batignolles district, less dramatic than Montmartre to the east but a distinct area in which the railway plays a considerable role. Pierced by the Rue de Rome and flanked by the Avenue de Clichy it culminates in the Rue Cardinet and the little Square des Batignolles; the ground falls away to the north overlooking the depots for the city's merchandise and the suburb of Clichy.

The poet Stephane Mallarmé, precursor and figurehead of the Symbolist movement lived at 89 Rue de Rome. He was an intimate friend of Manet, Degas and Renoir. His Tuesday evening gatherings here brought together many artists and writers of Impressionist, Symbolist and other schools in an influential private salon. He was also a personal friend of the painter Berthe Morisot, an admirer of the other-worldly prints of Odilon Redon and the translator of Whistler's *Ten o'clock* lecture. Manet illustrated Mallarmé's translation of *The Raven* by Edgar Allen Poe and in turn he was portrayed by Manet, Whistler, Gauguin and Edvard Munch. George Moore visited the Tuesday Salon: 'a few friends sitting round a hearth, the lamp on the table. I have met none whose conversation was so fruitful, but I never enjoyed his poetry, his early verses, of course, excepted.'[5] Mallarmé's later verse was fequently difficult and deliberately obscure. Although Degas found it baffling this did not prevent their friendship. A photograph by Degas provides a glimpse of Mallarmé with pointed beard relaxing in his apartment and testifies also to his friendship with Renoir (Plate 193); his study contained a river scene by Monet, a print by Redon and a print by Manet of Lola de Valence.

Further along the Rue de Rome, No. 62 was occupied by numerous artists. Georges Clairin, whose career was inextricably intertwined with that of Sarah Bernhardt, was here in the 1890s (Plate 194). His decorative commissions included three ceilings and six panels for the Opéra, (where in 1874 he had completed the decoration of the staircase after the death of the painter Pils), decorations at the Bourse, Sorbonne, Hôtel de Ville and two ceilings at the Eden Theatre. Louis Anquetin was another occupant with a studio at this address, his paintings filling the walls above the corner settee and striped cushions with portraits, landscapes and profiles of horses (Plate 195).

In the later 1880s the painter Henri Gervex was here, a specialist in female portraits and scenes with an eighteenth-century inspiration. A friend of Renoir and Monet, Gervex had experimented with Impressionism, but was nonetheless a stalwart Salon exhibitor. 'Beauty for him,' wrote a commentator 'consists of lips easy of reach, laughing lips, with nothing severe about them.'[6] His large painting *Le Jury au Salon de Peinture* (Plate 54) was accepted by the Luxembourg Museum as was his major composition *Before the operation* of 1886–7 (Plate 197). A *chevalier* of the Légion d'Honneur in 1882, *officier* in 1889, he rose to *commandeur* in 1911 and he was eventually elected to the Institut in 1913. He was a founder member of the Société National des Beaux-Arts and executed many public commissions, amongst them decorations for the Opéra Comique and a ceiling at the Hôtel de Ville. For Gervex a studio was both practical and a little exotic (Plate 196). A posed photograph shows him perched on a three-legged stool before a canvas depiciting an idyllic landscape with a nude. The room contains no mess whatsoever and his procedure appears meticulous. The polished floorboards are covered with a few oriental rugs, the furniture, even to the full-length mirror, is elegant and stylish. Framed works line the walls between ceramic dishes and portait busts. Above the elegant seat a spectacular frame attests to this taste for fine objects.

Also here in 1889 was the painter Norbert Goeneutte who like Clairin had been a

194. Georges Clairin, *Portrait of Sarah Bernhardt*, oil on canvas, 250 × 201 cm., Petit Palais, Paris.

195. Louis Anquetin's studio at 62 Rue de Rome, photograph from *c.* 1891–2.

196. Henri Gervex in his studio, photograph from *c.* 1895.

197. Henri Gervex *Before the Operation. Doctor Péan teaching at the Hôpital St. Louis, Paris,* Salon of 1887, oil on canvas, 242 × 188 cm., Musée d'Orsay, Paris.

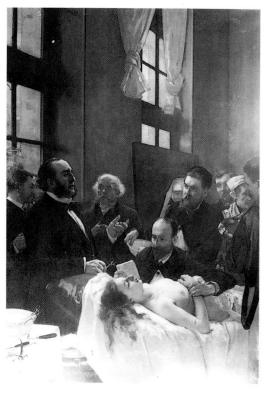

pupil of Pils. Goeneutte specialised in views of Paris, of which his view of the Boulevard de Clichy is the most celebrated example. He was an organiser of the Expositions des Peintres-Graveurs and an active printmaker. On the opposite side of the railway lines in the Rue d'Amsterdam Manet occupied No. 77 at the end of his life (1879–83) and in 1889 the successful painter J.J. Weerts was here.

The Rue Lemercier cuts north-west through the Batignolles area. Hector Leroux occupied No. 26 in the 1890s, whilst in a parallel street to the west, the Rue Truffaut, Edouard Vuillard was to occupy No. 28. A pupil of Gérôme at the Ecole des Beaux-Arts, Vuillard also studied under Bouguereau at the Académie Julian where he met Sérusier, Bonnard, Vallotton and others who were to form the core of the Nabis group, Vuillard translating the lessons of Gauguin's expressive decoration into an urban and Parisian art of brilliantly original decorativeness. Paris was as important a subject for Vuillard as for Bonnard. His large scale canvases of the parks of Paris, just as much as his interiors, in their restrained tuning of colours and in their dedication to flattened areas of pattern, made Vuillard amongst the most subtle of colourist-decorators, far removed in his approach and far exceeding in his originality the solutions of the Salons.

In the eastern part of Les Batignolles the streets lead up to Montmartre placing the studios of Angrand, Anquetin and Vuillard within easy reach of Signac, Seurat, Lautrec, and, a little further away, Bonnard. The Place de Clichy is where these areas meet, as the models who made up the 'model-market' in the Place de Clichy well understood.

Moving north from the Place de Clichy, the Avenue de Clichy, with Les Batignolles to the left and Montmartre to the right, veers towards the suburb of Clichy itself, beyond the depots for merchandise to the railway lines and the gasometers.[7] In the 1880s the industrial suburbs increasingly attracted painters turning their back upon the opportunities and demands of Institut and Salon or the architectural splendours of the city of Paris. Pointillistes associated with the juryless Salon des Indépendents and holding radical political views analysed the unbiased light which illuminated gasometer and Louvre without discrimination. Signac's *Gas Tanks at Clichy* focusses attention upon

168

198. Paul Signac, *Gas Tanks at Clichy*, 1886, oil on canvas, 65 × 81 cm., National Gallery of Victoria (Felton Bequest, 1948), Melbourne, Australia.

the mundane and emphatically ordinary spectacle of a house trapped in the centre of a ring of gasometers, an unpretentious dwelling extended by lean-to buildings and sheds, enclosed in a wooden fence on a scrap of free ground amongst the city's gas supply (Plate 198). The perspective and central placing of the image of the house in Signac's painting stress its importance, an importance which has significance in the look which selected the motif as much as in its depiction. The focus of Signac's attention is inelegant with no trace of fashionable Paris. He draws attention to a way of life, and a material context of existence, an essential adjunct of the city that is ignored by the decorators of the Opéra or Hôtel de Ville and is unconnected with civic pride. It is a pointer to Signac's own commitments, rejecting respected and honoured means of painting exemplified by Salon stars, their success and frequent reversion to historical themes or compositional devices from the distant past, in favour of an art that dispassionately reflects the commonplace in paintings for exhibition at an open Salon that had relinquished selection and honours.

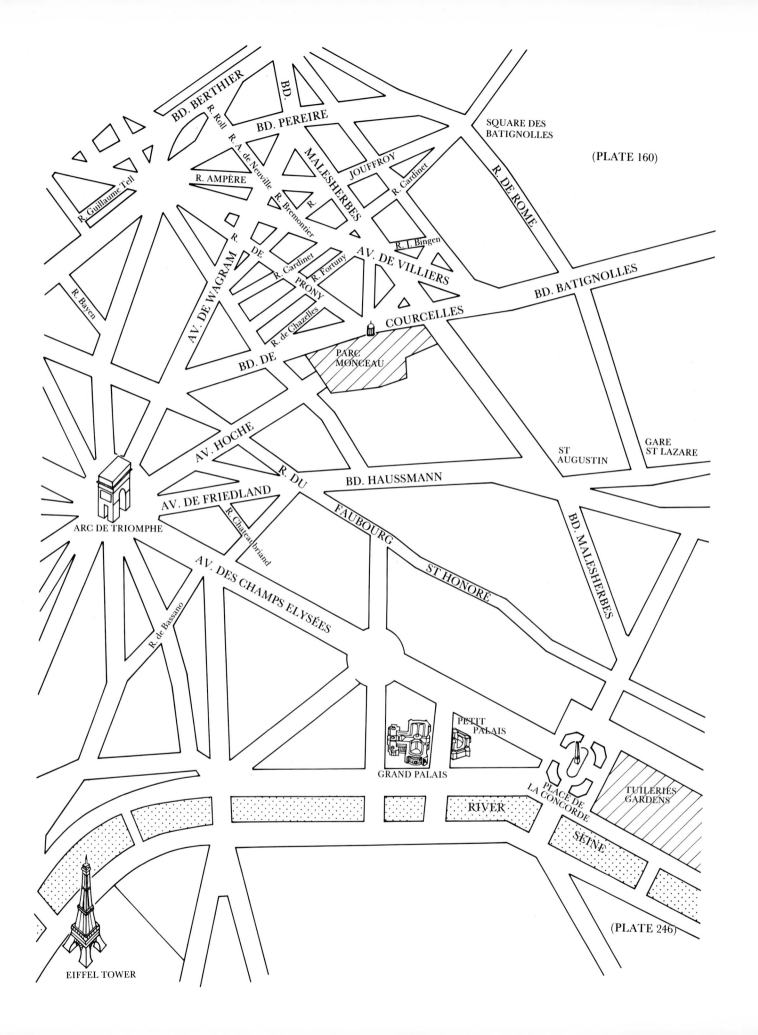

(PLATE 160)

BD. BERTHIER
R. Roll
BD.
BD. PEREIRE
R. A. de Neuville
R. Guillaume Tell
R. AMPÈRE
R. Bremontier
MALESHERBES
JOUFFROY
R. Cardinet
SQUARE DES
BATIGNOLLES
R. DE ROME
R. Bayen
AV. DE WAGRAM
R.
DE
R. Cardinet
R. Fortuny
R.
PRONY
AV. DE VILLIERS
R. I. Bingen
R. de Chazelles
COURCELLES
BD. BATIGNOLLES
PARC
MONCEAU
BD. DE
AV. HOCHE
R. DU
BD. HAUSSMANN
ST
AUGUSTIN
GARE
ST LAZARE
AV. DE FRIEDLAND
R. Chateaubriand
FAUBOURG
BD. MALESHERBES
ARC DE TRIOMPHE
AV. DES CHAMPS ELYSÉES
ST HONORÉ
R. de Bassano
PETIT
PALAIS
GRAND PALAIS
PLACE DE
LA CONCORDE
TUILERIÉS
GARDENS
RIVER
SEINE
(PLATE 246)
EIFFEL TOWER

# 7. *Around the Arc de Triomphe*

'"Say do any of you fellows know of an atelier?" questions Johnson at length. And after a pause someone suggests, not without a gentle sarcasm, that D--'s studio is at liberty in the street at the back of the Rue de la Grande Chaumière.

There is a roar of laughter, because D-- is one of the most famous exhibitors at the Salon, and his *atelier*, discarded in favour of one he has built over near the Parc Monceaux, is such as only D-- would require.'[1]

The Parc Monceaux and the Plaine Monceaux around it contains the studios of many the wealthiest and most successful, artists of the period 1880–1900, some of whose names along with those of predecessors have been adopted for its streets: the Rue Meissonier, Rue Edouard-Detaille, Rue Jouffroy, Rue Barye, Rue Léon-Cogniet and the Rue Ribot. They circle around the area north of the Parc Monceaux along the Avenue de Villiers and the Boulevard Malesherbes in answer to the Rue Rembrandt, Rue Murillo, Avenue Van Dyck and the Avenue Ruysdael to the south of the park. To the east lie Les Batignolles and Montmartre, but here civic splendour has reasserted itself. Beyond the Boulevard Haussmann to the south lies the Champs-Elysèes and from 1889 the great exhibition halls of the Exposition Universelle, the Grand Palais and Petit Palais. Southwest the wide imposing Avenue de Wagram descends through a steep perspective of massive and elegant apartment buildings in a precise straight line to the Arc de Triomphe, the immense monumental arch of victory that ends the vista of eleven radiating major thoroughfares, amongst them the great east-west axis of Paris which aligns the Arc de Triomphe with the Rue de Rivoli, the Tuileries gardens and the Louvre (Plate 200).

199. Map: Around the Arc de Triomphe from the Avenue de Villiers to Auteuil.

200. Pierre Bonnard, *The Arc de Triomphe*, 1899, lithograph, 32 × 47 cm., from the series *Quelques aspects de la vie de Paris*, Cabinet des Estampes, Bibliothèque Nationale, Paris.

The Avenue de Villiers formed the densest concentration of art and wealth in Paris. Insofar as such success demanded patronage, to attract it meant to be fashionable. 'Paris pours in there before going to the Bois,' commented the critic Albert Wolff in 1886, 'everyone pays a visit to his painter; in every house in the Monceau quarter there is a studio... The standing of a painter can be gauged by the number of vehicles parked in front of his hôtel on Fridays.'[2] Friday was the day usually reserved by artists for their visiting clientèle, potential patrons and admirers rather than friends, a day of social politeness concealing the hard-headed attitudes of business.

When Zola's courtesan Nana, sought the ultimate signs of success, the most extreme achievement of her plans to cause the finanical ruin and humiliation of her suitors, it was to this area that her ambitions led her:

> He started walking towards the door. But as he was leaving the room she took him in her arms again and turned meek and coaxing, looking up at him and rubbing her chin against his waistcoat like a cat. 'Where's the big house?' she whispered, with the laughing embarrassment of a little girl returning to the good things she had previously refused.
> 'In the Avenue de Villiers.'
> 'And there are carriages?'
> 'Yes'
> 'Lace? Diamonds?'
> 'Yes'[3]

Later in the novel Zola described the house 'in the luxurious quarter which was springing up on the waste ground which had once been the Monceau plain'.[4] Significantly Zola describes the typical house of a successful young artist in order to characterise the area:

> Built in the Renaissance style by a young painter intoxicated by his first success, who had been forced to sell it as soon as it was ready, it was a palatial building designed on original lines, with modern facilities in a deliberately eccentric setting. The Comte Muffaut had bought the house ready furnished, full of hosts of knick-knacks, beautiful eastern hangings, old sideboards and big Louis XIII chairs, so that Nana had come into a setting of the choicest furniture from a wide variety of periods.[5]

The central studio however was useless to Nana.

The studios spread out from a triangle formed by the Avenue de Villiers, the Boulevard Malesherbes and the Avenue Wagram, stretching south to the Boulevard de Courcelles and north between the Boulevard Pereire and Boulevard Berthier; they became less fashionable and more practical with the increasing distance. The writer, painter and sculptor Zacharie Astruc lived on the edge of this fashionable triangle at 75 bis Avenue de Wagram. Most successful as a sculptor, he exhibited at the Salon from 1871 up to his death in 1907. His most celebrated sculpture *The Mask Seller*, exhibited in plaster at the Salon of 1880 and bronze in 1883, was subsequently erected in the Luxembourg Gardens. The masks are portraits of Barbey d'Aurevilly, Berlioz, Carpeaux, Corot, Delacroix, Dumas the younger, Faure, Gambetta, Gounod and Victor Hugo. Astruc exhibited a bust of Manet at the Salon in 1881 and of the organiser of the Rosicrucian Salons, Le Sâr Péladan, at the Salon of 1899. In 1889 his figure of St Francis of Assissi was installed at Sacré-Coeur.

The geographical epicentre of success lay at the point where Gustave Doré's *Monument to Alexandre Dumas* marks the crossing of the Avenue de Villiers and the Boulevard Malesherbes. Here two of the most successful of Parisian painters raised their studios; they were Ernest Meissonier and his former pupil Edouard Detaille. Detaille occupied 129 Boulevard Malesherbes (Plate 201); Meissonier was at No. 131. Both were battle painters, articulate manipulators of the country's self-image and historical awareness.

201. A. Leveille, *Edouard Detaille in his studio*, 1885, wood engraving for the *Revue Illustré*.

Detaille painted themes of the Franco-Prussian War of 1870, although his first Salon exhibit predated that war by three years, significantly it was *A Corner of Meissonier's Studio*; he had begun to study under Meissonier at the age of seventeen. He fought in the war, and after it his ascent to success began: made a *chevalier* of the Légion d'Honneur in 1872, he was promoted to the rank of *officier* in 1881 and *commandeur* in 1897. Elected to the Institut in 1892, he also became Honorary President of the Société des Artistes Français. *The Dream* (Le Rêve) of 1888, with its minutely precise evocation of a vision of

202. J-B Edouard Detaille, *The Dream*, 1888, oil on canvas, 300 × 390 cm., Musée d'Orsay, Paris.

203. The cloisters of Meissonier's house in Paris.

204. The studio façade in the courtyard of Meissonier's house in Paris.

military victory, invoked the glory of Napoleon's military achievements haunting the modern French army (Plate 202); it became a popular success as an engraving after winning the Salon medal for 1888. Detaille executed decorations for the Hôtel de Ville and the Panthéon but was popular too by virtue of his work on panoramas with de Neuville at the Panorama de Champigny and the Panorama de Rezonville.[6]

The studio and dwelling of Detaille's tutor and inspiration Jean-Louis-Ernest Meissonier was unsurpassed as the most substantial and spectacular in Paris (Plates 203–4). At 131 Boulevard Malesherbes, Meissonier constructed a vast building in stone, with loggia and courtyard of finely cut architectural motifs eloquently proclaiming his erudition, taste, wealth, respectability and sheer worldly success. Not the least amazing aspect of this's success is that his paintings were usually very small indeed particularly by Salon standards. He inadequately supplied his market, managing to sell relatively few works at, as we have seen, some of the highest recorded prices. Demand, far exceeding the supply, greatly increased the prices attainable. Such a manoeuvre was inaccessible to all but the most successful and sought-after artist of the day. Meissonier was that artist. A photograph shows him clad in a kaftan and soft slippers; Meissonier in old age, his white beard straggling in two strands down his chest but his hair cropped short, stares imperiously from an imposing throne-like chair (Plate 206). He also had a house at Poissy outside Paris which he bought for 26,000 francs but upon which he spent a further 1,000,000 francs adjusting it to his taste. His plans for the Paris house were grandiose in the extreme yet within the bounds of possibility for Meissonier: 'How I should like to turn my house in Paris into a Foundation, a sort of Museum and School of Art. The very details of the architecture suit the idea.'[7]

To Albert Wolff it appeared a palace of bizarre construction with the air of a cloister amongst the new buildings. 'Rooms, properly speaking, do not exist in this artist's habitation; they are replaced by two studios which connect with each other and occupy the whole width of the first floor; there one of the greatest artists of this century is bent

205. Part of Meissonier's studio with sculptural maquettes and miniature cannons. The maquettes were studies for paintings. The *Wounded Horse* (see Plate 208) is visible right of centre.

206. Ernest Meissonier in his Paris studio, photograph, of 1890.

over a labour, which has lasted for fifty years, with the same commitment and passion.'[8]

Meissonier's assiduous and scrupulous attention to detail deeply impressed many of his contemporaries. His thoroughness and meticulous erudition appeared the antithesis of more painterly tendencies. The painter Jules Breton found in his work 'in contrast with Courbet...absolute conscienciousness and marvellous clearness of vision'.[9] Similarly Albert Wolff pointed out that a

panel by Monsieur Meissonier is the result of numerous researches and endless studies. The walls of his studio bear witness to his conscienciousness; all around the two studios...are the proofs of his constant efforts...sketches, painted studies, wax models have preceded the definitive evolution of the work...for the least figure, Monsieur Meissonier makes numerous preparatory studies.[10]

He would destroy unsatisfactory works with a knife in spite of their market value.

Meissonier received almost every available honour, but he rose to this position from a childhood of poverty. He studied briefly under Cogniet and copied Dutch and Flemish paintings in the Louvre. His Salon début was in 1834. He became friendly with Daubigny and he admired Delacroix. By 1859 Meissonier's fame was such that Napoleon III invited him to attend the battle of Solferino in which 300,000 soldiers were engaged. The experience horrified Meissonier but in his work the military ventures of Napoleon III and increasingly of Napoleon I, preoccupied him for many years. His paintings devoted to Napoleon Bonaparte were given dates for titles (*1796, 1807, 1810, 1814, 1815*) and comprise a succinct historical profile which appealed to patriotic memory and imagination. In his search for authentic detail he ammassed a collection of military regalia, uniforms, arms and models which was exhibited at Les Invalides in 1889. Military models may be glimpsed in photographs of his studio (Plate 205). Edmond de Goncourt recorded in his journal that

Gérôme was speaking this evening about Meissonier painting the great Emperor and

175

207. J-L. Ernest Meissonier, *Paris 1870–71. The Seige of Paris*, 1884, oil on canvas, 68 × 57 cm., Musée d'Orsay, Paris.

so assimilating himself to his model that he would make studies from himself, dressed in the historic riding coat, and even in a state of nature, persuaded that he was of the same height and the same physical stature.[11]

Meissonier's meticulousness, ridiculed with relish by Edmond de Goncourt, was a source of his popular success even before his concentration upon themes of history that impinged upon the nation's self-esteem. It was particularly evident in his study of horses: 'The innumerable studies of horses made before the first cavalryman was painted have to be seen in the studio of the master.'[12] Meissonier established his own stable, frequently working direct from the horses as part of his research, drawing, painting and modelling them. Meissonier's *Paris 1870–1871* depicts a mawled but proud section of the French army during the Seige of Paris (Plate 207). In the foreground lies a wounded horse. The painting measures a mere 51 by 68 centimetres, yet every detail was the result of intricate studies. Meissonier executed a model of a horse he observed dying, and worked from this to provide the wounded horse in the painting (Plate 208). With a directness of observation worthy of Degas, he recorded its awkward collapsing pose, a sculpture of unalloyed originality which for Meissonier was but one step in the production of his patriotic and detailed painting.

Meissonier's exhibited paintings could measure less than 10 centimetres square, yet they resulted from hundreds of studies.[13] They exercised an extraordinary fascination upon the public. 'The prices of his works', noted Albert Wolff, 'have attained formidable proportions, never before known'[14] and yet Meissonier refused to sell his studies and released so few paintings that in some years he earned nothing. Wolff calculated that his signature could be worth 1,000,000 francs per year.

Whilst Meissonier's ambition to teach at the Ecole des Beaux-Arts was never realised, he received the fullest imaginable recognition. Within the Légion d'Honneur he was made *chevalier* in 1846, *officier* in 1856, *commandeur* in 1867, *grand officier* in 1878 and awarded the Grand Cross in 1889. Napoleon III had bought his painting *The Brawl* (Le Rixe) at the Exposition Universelle of 1855 and presented it to Queen Victoria. In 1890 Meissonier was a prime mover in the founding of the breakaway Société Nationale des Beaux-Arts and its first president. At the Secretan Sale of 1889 his *Les Cuirassier* realised 190,000 francs. He was the most famous artist of his day. Within a hundred years of his death his reputation has evaporated almost entirely.

Around the corner from Meissonier's studio, at 43 Avenue de Villiers is dedicated to Jean-Jacques Henner, bequeathed to the City of Paris by his nephew and nephew's wife, M. and Mme Jules Henner in 1924, and now the Musée Henner (Plate 209). The imposing facade of stone and pink brick incorporates amongst its classical motifs enormous studio windows on the third and fourth storeys. A bronze portrait bust of Henner is inserted above the entrance.

Born of peasant stock in Alsace Henner entered the Ecole des Beaux-Arts under Drolling and in 1858 won the Prix de Rome. He studied Venetian art in particular in Italy and made his Salon debut in 1863. He rose steadily within the Légion d'Honneur, and was elected to the Institut in 1889. Paul Mantz considered that he was haunted by the memory of the greatest dead masters, and discerned little development in his work.[15] Devoted to study in the Louvre, he was deeply impressed by Rembrandt as well as Titian, although he admired aspects of more recent French art too and asserted that 'If I had to choose two modern works I would take a Corot and an Ingres'.[16] Henner was an enthusiastic reader of classical literature and made use of his studies of Homer, Virgil, Horace and Ovid in paintings which ammassed him a considerable fortune. His studio has a balcony enclosed in a perforated wooden arab screen and there are indications of an exoticism as well as an eroticism in his work. His paintings gained in fashion in the 1880s and 1890s.

Closeby at 53 Avenue de Villiers was the studio of the Hungarian painter Munkacsy which, with its liveried servants and visitors from Parisian high society, was an epitome of Parisian elegance: 'It is Munkacsy who has the most elegant clientèle, not a Friday passes but fifty vehicles of the best people stop at his door'.[17]

Munkacsy moved to Paris in 1872 and was impressed by Barbizon painters and by Courbet's example. He exhibited at the Salon until 1878 when he was awarded the medal of honour for his painting of the blind Milton dictating. Thereafter his success permitted him to abandon the Salon and exhibit in his studio. He returned to contribute regularly to the Salon from 1889 until his death in 1900.

Just off the junction of the Avenue de Villiers and the Boulevard Malsherbes on the north side, the short Rue Jacques-Bingen has studios, purpose built and of some elegance at Nos. 10, 12 and 16. No. 10 in yellow and red brick was built by the architect Charles Le More in 1880. No. 12 beside it has a stone facade with a robust arched studio

208. J-L. Ernest Meissonier, *Wounded Horse*, 1884, bronze cast from the original red wax maquette, 26.5 × 44 × 36.5 cm. A study for the painting *Paris 1870–71*, Musée de la Peinture, Grenoble (gift of Mme Meissonier, 1899).

209. The Musée Jean-Jacques Henner at 43 Avenue de Villiers.

210. Studios at 7 bis Rue Edouard-Detaille.

211. The Hotel of Sarah Bernhardt, Rue Fortuny, in 1891, Cabinet des Estampes, Bibliothèque Nationale, Paris.

212. (*facing page*) *The Statue of Liberty towering over the surrounding Roads and Buildings*, Cabinet d'Estampes, Biblioteque Nationale, Paris.

213. (*facing page top*) Studios at 34 and 36 Rue Fortuny.

214. (*facing page middle*) Studio on the corner of 38 Rue de Prony and 28 Rue Fortuny.

215. (*facing page below*) Studio at 21 Rue de Prony.

window at the third floor, complete with stone mouldings, key-stone and a high roof space behind it. No. 16 is an elegantly restrained facade; its rectangular studio window has a neo-Greek cornice on the third floor.

Continuing up the Avenue de Villiers eastwards the Rue Cardinet on the left has studios at Nos. 46 (built 1911), 48 and 56, the later a two-bay top storey studio next-door to the house where Debussy lived in 1902 (No. 58). Between this street and the Avenue de Villiers run the Rue Edouard-Detaille (opened 1892) and the Rue Meissonier named after the painters. In a small extension of the Rue Edouard-Detaille, No, 7 is a colourful block of studios on which coloured tiles and sunflower motifs decorate the third and fourth storeys (Plate 210).

Across the square where the Boulevard Malesherbes and Avenue de Villiers intersect, the Rue Fortuny (named after the Spanish painter José Maria Fortuny, 1838–74, in 1877) cuts south-west to the Rue de Prony with its glimpse of the Parc Monceau. It was on the corner of the Avenue de Villiers and Rue Fortuny (at Nos. 35–7 Rue Fortuny) that Sarah Bernhardt constructed her studio house in 1877 at a cost of over 500,000 francs after she moved from the Montmartre area (Plate 211). The vast studio apartment contained many exotic objects including a divan covered in tiny tiger skins. In the interior 'the great square sky-light is veiled with an awning, life-size portraits of Mme Bernhardt and of her son are on the walls, and chairs of every possible form are used as easels to hold other frames, soldier-subjects by Detaille, a water-colour by Doré, birds by Giacomelli'.[18] In addition there were spears, antlers, leopard skins and enormous palms. She clearly felt that her standing demanded a major studio in the most fashionable area of the Avenue de Villiers. She left here without selling her house to begin another on the Boulevard Pereire. The house in Rue Fortuny was remodelled by Chéret in 1891. No. 37 was demolished *c.* 1960 and No. 35 stripped of its décor in a public sale on 28 February 1970.[19]

The Rue Fortuny preserves numerous splendid studio-houses, some with immense studios concealed in the roof-space and top lit, others, including Nos. 34 and 36, with their large north-lights incorporated fully into stylish façades and staring directly into the street (Plate 213). 48 Rue Fortuny was occupied by the highly successful sculptor Louis-Ernest Barrias who had studied under Jouffroy. He worked for numerous architectural projects, providing sculpture for the Opéra, Hôtel de Ville, the Louvre, the Mairie at Neuilly and the Sorbonne. He rose to *commandeur* in the Légion d'Honneur in 1900 and was elected to the Institut in 1884; he taught at the Ecole des Beaux-Arts, was a member of the Commission des Musées nationaux and the Conseil supèrieur des Beaux-Arts. A bust of Munkacsy by Barrias was exhibited at the Salon of 1879 and he received major commissions for the Expositions Universelles of 1889 (where his *Electricité* featured in the Galerie des Machines) and 1900 (groups on the Grand Palais). His marble group *Les Premières Funérailles*, shown at the Salon of 1883 and the Exposition Universelle of 1889, was bought by the City of Paris. Numerous marble copies of this were made, including one for Munkacsy in 1887. The Barbedienne process was used by Barrias to make reduced copies of sculptures for the more popular market. His bronze *Monument to Victor Hugo*, 11 metres high, was erected at a total cost of 250,000 francs in the Place Victor-Hugo and inaugurated in 1902.[20]

An impressive corner-studio stands at 28 Rue Fortuny and 38 Rue de Prony with large vertical studio lights in both streets flanking the corner façade at roof level (Plate 214). A characteristic studio house in this area is the imposing building at 21 Rue de Prony which towers above adjacant buildings by virtue of the immense two-storey height of the studio built into its roof (Plate 215). Above the third storey behind a balcony which surmounts a cornice, the huge double-height window rises to the roofline, consuming half of the width of the façade, its curved stone moulding emerging from almost vertical roof slates above spacious and substantial living quarters.

Across the Rue Prony near the junction with the Rue Fortuny, tucked away in the

short Rue Jadin, is the cheaper accommodation in this expensive and luxurious area. 5 bis Rue Jadin is a block of four studios rising through eight floors with one bay of small windows to the left and a mass of double-height studio windows to the right. The façade is decorated in red, blue and emerald green.

The Rue Jadin leads into the Rue de Chazelles which in turn leads down to the Boulevard de Courcelles near the Parc Monceau. In 1883 this point in Paris witnessed an astonishing visual spectacle when the immense form of Bartholdi's *Liberty Enlightening the World* towered above the buildings, rising in scaffolding from the workshops of Gaget Gauthier et Compagnie at 25 Rue de Chazelles (Plate 212), dwarfing spectators and buildings alike before its dedication and transfer to New York Harbour.

216. Studios at 59 Rue Ampère.

There are many studios to the north of the Avenue de Villiers and parts of the Rue Ampère are almost entirely studios (Plate 216). The Rue Ampère is reached via the Rue Brémontier where Marie Bashkirtseff had a *hôtel* and where the painter Alfred Pierre Roll occupied No. 53 (Plate 217). Roll's painting achieved popular success at the Salon of 1888. Employing bright colour and loose handling derived ultimately from Impressionist precedent, Roll incorporated the nude into this context with some success. Paul Mantz admired his work particularly for its abolition of shadows in the painting *En Eté* seen at the Salon of 1889: 'Thus taken up with his triumphs, M. Roll cannot retrace his steps... He affirms his faith anew and says that his palette has been clarified for good.'[21] The *Studio* Magazine in 1896 noted that 'in his nude studies, in his women stretched on the grass in the sunshine, he triumphs indeed'.[22] He later moved to a studio in the nearby Rue Alphonse de Neuville. There his studio walls were filled cheek by jowl with his paintings. A photograph shows Roll at an elegant carpeted table, a tiger skin on the parquet floor and a framed painting with corners padded ready for transport, leaning against a studio stove. Roll's success was not short-lived. He had studied under Gérôme, Bonnat and Harpignies and made his Salon debut in 1870. Recognition followed with a steady ascent through the ranks of the Légion d'Honneur from 1883 to *comandeur* in 1900 and *grand officier* in 1913. He was president of the Société Nationale des Beaux-Arts from 1905 and had been amongst its founder members. His blend of Impressionism with techniques encouraged by the Salon, bridged the widening gap, combining brilliant colour with familiar themes, particularly the female nude displayed in the open air, in a manner that appeared at once both adventurously new and respectful in its development of what had long been respected and popular. Luridly colourful ceiling paintings by Roll, including the *Glorification of Berlioz* (1919), decorate the Petit Palais and testify to his continued success.

The Rue Brémontier meets the Rue Ampère where it crosses the luxurious Avenue de Wagram. Amongst the numerous studios of the Rue Ampère, the painter Flameng occupied No. 61.[23] To the north the Rue Puvis de Chavannes and Rue Gustave Doré open into the wide Boulevard Pereire (Plate 218) where Bernhardt's final vast Parisian home was situated at No. 56. Beyond this Boulevard the Rue Alfred Roll connects with

217. Alfred-Philippe Roll in his studio, photograph *c.* 1895.

the Boulevard Berthier at the edge of central Paris.[24] Near here was the Symbolist painter Paul Chabas, at 23 Boulevard Berthier, whose work has features in common with that of Roll but who also designed posters for the Rosicrucian Salons. His career flourished in the 1890s: he was awarded the Prix Nationale at the Salon of 1899 and a gold medal at the Exposition Universelle of 1900. The Boulevard Berthier is extremely wide with the buildings on its south side receiving maximum north light and ideal sites for studios. Every odd number had its studio as a result (Plate 219–25). The American John Singer Sargent had a studio at No. 41. A photograph shows him here, seated on a corner settle beside the model's dias (Plate 226). Oriental carpets add richness to the sparse and practical interior and amidst the copies after Rembrandt and Hals, his painting *The Breakfast Table* can be seen in progress on the easel. In the corner of the room is a concave circular object which may be a form of spotlight designed to accentuate the light and shade on his model. Sargent experienced great demand as a society portrait painter and other artists tapping this market were alarmed at his brilliant facility and success. Jacques-Emile Blanche was amongst them. 'Whether he liked it or not,' Blanche later recalled, 'Sargent was an artist of the Plaine Monceau'.[26] Both Blanche and Sargent had close contacts with Impressionist painters, both also wished to develop the elegant portrait for it led to further commissions and through them to wealth. Sargent achieved real originality and his portraits were frequently virtuoso performances in the handling of paint going beyond the requirements of commissions. On the other hand, the demands and practicalities of arranging sittings, in London as well as in Paris, scarcely left him time to eat according to Blanche: 'During the season, at the grill-room of the Hyde Park Hotel he devoured his meals and gulped down his wine, his watch on the table in front of him.'[27] The same would apply in Paris.

The Italian society portrait painter Giovanni Boldini took over 41 Boulevard Berthier from Sargent in 1886 and Sargent's technique can only have impressed him. Trained under the Macchiaoli painters in Florence, he settled in Paris in 1871 and was a life-long friend of Degas. He also knew Whistler, whom he painted, and he admired Anders Zorn. He had moved here from the vicinity of the Boulevard de Clichy. He painted many of the celebrated figures of high society as well as painters and writers of his day,

218. Studios at 95 Boulevard Pereire.

219. Studios at 105 Boulevard Berthier.

220. Rooftop studios at 3 and 5 (brick) Rue Bremontier.

221. Studio block at 29 and 31 Boulevard Berthier.

222. Studio group at 43, 45 (pediment) and 47 Boulevard Berthier.

223. Studios at 59, 61, 63 and 65 (roundel over door) Boulevard Berthier.

224. Studios at 75 and 77 (with skylight) Boulevard Berthier.

225. Studios at 93 Boulevard Berthier.

226. John Singer Sargent in his studio at 41 Boulevard Berthier, photograph of *c.* 1883–84, Collection Ormond Family, London. On the easel at left is *The Breakfast Table*.

including the spectacular and sometimes bizarre comte Robert de Montesquiou-Fezensac whose exotic life-style inspired both Marcel Proust and Joris-Karl Huysmans for characters in their novels.

Further along the Boulevard Berthier No. 61 was occupied by the Salon painter Georges Rochegrosse whose exhibits frequently depicted a lugubrious, violent and nightmare imagery that could scarcely be missed by the Salon visitor (Plate 227). He was, as Paul Mantz noted, 'always careful to choose subjects of a kind to interest the crowd'.[28] He had been a prodigal student at the Académie Julian. At No. 93 the great tenor singer Caruso had his appartment.

227. Georges-Antoine Rochegrosse, *Andromaque*, salon of 1883, oil on canvas, 470 × 335 cm., Musée des Beaux-Arts, Rouen. 'After the capture of the town, the royal prince Astynax is, on the orders of Ulysses, torn from the arms of his mother Andromaque, to be thrown from the ramparts."

228. Albert Besnard in his studio, photograph of *c.* 1895.

The Boulevard Berthier flows south-west into the Avenue de Villiers, beyond which further groups of studios are to be found. In the Rue Guillaume-Tell, Paul-Albert Besnard was at No. 17 in a house built to his own designs with the studio window extended into a bay forming a conservatory within the great height of the room (Plate 228). Besnard's mural decorations could be enormous and the studio contained moveable scaffolding for him to work on these commissions. He had studied at the Ecole des Beaux-Arts and won the Prix de Rome in 1874. He studied etching in London under Legros and admired the fluency achieved by Anders Zorn in this medium (Plate 230). His murals were loosely handled and highly coloured, revealing a debt to both his formal training and the new strength of colour which Impressionism had first released. They included commissions for the Ecole de Pharmacie (1883), the Mairie of the First Arrondissement (1887), a ceiling at the Hôtel de Ville (1890), another at the Comédie Française (1905–13) and a cupola at the Petit Palais (1907–10). His success continued well into the twentieth century. Elected to the Institut in 1912, he later became Director of the French Academy in Rome (1913–21) and Director of the Ecole des Beaux-Arts (from 1922). The ultimate accolade was his state funeral in the Louvre. 'Physically', wrote a visitor to his studio, 'not at all the man one would imagine from his works. Not a trace of *nervosité*, no sign of subtlety or over-refinement in this tall, thickly-built form, in which everything proclaims the true sanguine temperament.'[29] He was highly successful, lived in an area of Paris which proclaimed him to be so and he had a summer villa on the Lac d'Annecy.

There were more studios in the Rue Bayen to the south-west. Jules Chéret at one time occupied No. 41 and the Symbolist painter of twilight Henri Le Sidaner occupied 5 Rue Emile-Allez in this area. In the 1890s Le Sidaner was considered 'a landscapist of rare and delicate sensibility and very original gifts'.[30]

In stark contrast to the elegance of these studios and their clientèle, was the work of Jean-François Raffaëlli who had lived in the industrial suburb of Asnières but who in 1900 was at 202 Rue de Courcelles. Paul Mantz called him 'the official painter of rag-pickers and beggers',[31] whilst Edmond de Goncourt in his *Journal*, for the 27 March 1884, written after visiting a Raffaëlli exhibition, noted that his work resembled 'a curiously exact photography of the façades of suburban townhalls and wine merchants and the ridiculous interiors of the petits bourgeois'.[32] Raffaëlli studied briefly under Gérôme; he also became a friend of Degas and attended the Café Guerbois. Degas invited him to exhibit at the Impressionist group exhibitions of 1880 and 1881. The realist trait in his work remained forceful and original, and with Forain, whose cynicism he shared, he illustrated J.K. Huysmans' book *Croquis parisiens*. He was made a *chevalier* of the Légion d'Honneur in 1889 and promoted to *officier* in 1906.

The Rue de Courcelles crosses the Avenue de Wagram, that streams south to the Arc de Triomphe, at its great nexus of roads and the axis of the Champs-Elysées. A few artists worked off the Champs-Elysées itself in areas of the grandest and most reserved splendour. Jean Gigoux, friend of Nadar and of Balzac, occupied 17 Rue de Chateaubriand, and south, off the Champs-Elysées, in the Rue Bassano, No. 48, was Léon Bonnat,[33] one of the brightest of the Salon stars, a respected and highly sought-after portraitist, a professional in the fullest sense, an exemplar of academic control in painting and a man heavily loaded with honours (Plate 231). Bonnat was brought up in Spain and first studied there. The decisive chiaroscuro of Caravaggio and Ribera impressed him deeply. Later, he studied in Paris under Cogniet and travelled in Italy. He became a life-long friend of Degas. It was a portrait of Cogniet that initiated his success in 1875. By 1881 he was a member of the Institut and by 1888 a professor at the Ecole des Beaux-Arts His rise through the Légion d'Honneur was unparalleled culminating in the Grand Cross in 1900. A member of the juries of both Expositions Universelles in 1889 and 1900, he was a formidable influence upon the Salon too. In 1905 he was appointed to the directorship of the Ecole des Beaux-Arts. He was in

230. Anders Zorn, *Albert Besnard and his model*, 1896, etching.

229. Paul-Albert Besnard, *Portrait or Mme Roger Jourdain*, 1886, oil on canvas, 200 × 155 cm., Musée des Arts Decoratifs, Paris.

231. Léon Bonnat, *The Beheading of St Denis*, oil on canvas, Panthéon, Paris.

232. Léon Bonnat in his studio, photograph *c.* 1895.

addition an avid collector and he left his collection to the city of Bayonne where it is preserved in the Musée Bonnat. Amongst his numerous public commissions was his painting of *The Beheading of St Denis* for the Panthéon, which depicts with gruesome academic precision the moment at which the newly-beheaded saint astonishes his tormentors by picking up his severed head to carry it into Paris (Plate 231). The first monograph on him, *Léon Bonnat, the First Part of his Life and Works* by A.L. Fouquier, appeared as early as 1879 when Bonnat was 46 years old. His career was the epitome of a successful professionalism reaching beyond the vagaries of fashion, although post-humously his reputation has much diminished in the face of radical reassessments and changing views in the twentieth century.

233. Jean Béraud in his studio.

Less successful but very fashionable was Bonnat's pupil Jean Béraud, a little further south at 5 Rue Clémont-Marot (Plate 233). Beraud, a well-born dandy, specialised in depicting modern Parisian life in the elegance of the theatres and streets of central Paris; he did so with an amused and able eye, for Béraud was able to incorporate minute portraits, as could Degas, into his city scenes, emphasising the public persona of the street's individuals and analyzing the crowd in the process. The acidic bite of his paintings was equally evident in calculatedly shocking depictions of Christ in scenes of modern dress, incorporating recognisable portraits of public figures in major roles of the narrative. Other works by Béraud emphasise fashionable aspects of Paris as well as the vitality of its nightlife and entertainments.

Béraud's Salon debut was made in 1873; the modernity of Degas, Forain, Raffaëlli and others is reflected in his attitude to painting the city as a communal human organism and although he tended to focus upon the grands boulevards the faces presented by their inhabitants were more important to Béraud than those of the city's buildings. He was a founder member of the Salon of the Société Nationale des Beaux-Arts in 1890.

Béraud's address was close to the Seine. To the west lies the district of Passy. Here stood the Trocadéro Palace, which formerly faced the Champs de Mars across the river, where the Palais des Beaux-Arts, Palais des Arts Libéraux and Palais des Machines were installed at the foot of the Eiffel Tower. In the small Passy cemetery that opened onto the Place du Trocadéro Manet lies buried in a tomb with his brother Eugène and sister-in-law, the Impressionist painter, Berthe Morisot. Her home for many years was in the Rue Villejuste (now the Rue Paul-Valéry). Morisot's studio, at 40 Rue Villejuste was a focal point for many of the artistic and literary figures of her day, particularly for Manet, Mallarmé and her Impressionist friends. Morisot died in 1895, and from 1902 the house became the home of the writer Paul Valéry whose name the street has since assumed. Morisot had worked with Corot but subsequently responded to Manet and the Impressionists, contributing to seven of their group exhibitions.

South-west of the Passy cemetery is the Rue de la Tour where Frémiet, the most celebrated animal sculptor of the later nineteenth century, occupied No. 70. In a bronze by Henri Gréber, Frémiet is portrayed in greatcoat, cloak and top hat, his shoes appearing as if cast directly from the actual objects (Plate 234). Gréber's only departure from this mundane view of the man of the city is the skull of a horse, also possibly cast direct, which lies behind the legs of the figure. This distinguishes the figure as Frémiet. The nephew of François Rude, who sculpted the gigantic *Marseillaise* relief on the Arc de Triomphe, Frémiet began his career without adequate funds and was obliged to earn a living as painter to the Paris morgue. Later, he received lessons from Rude in his studio on the Rue d' Enfer in Montparnasse. He also studied animals intensively in the Jardin des Plantes. His Salon début was made in 1843 and success steadily followed. He received a curious if exacting commission from Napoleon III who requested fifty-five statuettes showing all the uniforms of the army. In 1874 his *Joan of Arc* was erected in the Rue de Rivoli at a cost of 24,000 francs,[34] replaced by a later version in 1899, and the following year his *Stone Age Man* was installed in the Jardin des Plantes. He was awarded

234. Henri Gréber, *The Sculptor Frémiet*, bronze, Musée d' Orsay, Paris (formerly Luxembourg Museum). The medallion on the base depicts Frémiet's *Joan of Arc* (see Plate 112).

many honours, rising ultimately to *grand officier* of the Légion d'Honneur, and in 1892 he was elected to the Institut. He supplied groups for the Pont Alexandre III, and he was instrumental in teaching Gérôme to sculpt. At the Ecole de Medecine he had acquired a detailed knowledge of anatomy, and produced anatomical models for a museum. From this he moved on to producing zoological models for the Jardin des Plantes and his career as an *animalier* was launched. Amongst his most grotesque and popular sculptures was the startingly credible and erotic sculpture of 1888 *Gorilla carrying off a Woman* (see Plate 85).

235. The studio of Puvis de Chavannes at Neuilly.

236. The entrance to the studio of Puvis de Chavannes at Neuilly with special door for the removal of mural paintings.

\*     \*     \*

237. Gaston La Touche, *Portrait of Puvis de Chavannes*, oil on canvas, whereabouts unknown.

The immensely long axis that divides Paris in a straight east-west line from the Louvre to the Arc de Triomphe continues uninterrupted beyond the old fortifications of the city, through the suburb of Neuilly to the curving Seine and the suburb of Courbevoie beyond. It was in spacious and newly developed Neuilly that Puvis de Chavannes constructed his vast mural painting studio, a single-storey hangar, top lit by sky-lights along its whole length and with double-height doors, opening into the trees and flower beds of the garden (Plate 235–6). These permitted the passage of his colossal paintings for the town halls of France, the Sorbonne and the Boston Library. When engaged upon major commissions Puvis quit Paris for Neuilly:

> Puvis works but little in his Place Pigalle home. His real working studio is at Neuilly, outside the fortifications, a vast bare room, with plenty of space for his enormous canvases. He goes every morning at nine o'clock and remains until evening, working alone all day on the ladder without the assistance of a pupil.[35]

His stretchers for canvases reached the roof and only the relevent studies for his major paintings stood on easels for reference. Across its immense floor, the studio had few comforts, an easy chair, a minimum of light-weight tables that could easily be moved, a turntable with the model of a figure on it (possibly a small dressed lay figure) and no clutter or confusion whatsoever. As the *Portrait of Puvis de Chavannes* by Gaston La Touche reveals, he was dwarfed by his mural compositions, and the sheer physical task of painting them was heroic (Plate 237). No confusion could be permitted with such projects and Puvis' process of painting was as closely controlled as his working environment. He would evolve a synthesis from numerous *croquis*, or first thoughts and studies; this comprised the *esquisse*, a compositional drawing establishing the general disposition of forms. There followed an *ébauche*, a colour study based upon this composition, fixing local colours and the overall coherence of colour for the major canvas. In his preparatory studies Puvis isolated and refined quite separately the elements of composition, drawing, colour and tone. The later colour studies define the colour-structure for the large canvas and contained a limited set of particular points of colour which maintained control across the wide area to be painted: they provided a constant guide during the execution of the commission, whereas painting direct from the model would cause an undesirable attention to particular traits and effects of light Colour, though restrained, was mixed as little as possible. Puvis adivsed that the painter should 'have a horror of useless mixtures which become like glue, darken, form a bloom and become heavy'.[36] Puvis distinguished clearly between the studies and the major work itself: there was nothing of the dilettante in his approach: 'The drawing,' according to Puvis, 'that is the libretto; the painting, that is the opera.'[37] He did indeed, in a sense, put his figures on stage within the picture-space of his canvas, squaring up his drawings for transfer on a scale appropriate to the final work. Every feature was refined and edited down to its essential traits to fit its role within the painting. As with his studio so with his paintings, Puvis relied upon the sparsest of means to produce the maximum effect. He rarely drew from the model except to use the drawing in evolving a composition, but in that process of evolution he used life-drawing constantly and a stream of models young and old were called to his studio. The gigantic canvases were manipulated by a system of pulleys and counterweights devised by Puvis.

The studio of Dagnan-Bouveret, who also lived at Neuilly, was a different world, filled with screens, hangings, potted palms, elegant furniture and Salon paintings (Plate 238). The artist posed for a photograph clad in a velvet suit, his brushes, mahl-stick and palette in hand. On the easel is a painting rested against the moulding of a frame too large for it. Formerly an inhabitant of the Avenue de Villiers, Dagnan-Bouveret was at Neuilly by 1900 at 73 Boulevard Bineau. His success flourished in the shadow of Bastien-Lepage's early death, as he was seen by many as a potential inheritor of his reputation. In 1879 his *Wedding at the Photographers* made him a popular artist. The Salon critic Paul Mantz did not approve of it however, calling it 'a painting where the spirit of observation with which the author is so generously gifted, was used to achieve a comic effect and vulgar laughter. This painter, dedicated to the great Sunday public, irritates us profoundly.'[38] By contrast *Bretons at a Pardon* at the Salon of 1889 showed his talents used to more serious purpose (Plate 239). 'This sober, concentrated, essentially French painting', wrote Mantz, 'is the most expressive painting at the Salon and the most advanced.'[39] The words of critics could create stars in the firmament of Parisian art. Here was one in the making for 'we expect much of M. Dagnan'[40] was an invitation to follow his talents in a particular way. With its implied promise of support and recognition it was difficult to resist the invitation. Dagnan-Bouveret who had studied under Gérôme and Corot, showed control and originality. He won the Prix de Rome in 1876, was made *chevalier* (1885) and *officier* (1892) of the Légion d'Honneur and was elected to the Institut in 1900.

In the river Seine near Neuilly are several small and elongated islands, the biggest of which, the Ile de la Grande Jatte, was a popular resort for picnics, sunbathing and summer pleasures in the late nineteenth century. Here Seurat made numerous little studies for the large composition *A Sunday Afternoon on the Ile de la Grande Jatte*, visible on his studio walls in his painting *Les Poseuses*. The art student Shirley Fox writing in 1909 regretted the development of the island, and the scene he described is recognisably that witnessed by Seurat:

The Ile de la Grande Jatte was in those days very different from what it is now. Many parts of it were practically wild, and cafés, restaurants, landing stages and mai-

238. Pascal-Adolphe-Jean Dagnan-Bouveret in his studio, photograph of *c.* 1895.

239. P.-A.-J. Dagnan-Bouveret, *Bretons at a Pardon*, 1887, oil on canvas, 125 × 141 cm., Calouste Gulbenkian Foundation, Lisbon.

sonnettes few and far between. Now the whole place is built over and covered with roads and enclosures and has lost for ever its old unsophisticated character. We nearly always used to row down the narrower portion of the river on the south side of the island.[41]

Seurat's painting shows sailing and rowing in this part of the river with a scene of unsophisticated relaxation in the foreground. The limpid water flows quietly, reflecting the light. What is unrelaxed and formal is Seurat's composition of strict profiles, front and back views of figures who appear motionless even when running. His depiction of light, owing much to Impressionism, is nonetheless now systematised, analytical and slowly executed with small points of colour. Foresaking the immediacy of handling evolved by Monet, Pissarro, Sisley and Renoir, Seurat returned the act of painting light into the studio, to be worked up from small studies, a process comparable with that of Puvis, producing likewise a large canvas of controlled intervals with no haphazard detail. This resulted in a considered gravity which is not dispelled by the spiral-tailed monkey, the leaping dog or the running girl. Yet Seurat is here committed to painting modern life and like Signac is attracted to the suburbs for his subject. George Moore had heard about the painting whilst still a practising art student at Julian's, although his friend Marshall's description of it was scarcely accurate:

Today is the opening of the exhibition of the Impressionists. We'll breakfast round the corner...and go on there. I hear that Bedlam is nothing to it; at one end of the room there is a canvas twenty feet square and in three tints: pale yellow for sunlight, brown

240. Georges Seurat, *Bathing at Asnières*, 1883–4, oil on canvas, 201 × 301 cm., National Gallery, London.

241. Georges Seurat, *The Bridge at Courbevoie*, 1886–87, oil on canvas, 45.7 × 54.7 cm., Courtauld Institute Galleries, London.

for the shadows, and all the rest is sky-blue. A large woman walks, I am told, in the foreground with a ring-tailed monkey, and the tail is said to be three yards long.[42]

On the edge of Paris the Seine took on a different aspect; the ancient and grandiose buildings of central Paris were exchanged for woods and factories which Seurat had recorded in his first major painting, the *Baignade à Asnières* (Plate 240). The figures he recorded were similarly stripped of the fashionable pretentions of the central boulevards and unselfconsciously relaxed in the sun in poses which for Seurat recalled respected Renaissance works in a setting that remained modern Paris. This allowed his erudite love of composition to combine with a systematic analysis of light which paid no heed to the formulas of the Salon painters. The river remained important for Seurat as a shifting mirror of the sky's light, just as it did for Monet. Here the Seine was still part of Paris but seen in a different context away from the press and business of the city, meandering and glittering with a fresh independence. Seurat's painting of the Seine at Courbevoie is an image of melancholy, quiet movement in opalescent light, the painter's eye observing astutely the constituents of its colour (Plate 241). The foreground figures are themselves watching, quite still, on the river bank. Masts of boats and the fading arches of the Courbevoie bridge mark out rhythms across the painting; movements are restricted to the slightest — a man shifts his pose in the middle distance, smoke rises diagonally from the chimney of a factory and disperses, the tree at right spreads its branches. This is the antithesis of the seething, active Paris of Degas, Lautrec, Béraud, Monet or Pissarro when painting in the city centre.

Seurat's brief painting career was soon in fact to embrace subjects of rapid action at the cabaret and circus, closer in theme to those of Degas and Lautrec, but an important influence in these works lived at Courbevoie. This was the poster-designer and painter Jules Chéret whose effervescent lithographs decorated the gable-ends and hoardings of Paris. His innovative techniques with colour lithography, particularly the blending of colour optically by superimposing hazy effects in different colours, and the vitality of his designs, also inspired Lautrec and Bonnard. His posters were collected as artworks but were cheaply mass-produced. Edmond de Goncourt visiting a friend's newly decorated apartment in Paris in 1888 noted that 'he had had the idea of installing two screens which he had covered in posters by Chéret, the colours of which mix well with the japonaiserie of the walls'.[43]

Chéret lived at 156 Rue St Denis at Courbevoie beyond the bustle of the city that his posters decorated with enthusiastic exhortations to visit balls, ice-rinks and other events (Plate 242). He began at the age of thirteen by drawing lettering for a lithographer and his own posters integrated hand-drawn lettering into the design. He founded his own printing works in 1866. In 1889 he executed posters for the Moulin Rouge and in 1893 advertised Loïe Fuller's dances at the Folies Bergère. His dynamic, explosive compositions for posters did much to create an image of Paris the optimistic vitality of which was as much due to Chéret's personality as to the events which his posters promoted.

Asnières, an industrial suburb close to Courbevoie and visible in Seurat's *Baignade*, was painted by Van Gogh, Emile Bernard and Anquetin. Bernard lived there in 1889 at 5 Avenue Beaulieu. His studies with Van Gogh, Anquetin and Lautrec in the studio of Cormon were counterbalanced by his meeting with Gauguin in 1886. He also experimented with pointillist works, but these were destroyed after a disagreement with Signac in 1886–7. He worked closely with Gauguin from 1888 in Brittany, the year he was also painting with Van Gogh at Asnières. He was an inventor of the *cloisonniste* technique of painting which stressed the picture surface with flat areas of colour separated by even, rhythmically placed lines of dark blue, decorating the painting to expressive effect, in keeping with suggestive and symbolic Breton subjects. Bernard had links with the Nabi painters too and visited Cézanne with Maurice Denis in the South

242. Jacques-Emile Blanche, *Portrait of Jules Chéret*, 1892, oil on canvas, 200 × 179 cm., Petit Palais, Paris (gift of the artist, 1902).

243. Jacques-Emile Blanche, *The Painter Fritz Thaulow and Family*, 1895, oil on canvas, 180 × 200 cm., Musée d'Orsay, Paris.

of France. The painter Raffaëlli also lived for some time at Asnieres at 19 Rue de la Bibliothèque.

South of Neuilly spreads the Bois de Boulogne where the collector Sir Richard Wallace had his mansion at the Bagatelle and where Degas studied the crowds at Longchamps racecourse. Zola described the scene in *Nana* in terms that emphasised the dislocated sense of direction in the crowd and the horses before the race in a manner so close to Degas' impression as to suggest that he may have had Degas' paintings of the races in mind:

> carriages stood about separately in complete disorder, looking as if they had been stranded on the grass. Wheels and horses were pointing in all directions, side by side, askew, at right angles or head to head. On such stretches of turf as remained unoccupied riders kept trotting, and dark clusters of pedestrians moved continually.[44]

Between the Bois de Boulogne and the Seine looping south from central Paris, elegant streets reach south to the suburb of St Cloud all the way from the Arc de Triomphe. The painter James Tissot lived near the Arc de Triomphe in a house he owned at 64 Avenue du Bois de Boulogne (formerly the Avenue de l'Impératrice) from 1867 until his death. After fighting in the Franco-Prussian war, Tissot settled in London where he studied etching under Seymour Haden. His work is in two distinct phases; there are paintings of elegantly dressed and beautiful young women that consciously emphasise fine materials and the life of the wealthy young woman in Paris and London, and there is an enormous sequence of paintings executed after his religious conversion. In 1895 Tissot exhibited in Paris no less than 350 watercolours on New Testament themes. They were highly successful sold as reproductions. Tissot joined the community at the Abbaye de Bullan where he worked upon an ambitious cycle of Old Testament paintings uncompleted at his death in 1902.

Further south at 11 Rue Weber was the history, battle and portrait painter Aimé Morot; much honoured, he replaced Gustave Moreau at the Institut in 1898.

At the southern end of the Bois de Boulogne lies the suburb of St Cloud, whilst within the city boundary, between the Bois de Boulogne to the west and the Seine to the east lies the residential area of Auteuil. Degas lived at Auteuil at the end of his life, and Jacques-Emile Blanche had a family home here in the Rue des Fontis. A brick studio was constructed for him in the garden with sash-windows in the English style, although he spent much time at Dieppe on the Channel coast where his studio, which according to Blanche was 'a movable shed made of wood and iron, of quite inexcusable hideosity'[45] became a focal point for visiting atists. A pupil of Gervex and Humbert, Jacques-Emile Blanche was, like Whistler, Sickert and Sargent, active in both London and Paris. As a portrait painter he painted, as well as society portraits, many of the celebrated literary and artistic figures of his day, amongst them Viélé-Griffin, Paul Adam, Charles Cottet, Aubrey Beardsley and Marcel Proust. His complex and psychologically subtle group-portrait of *The Painter Fritz Thaulow and his Family* exemplifies his analysis of character and was highly esteemed (Plate 243). Degas and Sickert were amongst his prolific circle of contacts and friends and Degas portrayed Blanche together with Sickert and Gervex in a pastel group portrait in 1887.

Beyond the city boundary in the suburb of St Cloud at 15 Rue de Calvaire an extraordinary studio house was constructed to the designs of the painter Gaston La Touche (Plate 244). Unlike any other Parisian studio of its date, it ressembled an enormous country cottage, half timbered in part with a complicated assemblage of bay windows, conservatories and roofs at different levels. With an evident enthusiasm for the qualities of different materials Gaston La Touche constructed a large studio held up by exposed brick piers joined by arches through the wide open space of which was an anteroom lit by a sequence of large arched windows. He even hung paintings against the bare brickwork which was left exposed for its own material qualities to be displayed. On

244. Studio house of Gaston La Touche at Saint-Cloud, photograph of *c.* 1898.

245. Gaston La Touche in his studio at Saint-Cloud, photograph of *c.* 1898.

the bare floor of wooden boards stood a simple wooden table and an elaborate bentwood rocking chair by Thonet. The setting for his paintings was airy, unpretentious, practical and highly original for its date (Plate 245). He was a founder member of the breakaway Salon of the Société Nationale des Beaux-Arts with Puvis de Chavannes, Meissonier and others in 1890. He was awarded a gold medal at the Exposition Universelle in 1900, made a *chevalier* of the Légion d'Honneur the same year and promoted to *officier* in 1909.

\*     \*     \*

Auteuil and St Cloud border the Seine which in south-west Paris begins its great loop north again to the Ile de la Grande Jatte, Courbevoie and Asnières. The Seine is at the heart of Paris. In the centre of the modern city the island upon which the massive bulk of Notre-Dame rises is a testament to the long history of Paris and the core from which the city grew from ancient Lutèce to sprawling modern Paris. The city is divided and embraced by the Seine which gave it its origins. Linked by a multitude of splendid and varied bridges the north and south of Paris evolved differently. For artists, the great palace of the Louvre dominating the right-bank was reflected in the great north-light windows of Ecole des Beaux-Arts which face it across the Quai Malaquais as if the aims and ambitions of the practising painter and sculptor had necessarily to keep in view the vast treasure-house of past achievements in art. They were joined by the lightest and least substantial of physical links, the iron footbridge of the Pont des Arts from which the river Seine could be viewed in peace in its most spectacular setting, flowing ceaslessly around the prow of the Ile de la Cité.

196

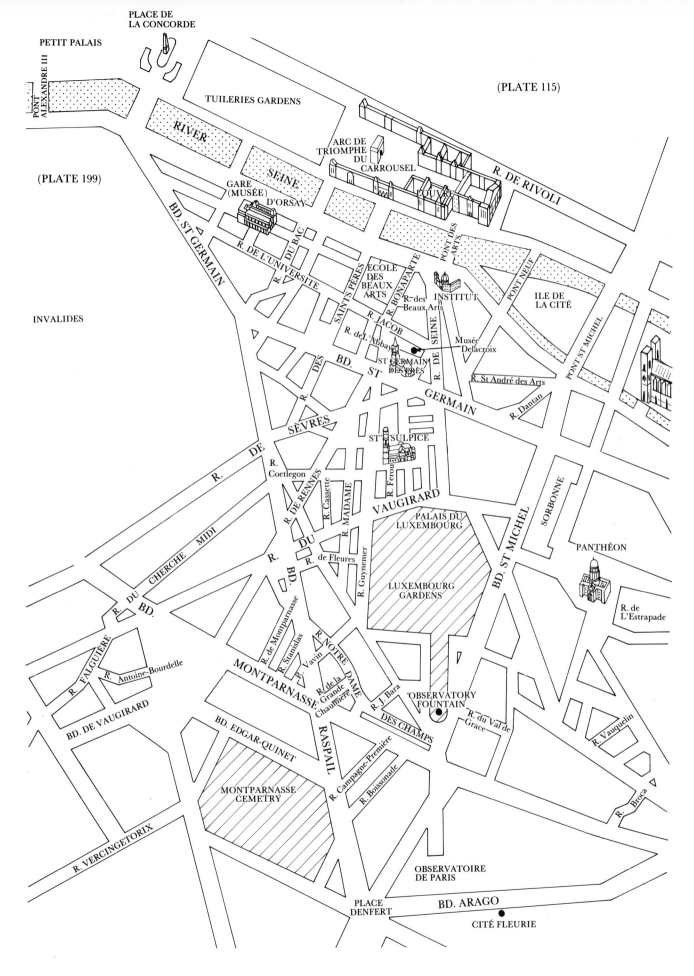

246. Map of central southern Paris from the Quartier Latin to Montparnasse.

247. John Singer Sargent, *The Luxembourg Gardens at Twilight*, *c.* 1879, oil on canvas, 73 × 93 cm., Minneapolis Institute of Arts.

# 8. The Left Bank: Quartier Latin

For artists, the Left Bank of Paris, south of the Seine, had a natural focus in the Ecole des Beaux-Arts. A multitude of studios occupy the narrow streets around it, usually installed high up at roof level on the seventh or eighth floor facing north as best they could in this densely populated central area between the river and the Boulevard St Germain which forms the prime east-west artery of central Paris south of the Seine. From here the studios spread south to the Jardin du Luxembourg, amongst the most splendid parks of Paris, and continue beyond to Montparnasse and the southern limits of the city in a broad swathe of artistic endeavour and ambition until they fade away on the edges of the metropolis. As we have seen it was on this river bank that stood the sites of success; appointment as professor at the Ecole des Beaux-Arts was a much sought and rarely attained sign of recognition, a practical accolade yet a position of high honour and accompanied by other honours too. Alongside the Ecole des Beaux-Arts stands the Institut whose Académie des Beaux-Arts was so esteemed and so despised by different sections of the Parisian population of artists, for both its ideals and its power. A third site, just to the south, was the Musée du Luxembourg set in splendid gardens, the museum of living artists' work; its evolving display publicly proclaimed recognition and respect. Works acquired by the Luxembourg Museum were transferred ten years after the artist's death to provincial museums or to the Louvre, a credible glimpse of a reputation beyond the grave.

In the Luxembourg Gardens sculpture abounded, and the public gardens themselves attracted painters not represented in the Museum, as an oasis amongst the desert of activity and traffic, a landscape within the city that lured the painters from their high roof-top studios to paint or to relax. Here were the 'exquisite tree-shaded gardens, in which the students and their *amies*, models, *bonnes*, poets and bourgeoisie gather of an afternoon to gossip, quiz their neighbours, and listen to the band.' (Plates 247–9)[1] Whistler, Sargent and many other artists worked here, especially on the terrace with its boating pond, balustrades and distant view of the Pantheon's dome above the trees.

The Luxembourg Palace was built for Marie de Medici in 1615–27 by the architect Salomon de Brosse, was altered in 1804 and enlarged in 1831–44. Delacroix executed paintings for the library and the Musée du Luxembourg occupied the Orangery until 1945. The sculptures in the garden include Dalou's baroque *Monument to Delacroix*, his *Triumph of Silenus* and many other sculptors' work including Denys Puech's *Leconte de Lisle* and *Saint-Beuve*, and *Paul Verlaine* by Niederhausen-Rodo. The central axis of the gardens extends south in a long tree-shaded spur down the Avenue de l'Observatoire populated with white sculptures by Jouffroy which stand in flower-beds and contrast starkly with the continuous leafage of the long straight avenue of chestnut trees. At the culmination stands the *Fontaine de l'Observatoire* encompassed by Frémiet's pared sea-stallions, dolphins and turtles and surmounted by Carpeaux's bronze nudes marking north, south, east and west and holding above them a bronze globe of the planet caged in a zodiacal sphere (Plates 251–2). Here roof-top double-height studios appear on the Boulevard St Michel at Nos. 113 and No. 115 where Mercié worked (Plate 250). The studios stretch from the Seine south to the limits of Paris.

One artist had a spectacular studio apart from all this on the southern side of the Seine. His position, like his career and his talent, was exceptional:

248. Clive Holland, *In the Luxembourg Gardens*, photograph of 1901.

199

249. James A. McN. Whistler, *Nursemaids in the Luxembourg Gardens*, 1894, lithograph, 19.8 × 15.5 cm., The Print Room, British Museum, London.

250. Rooftop studios at 113 and 115 Boulevard St Michel.

251. Albert Maignan, *Carpeaux*, 1892, oil on canvas, 350 × 445 cm., Musée des Beaux-Arts, Amiens.

252. Jean-Baptiste Carpeaux (figures), Emmanuel Frémiet (horses) and Davioud (architect), *The Observatory Fountain*, 1875, bronze and stone, Luxembourg Gardens

At the end of the long Rue de l'Université, close to the Champs de Mars, in a corner, so deserted and monastic that you might think yourself in the provinces, is the Dépôt des Marbres. Here in a great grass-grown court sleep heavy greyish blocks, presenting in places fresh breaks of frosted whiteness. These are the marbles reserved by the State for the sculptors whom she honours with her orders. Along one side of this courtyard is a row of a dozen ateliers which have been granted to different sculptors. A little artist city, marvellously tranquil, it seems the fraternity house of a new order. Rodin occupies two of these cells; in one he houses the plaster cast of his Gate of Hell.[2]

In addition Rodin had a studio in the Boulevard de Vaugirard in Montparnasse. Edmond de Goncourt visited him in both places in 1886:

This afternoon Bracquemond took me to see the sculptor Rodin. He is a man of common features, a fleshy-nose, bright eyes flashing beneath unhealthy red lids, a long yellow beard, hair cut short and brushed back, and a round head, a head suggesting gentle, stubborn obstinacy — a man such as I imagine Christ's disciples looked like. We found him in his studio on the Boulevard Vaugirard, an ordinary sculptor's studio with its walls splashed with plaster, its wretched little cast-iron stove, the damp chill emanating from all the big compositions in wet clay wrapped in rags, and a litter of heads, arms, legs in the midst of which two emaciated cats were posing like fantastic griffins. (Plate 253)[3]

Rodin was to have several studios including a vast one at Meudon outside Paris:

Approaching, you find that the main buildings are three. The first, a Louis XIII pavilion of red brick and freestone with a high gabled roof, serves as his dwelling. Close by stands a great rotunda, entered through a columned portico, which is the one that in 1900 sheltered the special exhibition of Rodin's work at the angle of the Pont de l'Alma in Paris.[4]

202

253. Fragments of plaster limbs in a drawer at Rodin's studio at Meudon.

As well as his own casts, studies and plasters Rodin assembled a collection of sculpture here, particularly Greek and Roman carvings. He also collected fragments, pieces of figures produced in the casting of his works and sketches of limbs. He was a prolific artist and needed extensive storage as well as working space.

Perhaps the most celebrated and even notorious of Parisian sculptors by the turn of the century, Rodin had been at odds with the customary structure of tuition, patronage and recognition throughout his career. Three times rejected by the Ecole des Beaux-Arts, he studied under Lecoq de Boisbaudran at the Ecole des Arts Décoratifs. He met Whistler, Fantin-Latour and Legros at this time and had several lessons in modelling from Carpeaux. He also assiduously studied sculpture in the Louvre collections. Subsequently, he worked for the ornamentalist sculptor Carrier-Belleuse and also upon architectural projects. In 1877 his anatomically precise *Age of Bronze* caused a furore as Rodin was accused of casting his figure from the life-model. Amongst his supporters in the ensuing investigation were Paul Dubois, Chapu, Carrier-Belleuse and Falguière. Both the *Age of Bronze* and *St John the Baptist Preaching* were exhibited at the Salon of 1880 and were later acquired by the Luxembourg Museum. But all of his major public commissions ran into difficulties, including the *Burghers of Calais*, *The Gates of Hell* and the *Victor Hugo Monument* which was commissioned for the Panthéon. In 1898 Rodin withdrew his *Balzac* from the Salon National des Beaux-Arts in the face of criticism and it was not until his exhibition in his own pavilion at the Place de l'Alma in 1900 that his colossal success finally crystalised. Rodin left his works to the state in 1917 on condition that they be housed in the Hôtel Biron where he had worked in Paris (Plate 254). This

254. The Hôtel Biron, Rue de Varenne.

now forms the Musée Rodin. His work, for all his profound respect for the achievements of the past in sculpture, was difficult for many to accept during the major part of his career. His immense skill was allied to a ruthless imagination that must have appeared uncontrolled in its use of fragmented, dramatic and anatomically exaggerated forms. His use of drawing was incessant, particularly drawings from the moving model, and they often appeared loose and unfinished. The drawings and sculpture are accepted now for their own mastery of movement and surface although Rodin's knowledge of anatomy was always beyond doubt. His originality was such that he demanded new canons of assessment which were only reluctantly and spasmodically applied before 1900, and his public monuments unfailingly outraged expectations.

A contrasting case is that of the far less inventive or able but nonetheless prolific sculptor Henri Chapu, a pupil of Pradier, Duret and Cogniet at the Ecole des Beaux-Arts and a winner of the Prix de Rome who acquired Salon medals regularly from 1863, and was elected to the Institut in 1880. He produced many portrait medals including those of Léon Bonnat, Elie Delaunay, Tony Robert-Fleury as well as busts of the bronze-founders Victor Thiébaut (1875) and Ferdinand Barbedienne (1882). In contrast with Rodin, his public works were not problematic; they included the Four Seasons for the main facade of the *Printemps* store in Paris (1882, stone), a colossal medallion of the painters Jean-François Millet and Theodore Rousseau for the rustic monument erected at Barbizon (1884), and *Painting* executed in marble for the central pavilion of the Musée Galliera in Paris (exhibited 1889). Chapu lived at 14 Cité Vaneau not far from the Rodin studio at the Hôtel Biron.

The Luxembourg Gardens are skirted on the west by the long Rue d'Assas where Falguière had his studio at No. 68 for more than forty years. Falguière knew great success and fame; he was both a friend and a competitor of Rodin. 'It was when the Société des Gens de Lettres refused my Balzac,' commented Rodin to Paul Gsell, '[that] Falguière, to whom the order was then given, insisted on showing me, by his friendship,

255. Bartholdi in his studio, Rue Vavin, photograph from *c.* 1890, Bartholdi Museum, Colmar.

256. Fantin-Latour in his studio, photograph from *c*. 1900, Cabinet des Estampes, Bibliothèque Nationale, Paris.

that he did not at all agree with my detractors. Actuated by sympathy, I offered to do his bust'.[5] Falguière in turn executed a bust of Rodin. Falguière had studied under Jouffroy at the Ecole des Beaux-Arts and won the medal of honour at the Salon of 1868. In the National Guard with other painters and sculptors in the Seige of Paris he erected a sculpture *Resistance* made out of snow on the eighty-fifth bastion. Between 1881 and 1886 his colossal group *The Triumph of the Revolution* surmounted the Arc de Triomphe. He received many honours, and in 1882 became a professor at the Ecole des Beaux-Arts and was elected to the Institut. Amongst those giving orations at his funeral at the Père Lachaise cemetry in 1900 were Paul Dubois, J.P. Laurens and Mercié. His seated figure of Balzac was erected on the Avenue Friedland in 1902 and a retrospective memorial exhibition was held at the Ecole des Beaux-Arts the same year.

Further along the Rue d'Assas No. 82 was occupied by Bartholdi who died there at the age of 80. He earlier had a studio in Rue Vavin nearby (Plate 255). At No. 86 was the sculptor Morice whose *Monument to the Republic* stands in the Place de la République.[6]

In the tight streets around the Ecole des Beaux-Arts itself the printmaker and painter Fantin-Latour, a friend of Manet, Whistler and the Impressionists, occupied No. 8 in the Rue des Beaux-Arts with a studio on the ground floor. Jacques-Emile Blanche visited him here: 'Timid and pessimistic, Fantin, who poured contempt on the Institut, on the academicians of the official Salon where he exhibited nevertheless refused to join the Impressionists.' The studio, where Blanche would watch Fantin-Latour paint 'stood at the end of a courtyard which had an air of hopelessness' (Plate 256). The Fantins 'lived in a sort of wooden barn painted red, white and blue, which Degas called Fantin's

257. Henri Harpignies in his studio.

258. James A. McN. Whistler, *The Rue Furstenberg*, 1894, lithograph, 12 × 16 cm., The Print Room, British Museum, London.

"Orleanist tent", though he was a republican, anti-clericalist and anti-militarist'.[7] Fantin-Latour had studied under Lecoq de Boisbaudran and Courbet and had worked as a copyist in the Louvre. His *Hommage à Delacroix* of 1864 included portraits of Manet and Whistler. Delacroix had had a studio nearby which still survives as the Delacroix Museum, off the Rue Furstenberg (Plate 258), and his enormous late murals of *Jacob Wrestling with the Angel* and *The Expulsion of Heliodorus from the Temple* were readily available for inspection in the nearby church of St Sulpice. Many of Fantin-Latour's prints and later paintings reflect his love of music, particularly that of Berlioz and Wagner. He was also a brilliant painter of flowers and still-lifes which found a ready market for the domestic interior. In earlier years the sculptor Pradier had occupied No. 4 Rue des Beaux-Arts, the poet Gérard de Nerval No. 5, Corot No. 10, and in the hotel at No. 13 Oscar Wilde died in 1900.

The Rue des Beaux-Arts ends at the courtyard entrance of the Ecole des Beaux-Arts across the Rue Bonaparte. At 31 Rue Bonaparte the Salon des Cent and Salon de la Plume held their exhibitions. Further south the Rue Bonaparte encounters the romanesque church of St Germain-des-Prés, and just behind it in the Rue de l'Abbaye at No. 14 was the landscape painter Henri-Joseph Harpignies (Plate 257). As it continues south, the Rue Bonaparte passes numerous streets with studios and enters the Place St Sulpice and the gaunt massive towers of its church. From the south of St Sulpice runs the Rue Servandoni where the painter Guillaumin occupied No. 20; a friend of various Impressionists he contributed to many of their group exhibitions. He was also a friend of Van Gogh, yet only in 1891 after winning 100,000 francs in a lottery did he give up his employment as a city clerk to devote himself full-time to painting. The painter Paul Flandrin lived in the next street, the Rue Garancière, at No. 10.

Across the Rue Bonaparte to the west there were further studios in the Rue Madame and the Rue Fleurus. The Rue Bonaparte ends where it meets the Rue de Vaugirard and

259. Jean-Charles Cazin in his studio, photograph from *c.*, 1895.

260. Jean-Charles Cazin, *Agar and Ishmaël*, Salon of 1880, oil on canvas, 252 × 202 cm., Musée des Beaux-Arts, Tours (formerly Luxembourg Museum).

the Luxembourg Gardens. Its line continues in the Rue Guynemer (formerly Rue du Luxembourg) where the Cazin family of painters lived at No. 40 overlooking the gardens of the Luxembourg (Plate 259). Charles Cazin, painter, printmaker and ceramicist studied under Lecoq de Boisbaudran (Plate 260). During the Franco-Prussian War Cazin moved to England where he knew Legros. After the death of Puvis de Chavannes, it was Cazin who undertook to complete his murals at the Panthéon. He was awarded a gold medal at the 1889 Exposition Universelle and Grand Prix at that of 1900.

261. James A. McN. Whistler. *The Panthéon from the Terrace of the Luxembourg Gardens*, 1893, lithograph, 18 × 16 cm., The Print Room, The British Museum, London.

Studios continue east as far as the Sorbonne with its murals by Puvis de Chavannes, Lhermitte, Henri Martin and others. Studio windows can be seen staring at the great dome of the Panthéon in the Place du Panthéon on its southern side (Plate 261–2). In the Rue Monsieur-le-Prince was the Spanish Symbolist painter Antonio de la Gandara. Southeast of the Luxembourg Gardens at 6 Rue Val-de-Grâce was the bohemian painter and poster designer Alphonse Mucha who moved to Paris to study under J.P. Laurens at the Académie Julian in 1887 and who within a few years attained popular success promoting Sarah Bernhardt in posters of lavish art-nouveau decoration.

Beyond the Val-de-Grâce hospital to the east lies the Rue Vauquelin where Lhermitte occupied No. 19. He had studied under Lecoq de Boisbaudran. Lhermitte began to work on Breton themes in the mid–1870s and became successful when the state bought his monumental *Harvesters' Payday* at the Salon of 1882. Commissions followed for the Sorbonne and the Hôtel de Ville. His work was widely bought in reproduction prints. In 1905 he replaced Henner at the Institut, and became the Vice-President of the Société Nationale des Beaux-Arts, of which he had been a founder member in 1890.

One street away from Rue Vauquelin lies the Rue de l'Arbalète running eastwards into the thoroughfare of the Rue Monge after crossing the Rue Mouffetard. Here was the painter Aman-Jean, friend of Seurat, with whom he had once shared a studio. He was a

262. Anders Zorn, *The Rue des Carmes and the Dome of the Panthéon*, 1881, water-colour, whereabouts unknown.

263. Edmond-François Aman-Jean in his studio, photograph of *c.* 1896.

decorative and highly original portraitist of the Symbolist tendency (Plate 264). Seurat drew him fine-featured and elegantly dressed, painting with care in a drawing in which black and white seem equally luminous. A photograph taken in his studio reveals the slender build and elegance of Aman-Jean seated in a bamboo chair before a rapturous and evocative portrait (Plate 263). He wears, as Meissonier did, rope-soled shoes for the studio. On the mantlepiece of his elegant studio apartment are modern vases, a sign of his love of decorative effects and a portrait hangs, as Mallarmé sometimes hung paintings, against a large mirror. The *Studio* magazine was won over by his painting in 1896 describing it as an 'art of delicacy and subtle refinement'.[8] Aman-Jean himself wrote for this periodical the same year reviewing the Royal Academy exhibition in

London where he noted Whistler, approved La Thangue but waxed lyrical over Sargent. Alma-Tadema's work by contrast he found to be 'laborious painting'.[9] He had been a fellow pupil with Seurat at the Ecole des Beaux-Arts studying under Lehmann. He exhibited regularly at the Salon Nationale des Beaux-Arts and with the Rosicrucian Salon in 1892 and 1893.

South and west of here lies Montparnasse, rich in studios of a more severely practical kind and less self-consciously or overtly associated with art than the Latin Quarter around the Ecole des Beaux-Arts and the Luxembourg Gardens. The studios were fecund and important but are not easily found. The further south the artist moved the cheaper his accommodation became.

In 1923 Andre Warnod wrote that Montparnasse, is 'a new quarter, without monuments, a long boulevard planted with trees'.[10] Despite its large population of artists, their studios were discreet. 'Montparnasse has nothing in its appearance to give it the air of an artists' quarter.'[11] But Montparnasse was in fact already a thriving, if impretentious, artists' quarter during the 1880s.

264. (*facing pages*), Edmond-François Aman-Jean, *The Girl with a Peacock*, 1895, oil on canvas, 150 × 104 cm., Musée des Arts Decoratifs, Paris.

# 9. *The Rue Notre Dame des Champs*

On 10 February 1905 the order was given for the piercing of the Boulevard Raspail through the Rue de Vaugirard to the Boulevard Montparnasse. This short stretch of boulevard, inaugurated in 1913, sliced through a triangle of land dense with artists studios, many of them associated with the Ecole des Beaux-Arts or the Institut but many independent and struggling. As recently as the 1970s when the massive Tour Maine-Montparnasse complex was built, it is estimated that five hundred studios were demolished.[1] In the intervening period the high apartment buildings steadily encroached upon streets of two-storey suburban houses. Yet some studios still remain, their windows overlooking gardens, or piled one upon another in courtyards, providing a glimpse of the area's past.

The triangle of land that formed the heart of this area is bounded by the Boulevard Montparnasse, the Rue d'Assas and the Rue du Cherche-Midi. Snaking through it the Rue Notre Dame des Champs accommodated more studios than any other street in Paris and they spread laterally into all of the small streets off it. Many were already here in the 1840s when Montparnasse was clearly separate from central Paris with local fairs, farms and stables. The painter Bonvin, for example, was at 53 Rue Notre Dame des Champs in the 1840s and Jules Breton hired a studio at this address in 1849.[2] By the 1880s there were many large studios here attracting, amongst many others, the Académie Rollins to its spacious facilities which were ideal for the commercial venture of a teaching atelier with an expanding clientèle, which here included the English sculptors Pomeroy and Frampton. The sculptor Chapu occupied No. 28. Some immense and imposing studios survive: at Nos. 57–9, for example, a vigorous symmetrical stone façade with heavy classical detailing is resolved at the top floor with a huge studio window flanked with stone architectural motifs and a stone mullioned doorway opening on to a small balcony set within the north light (Plate 265). This is a building of considerable architectural pretensions constructed on a grandiose scale.

Whilst Montparnasse provided a wealth of spacious, cheap studio accommodation in courtyard sheds and workshops, it also provided for wealthy and successful academicians who for one reason or another preferred unpretentious Montparnasse to the

265. Rooftop studio at 57–9 Rue Notre Dame des Champs.

266. John Sargent, *Portrait of Carolus-Duran*, 1879, oil on canvas, 116.9 × 96 cm., Stirling and Francine Clark Art Institute, Williamstown, Mass. Inscribed 'To my dear master M. Carolus Duran, his affectionate pupil John S. Sargent 1879'.

267. Carolus-Duran in his studio, photograph from *c*. 1895.

elegance of the Avenue de Villiers. The painter Carolus-Duran exemplifies this attitude. He occupied 58 Rue Notre Dame des Champs,[3] But, as Albert Wolff noted, it was an extraordinary achievement to draw wealthy society patrons to this area.[4]

John Sargent's *Portrait of Carolus-Duran* captures the forthcoming personality and the elegance of the pleated cuffs, soft necktie, the dramatically groomed hair and beard in 1879 (Plate 266). A photograph taken almost twenty years later, his mane now white, reveals a studio crammed with copies after Rubens and Spanish painters, filling the walls between the portraits (Plate 267). Everything is framed and ready for dispatch except the current portrait commission on the easel. Carolus-Duran had studied in Italy and Spain as well as Paris. His love of Spanish art was shared by Manet, Whistler and others. Salon success had begun in the 1860s and honours poured upon him with his increasing age and popularity. Within the Légion d'Honneur he was appointed *chevalier* in 1872, *officier* in 1878, *commandeur* in 1889 and in 1900 promoted to *grand officier*. He was on the jury of the Expositions Universelles of 1889 and 1900. A founder member of the Société Nationale des Beaux-Arts in 1890, he became its president eight years later. In 1905 he was appointed rector of the French Academy in Rome and a member of the Institut.

Further along the Rue Notre Dame des Champs, the robust painter of horses, Rosa Bonheur, had used No. 61 for her studio, although her real base was at Fontainebleau in the forest.

But No. 70 has a remarkable history (Plate 268). In 1889 the sculptor Moreau-Vauthier had his studio there (at 70 bis). In his book on Gérôme in 1906 he described the area and the history of No. 70: 'Forty years ago, this street with its long garden walls, with its stream flowing down the middle of its ill-paved carriageway, with its paths of beaten earth fringed with grass...merited its name more fully.'[5] Here, a few steps from the studios of the Passage Stanislas where Carolus-Duran later established himself, the painter Toulmouche constructed studios for himself and his artist friends in the garden behind his father's house. Their walls were distempered and ornamented with wood, giving the appearance of a gigantic box upon which were painted two chinamen. The appearance of the group of studios gave the name the *Boîte à Thé*, the Tea Caddy. Gérôme was amongst the inhabitants. The studios overlooked a garden in the seclusion of which models would relax naked or costumed amongst trees and sculpture. Lunch was arranged communally in the garden but with each artist paying for this own, and a puppet theatre was established in Gérôme's studio, the artists constructing the theatre, puppets and costumes. Many artists visited here including Hébert, Baudry and Cabanel. Gérôme's monkey sat at table dressed formally with a white cravate. If he was troublesome he was banned from table and re-attired as a ragpicker. Jules Breton met the monkey: 'I have been at gay banquets with those excellent companions,' at the Boîte à Thé, 'at which was also present, and not always without committing some misdemeanor, the monkey Jacques, a pet of Gérôme, and who sat at the table on a seat made like a child's chair.'[6] Gérôme was here from the 1850s before later settling in the Boulevard de Clichy in Montmartre. Closeby at No. 73 was a studio later used by Jean-Paul Laurens (Plate 269), amongst the most popular tutors of his day at the Académie Julian. He had made his Salon debut in 1863 and risen rapidly in honours and public

268. Studios at 70 and 70 bis Rue Notre Dame des Champs.

269. Jean-Paul Laurens in 1912 working on his painting *The Court of Love at Toulouse in the Fifteenth Century*.

270. Jean-Paul Laurens, *The Men of Holy Office*, 1877, oil on canvas, 146 × 202 cm., Musée de Moulins (formerly Luxembourg Museum).

271. William-Adolphe Bouguereau, *Virgin of Consolation*, 1877, oil on canvas, 204 × 148 cm., Musée des Beaux-Arts, Strasbourg.

272. Bouguereau in his studio, photograph from before 1905, Cabinet des Estampes (Sirot Collection), Bibliothèque Nationale, Paris.

esteem. *Chevalier* of the Lègion d'Honneur in 1874, he rose to *grand officier* in 1919. A Salon painter par excellence, he was elected to the Institut in 1891 where he replaced Meissonier. His Inquisition drama *The Men of the Holy Office* (Les Hommes du Saint-Office) was considered one of his finest works (Plate 270), many of which were popularised through prints and photographic reproductions. He also executed many public commissions, including paintings for the Hôtel de Ville and the Panthéon. His *Death of St Geneviève* at the Panthéon contains a portrait of Rodin in the role of a Merovingian soldier. They had long been friends and Laurens was instrumental in gaining the commission for the monument to the Burghers of Calais for Rodin. Next door at 75 Rue Notre Dame des Champs Adolphe-William Bouguereau worked in an immense studio surrounded by large canvases depicting his favourite models as Venus or the Virgin Mary (Plate 271). Bouguereau's studio with its heavy trundling easels rolling on castors their burden of alterpieces and Salon works in elaborate frames (Plate 272), was the nerve centre of a successful business enterprise supplying the churches and townhalls of France. He was efficient in his response to patrons and the market, working reliably to supply an insistent demand. 'Bouguereau is not a great artist,' asserted the *Art Journal* in 1885, 'it is likely enough that his work will be as little regarded in sixty years time as that of Benjamin West is now; but he is an excellent workman.'[7] Winning the Prix de Rome in 1850 from the Ecole des Beaux-Arts, gave Bouguereau the opportunity to study Raphael, Andrea del Sarto and Guido Reni over three years. Salon success established his reputation immediately upon his return. He knew almost every available honour, became a professor at the Ecole des Beaux-Arts in 1875, a longstanding Institut member from 1876, President of the Société des Artistes Français, jury member for the Expositions Universelles of 1889 and 1900 and ultimately *grand officier* in the Légion d'Honneur in 1903. He was the subject of two monographs during his lifetime, by R. Ménard in 1885 and by M. Vachon in 1900.

86 Rue Notre Dame des Champs is still a high pile of studios on four floors confronting the street with colossal studio lights which fill the entire wall overlooking the small adjacent yard. At this address both Whistler and Charles Cottet had studios (Plate 275). Whistler had studied under Gleyre, but became a friend of Courbet, Fantin-Latour, Degas, Legros and Bracquemond. He was successful in Paris after the debacle

273. Studios at 86 Rue Notre Dame des Champs.

274. Studios at 86 Rue Notre Dame des Champs.

275. Whistler in his studio at 86 Rue Notre Dame des Champs.

of his London career in the wake of his law-suit with Ruskin in 1878. Whilst he lived in the Rue du Bac, he kept the studio here at Rue Notre Dame des Champs from 1892 to 1901 when he sold both properties. He particularly pursued etching and lithography here. In 1889 he had won a gold medal at the Exposition Universelle and at that of 1900 was awarded the grand prix. Made a *chevalier* of the Légion d'Honneur in 1889, he was promoted to *officier* in 1891. His characteristically dandyish elegance is as apparent in the photograph as it is in Whistler's own writings. He sits perched on a settle, hand on hip, well dressed for the city, monacle in place, in a large, sparsely furnished studio containing a screen he evolved from his nocturnes of the Thames and redolent of his enthusiasm for Japanese decorative assymetry.

Charles Cottet, by contrast, much inspired by Gauguin, devoted much of his career to painting in Brittany, and whilst his art too stressed the flatness of the picture surface, his technique was indebted to the innovations of Gauguin and Bernard. He made his debut at the Salon in 1889 but the following year joined the Société Nationale des Beaux-Arts.

There are studios on four floors at 94 Rue Notre Dame des Champs arranged as a continuous projecting bay, and more studios project from No. 125. The street itself ends in a restaurant with a history. Now demure and reserved, the Closerie des Lilas 'used to be a merry low-ceilinged spot. Now alas it is no more. Thick with caporal smoke, it held much that was interesting within its old walls of an evening. How many a *nouveau* has begun an upward or downward course whilst sitting at those little tables.'[8] It became the setting for the *Vers et Prose* literary circle and was frequented by Paul Fort, Stuart Merrill, Alfred Jarry, Jean Moréas, Paul Verlaine.

Opposite the Closerie des Lilas on the Boulevard St Michel stands the monument to *Francis Garnier* by Denys Puech; a pupil of Jouffroy, Chapu and Falguière, he survived to become the successor to Besnard as Director of French Academy in Rome in 1933. He was a regular Salon contributor from 1875 and in 1905 was elected to the Institut. This monument characterises the taste of the 1890s and resembles in style the figures which clad the Alexandre III Bridge in Paris. Naked studio models pose as embodiments of rivers with urns and exotic animal skins around a Cambodian pedestal upon which rises the bust of the explorer. Its site marks the meeting point of the Boulevard Montparnasse, the Boulevard St Michel and the terminus of the Rue Notre Dame des Champs.

Returning up the Rue Notre Dame des Champs studios existed in all of the connecting streets, including the Rue Leverrier and Rue Joseph-Bara on the right. After the convent of Les Dames Augustines, a left turn leads to the Rue de la Grande Chaumière which runs through to the Boulevard Montparnasse. On the corner of the Boulevard Montparnasse a regular model's market look place every Monday. Models charged by the hour and artists could rely upon finding them here when they came out from their studios: 'if you want to pick up a model at any time they are right there on the *carrefour* — heaps of them — old Antonio, who sits for Shylock and old men; Paolo who's just fine for St John; that little devil of a Suzanne, who only comes when she feels like it; and a host of others.'[9] Like the model markets of the Place Clichy and the Rue Bonaparte this was a thriving concern dominated by Italian models (Plate 276–7).

There are roof-top studios overlooking gardens at 5 Rue de la Grande Chaumière, and Gauguin stayed at No. 8 on his return to Paris from his first Tahitian visit. At No. 10 was a thriving and important teaching academy much used by the artists of Montparnasse. This was the Académie Colarossi. Here many a newcomer began his career: 'Ultimately Colarossi's, in the Rue de la Grande Chaumière is decided upon. It is quite handy.'[10] It provided a complex of studios:

> space counts for a good deal at Colarossi's; and so when the *nouveau* a day or two later climbs the stairs...he finds them narrow, steep and leading past a veritable nest of

276. Clive Holland, *Italian Models*, photograph of *c.* 1901.

277. Edouard Cucuel, *Italian Models in front of the Atelier Colarossi, c.* 1889.

*ateliers*, located one above another... The life class was cosmopolitan enough, an Englishman or two, a few Americans, a couple of Japanese, a coloured gentleman, Poles, Austrians, French, Russians; girls and fellows all hard at work with the model posed (Plate 278).[11]

Subsequently an Académie de la Grande Chaumière opened in 1904 at No. 14 including

278. Clive Holland, *Life Class at the Académie Colarossi,* photograph of *c.* 1901.

Antoine Bourdelle, Despiau and eventually Zadkine amongst its tutors. Seventh floor studios crown No. 17 at roof level.

The next street off the Rue Notre Dame des Champs is the Rue Jules-Chaplain (formerly Passage Stanislas) where Carolus-Duran's studio flourished at No. 11. Overlooking a tree-filled garden at No. 6 is a two-storey window surmounted by gable, cornice and roundel. Whistler, whose own studio was just around the corner, established a teaching studio at No. 6 between 1892 and 1901. Whistler's contribution was intermittent and the *atelier* was under the direct supervision of his model Carmen Rossi and became known as the Académie Carmen.

A little further along the Rue Notre Dame des Champs is bisected by the Rue Vavin where until 1893 the sculptor of the *Statue of Liberty* (see Plate 215), Fréderic-Auguste Bartholdi occupied No. 40. He had travelled to the Near-East with Gérôme in the 1850s and made his salon debut in 1857. Originating in Alsace, Bartholdi's strong patriotism provoked by the Franco-Prussian War was expressed in colossal monuments. *Liberty* is an outstanding example, but was preceded by the *Lion of Belfort*, built between 1875 and 1880 at a scale of 22 metres wide by 11 metres high, a reduced version of which was bought by the City of Paris for 25,000 francs and inaugurated at the Place Denfer-Rochereau in 1880. *Liberty* was finally inaugurated in New York in 1886. Bartholdi rose to *commandeur* in the Légion d'Honneur in 1887, and was Vice-President of the Société des Artistes Francais from 1900 to 1903.

The Rue Vavin now empties into the junction of the Boulevard Raspail and the Boulevard Montparnasse. Rodin's *Balzac* was finally erected at this point. There are very many studios on the Boulevard Montparnasse. The Nabi artist Paul Ranson, friend of Bonnard, Vuillard and others held Saturday gatherings at his studio, the so-called Temple, at No. 25. Here Ranson operated a puppet-theatre for which he executed designs and wrote plays later published as *L'Abbé Prout, Guignol pour les Vieux Enfants*. He admired Gauguin's work and medieval art. Maillol inspired him to design tapestries executed by his wife 'la Lumière du Temple'. After Ranson's death she established the Académie Ranson in the nearby Rue Joseph-Bara, at No. 3, where the tutors included Bonnard, Denis, Maillol and Vallotton. The painter Alfred Guillou lived in this part of the long Boulevard Montparnasse at No. 161. Many more studios are found in the Rue de Vaugirard further north including that of a Symbolist pupil of Gustave Moreau, Edgard Maxence, at No. 71 bis, a regular contributor to both the Salon and the Rosicrucian Salon in the 1890s.

Beyond the Rue de Vaugirard, the long Rue du Cherche-Midi housed many artists and encloses the area of their greatest profusion in the triangle of streets around Rue Notre Dame des Champs. Here in the Rue du Cherche-Midi, the academician Ernest Hébert had a studio at No. 85 which is now preserved as a museum. He became a powerful influence at the Institut after serving as Director of the French Academy in Rome from 1867 to 1873. By 1900 he was *grand officier* of the Légion d'Honneur and in 1903 held the *grand croix*. He had studied under David d'Angers and Delaroche and won the Prix de Rome in 1839. He won almost every honour available, and from 1885 to 1891 was appointed for a second time as Director of the French Academy in Rome. The studio exhibits a restrained oppulence. His landscape studies recall Corot in their broad handling, creamy colours and meticulous tonal control; his major compositions are a model of academic procedure, evolving from mid-toned brown underpainting through cross-hatched strokes, building up gradually to develop stronger colour, decisive chiaroscuro and assured delicacy of modelling. He was responding to Pre-Raphaelite themes already in the 1850s, which reveals an astute interest in English art, rare at that time. He also made copies after Velasquez. His palette, preserved at the museum, reveals a strict organisation of colour progressing from a large area of white, along two neat and systematic sequences of pigment. The first proceeds from lemon yellow, via chrome yellow and olive green to numerous reds. The second row begins with orange then proceeds to blues and violets ending with blacks.

The street is still quiet, its central sundial marking out the light's transition through the hours and lending the street its name, although the atmosphere is now more urban than when Zola described it in *L'Oeuvre*:

> There is something pleasantly provincial about this particular bit of the broad, quiet Rue du Cherche-Midi, and even just the faintest odour of sanctity. There are great open gateways leading to long strings of courtyards, a cow-byre that sends out wafts of bedstraw and manure, and a convent wall that seems to go on for ever.[12]

# 10. The Southern Reaches of Montparnasse

'He resisted all Johnson's persuasive eloquence that he should go yet further along the endless Rue de Vaugirard to a nest of studios which usually let at two-thirds the rent asked for one in the Rue Falguière.'[1] Further into Montparnasse the studios were cheaper as grandeur was left far behind in the receding city centre. The Gare Montparnasse brought in cheap labour from Brittany and wine in Montparnasse was exempt from the heavy duty imposed on entry into Paris proper. As a result cheap bars, cafés and musical hall entertainments flourished in the Rue de la Gaité, amidst the spreading city's new buildings.[2]

Studios abounded along the Boulevard Montparnasse and in the streets leading off to the south-west (Plate 279). The sculptor Chapu, for example, occupied 19 Rue Montparnasse in 1886, and further along on the same side the Rue Campagne-Première and Rue Boissonade were full of studios. One of Bouguereau's favourite models, Rosalie Tobia who posed for his *Venus*, gained great popularity in the area when she opened a restaurant specialising in Italian cooking in the Rue Campagne-Première amongst the artists. At 9 Rue Campagne-Première was a curious *cité d'artistes* comprising over a hundred studios built from materials salvaged from exhibition buildings demolished after the 1889 Exposition Universelle.[3] No. 15 was occupied by the sculptor Jean-Auguste Dampt, an associate of the Symbolists and Rosicrucians and former pupil of Jouffroy and Paul Dubois. He executed work for the Hôtel de Ville and a sculpture of Bizet for the foyer of the Opéra Comique. He had considerable Salon success. In 1919 he was elected to the Institut. A wealthy man, he left a bequest of 600,000 francs to the Institut for a religious sculpture prize. His *Kiss of the Knight* executed in silver and ivory shows Dampt at his most bizarre, exotic and erotic.

The tradition of studios in this short street continued well into the twentieth century. A spectacular block of studios dating from 1910–11 now occupies No. 31 and 31 bis near the corner of the Boulevard Raspail (Plate 280). It has enormous studio windows on four floors, their great glass lights filling almost all of the five bays of the façade like a factory. Any surface that is not glass is covered in decorative tiles in dull yellow ochre, grey and red with motifs of flowers in relief. It is a building of remarkable splendour and inventiveness.

Older studios populate much of the parallel Rue Boissonade, providing a glimpse in parts of an earlier Montparnasse (Plate 281). Nos. 35 to 45 are all purpose-built studio houses. No. 41 has studios on three floors. No. 43 is a demurely stylish house of three floors with a studio at the top and caryatids above the entrance. Nos. 37 and 39 were

279. Clive Holland, *A Sculptor's Workshop*, photograph of *c.* 1901.

219

282. (*facing page*) The Cité Fleurie at 65 Boulevard Arago.

280. Studio at 31 and 31 bis Rue Campagne-Première.

281. Row of studios at 37, 39, 41, 43 (with carytids) and 47 Rue Boissonade.

built in 1880 by the architect Léon Bonnenfant. At least four studios cluster around the garden square at No. 47 and another opens onto the street here. Further east in the Avenue de l'Observatoire the sculptor Antonin Mercié occupied No. 15, convenient for teaching at the Académie Rollins. He knew great success before the age of 30 and was admitted to the Légion d'Honneur whilst still studying at the French Academy in Rome. His marble monument to Meissonier of 1895 was erected in the Tuileries Gardens near the Louvre. He replaced Chapu at the Institut in 1891. In 1900 he was appointed a professor at the Ecole des Beaux-Arts and made *grand officier* of the Légion d'Honneur. His monuments appear throughout France.

Apart from streets of studios, Montparnasse was rich too in whole groups of studios gathered around a courtyard and set back from the street. These *cités d'artistes* occurred in several parts of Montparnasse and some survive today. They comprised whole close-knit communities of artists. One of them, south of the Avenue de l'Observatoire was situated at 65 Boulevard Arago (Plate 282). This is the Cité Fleurie established in 1878 to accommodate twenty-four artists in single-storey wooden studios around its leafy central courts. The poster artist and decorative designer Eugène Grasset was amongst the inhabitants of the Cité Fleurie, which in 1974 was preserved from redevelopment by order of the state.[4] Its grounds incorporated sculpture from the Palais des Tuileries.[5] Other inhabitants included J.P. Laurens and Daniel de Monfried who was visited by his friend Gauguin there.

Just to the north-west of the Gare Montparnasse the Rue Falguière curves south-west off the Rue de Vaugirard. A small cluster of shed-like studios, which have recently been demolished, were hidden with a chain of yards leading off the Impasse de l'Astrolabe near this point. Destroyed in 1985, a wall plaque here recorded the importance of its yards and its bar to the artists of the neighbourhood. Moving south in the Rue Falguière other *cités d' artistes* appear (Plate 283), one of which was of considerable historical importance. Off the Rue Antoine-Bourdelle, and now occupied by the Musée Antoine

283. The Cité Falguière, Montparnasse.

Bourdelle, is an archway leading into a courtyard completely surrounded by practical factory-like studios on three floors, made of wood, brick and glass.[6] This was formerly the Impasse du Maine created in 1812. The studios became a source for some of the most significant works of late nineteenth century sculpture by Jules Dalou and Antoine Bourdelle. In addition, the sculptor Recipron whose *Quadrigas* surmount the Grand Palais, a creole sculptor José de Charmoy, and also the painters Jean-Paul Laurens (for a time), Jules Bastien-Lepage and Eugène Carrière worked here.

Bastien-Lepage had found sudden fame at the Vernissage of the 1874 Salon with an unconventional portrait of an old man. He considered that the expertise of technique taught at the Ecole des Beaux-Arts, where he studied under Cabanel, needed to be counterbalanced by the direct study of nature observed away from the city. He consequently left Paris periodically for his studio at the family home at Damvilliers in Lorraine (Plate 284). He frequently worked outside, and his tragically brief career, from success at 24 to his death at 36 years of age, occurred at precisely the time when Impressionism was asserting itself to the public eye through the group exhibitions. He was not an Impressionist at all however, and his *plein-air* painting was much more readily assimilated by press and public alike. His portrait of Sarah Bernhardt appeared at the Salon of 1879 (see Plate 150), a year after he had caused a sensation with his painting *Les Foins* (Plate 285). Millet's *Gleaners* are called to mind by the picture but it

284. Mihaly Munkacsy, *The Studio of Bastien-Lepage*,
*c.* 1885 ink drawing.

also struck a highly original note in the firm drawing and in the depiction of the peasants
who suggested to some critics that they were entranced by religious experience in the
midst of their poverty on the open field. 'During this rough day the soul will have its
interval, the infinite will have its quarter of an hour.' wrote Paul Mantz, 'I do not
exaggerate. Of all the paintings of the Salon, including the religious paintings, the
composition of Bastien-Lepage is the one which contains the most thought.'[7] The critic
Castagnary was equally enthusiastic: 'he has realised a pure masterpiece. The French
school will reserve a good place for *Les Foins* in its annals. What a piece of work! All the
art of Jules Breton pales before it, and since Courbet, no-one has struck so authentic, so
astonishing a note.'[8] The state acquired the painting for the Luxembourg Museum.

285. Jules Bastien-Lepage, *Les Foins*, 1878, oil on canvas, 180 × 195 cm. Musée d'Orsay, Paris.

Bastien-Lepage seemed to offer a middle way, reconciling the correct drawing of the Ecole des Beaux-Arts to the recent study of open-air painting. For Albert Wolff *Les Foins* was a great painting not because of its subject but for its composition and 'the soul which the young artist has put into it.'[9] For Wolff the originality and achievement lay in the successful translation of a subject-painting into the context of open-air painting. As he expressed it in *Le Figaro* 'the young man seems to indicate to painting the definitive path that it must pursue, after the long sustained conflict between the blankest

224

realism and the miseries of convention.'[10] He certainly had his followers amongst whom were the young Marie Bashkirtseff, George Clausen, La Thangue and many others. In Montparnasse he lived in some poverty at first, but found the area preferable to central Paris for in Montparnasse 'one sees a little and the existence of Paris is less overwhelming.'[11]

Bastien-Lepage rose to public and critical acclaim very fast. This constituted a kind of exchange, for success depends not solely upon the inherent abilities of the artist but upon its recipients also. Edmond de Goncourt's estimate of Bastien-Lepage's achievement is significant; he described his work as 'pre-Raphaelite painting applied to the motifs and compositions of Millet'.[12] Millet's paintings and drawings were rising rapidly in value in response to a growing demand. They reflected a shift in the posthumous assessment of Millet and of Barbizon painting as a whole. Rosa Bonheur, who continued to work in the Fontainebleau forest was able to benefit from this, and it provided also a highly sympathetic climate for the reception of Bastien-Lepage. To a degree the success of Jules Breton reflects the same shift of taste and also effectively prepared the ground for the success of Bastien-Lepage. By offering a resolution of open-air painting with techniques respected at the Salon, Bastien-Lepage appeared a more readily acceptable but still up-to-date alternative to the Impressionists whose paintings were still considered by many to be outrageously unconventional.

By 1881 he was already a member of the council of the Société des Artistes Français and elected to the Salon jury. The death of this young man in 1884 was received as a major tragedy for French culture. 'France', wrote Jules Breton, 'has lost her Holbein'.[13] Preparations began at once for a major memorial exhibition at the Hôtel Chimay, the newly opened annexe of the Ecole des Beaux-Arts. This posthumous accolade confirmed the recognition of Bastien-Lepage's achievement and importance, and also spread his influence. It received crowds of visitors day after day. Two monographs rapidly followed.[14]

Today the Impasse du Maine is devoted to the work of Antoine Bourdelle and houses the museum in his name. Its wood, brick and glass studios have expunged all trace of

286. Studio complex at the Impasse du Maine, now the Musée Antoine Bourdelle. Sculptures by Bourdelle.

the sculptor Jules Dalou who worked here at No. 18 towards the end of his career up to his death in 1902. But Dalou's checkered carrer flourished before that of Bourdelle reached prominence. It encompassed both exile and grand acclaim. Dalou, a pupil of Lecoq de Boisbaudran from 1852, subsequently studied under Duret at the Ecole des Beaux-Arts. He then undertook sculpture on architectural and decorative projects, working on the Hôtel Païva in the Champs-Elysées, the Hôtel Menier by the Parc Monceau, and the Hôtel André, later Eiffel's house, in the Rue Matignon. He was a political activist and joined the Commune in 1871. On 16 March 1871 the revolutionary government of the Commune delegated to Dalou, together with the painters Jules Herreu and Oudinot, responsibility for the Louvre Museum, an alarming and impossible responsibility during the period of street fighting and bloodshed. Dalou stayed at his post for approximately one week before escaping to London where his friend Alphonse Legros arranged for him to teach at the Royal College of Art. After an active period in London, Dalou returned to Paris on the amnesty of 1879. Dalou's reputation was secured by the commission for *The Triumph of the Republic*. In 1890 he became a founder member of the Salon Nationale des Beaux-Arts. Admitted to the Légion d'Honneur in 1883, he was promoted in 1889, and made *commandeur* in 1899.

*The Triumph of the Republic* (see Plate 90) stands 12 metres high. Its costs rose from 70,000 francs to 100,000 francs and in 1889 the city provided 250,000 francs for it to be cast in bronze. Its final inauguration in 1900 was attended by the President of the Republic. Dalou's *Triumph of Silenus* was acquired by the State in 1894 and erected in the Luxembourg Gardens, which also house his *Monument to Delacroix* (inaugurated 1890) (see Plates 87 and 89). Dalou was a prolific sculptor who also frequently executed works for architectural contexts. He made caryatids for the Théâtre de la Renaissance in 1881–2, figures above the proscenium of the Théâtre du Palais Royal (1881–2) and *Progress leading Commerce and Industry* for the façade of the department store Les Grands Magazins Dufayel between the Rue de Clignancourt and Boulevard Barbès. His bust of Albert Wolff (Salon Nationale des Beaux-Arts, 1891) surmounts the critic's tomb in Père Lachaise Cemetry, and a marble bust of Victor Hugo (1891) was executed for the foyer of the Comédie Française.

Dalou knew Rodin well and attended the dinner given in Rodin's honour in February 1888. Edmond de Goncourt, who presided at the dinner, described Dalou with characteristic brevity and bite in his Journal: 'Dalou, the sculptor: nothing frank, nothing open about him, a man of shrivelled and foxy appearance.'[15]

The sculptor Antoine Bourdelle was twenty-three years younger than Dalou. When he moved to the Impasse du Maine on arriving in Paris in 1884 fields of corn were visible from the windows stretching across to the Rue Falguière. Bourdelle studied under Falguière for three years although his handling owed more to the examples of Dalou and to Rodin. The ground floor studios of the Impasse du Maine are perfect for sculpture with maximum daylight and doors opening into the courtyard allowing heavy materials to be brought in and sculpture to be taken out from the courtyard to the street (Plates 286 and 288). The open-air space would allow the sculptors also to work on large-scale projects. There were balconies and cupboards for the storage of drawings and maquettes and a suite of rooms for living accommodation. The dust of plaster, stone and clay was easily swept out and water could he used in a manner problematic in any studios above ground level or opening into a central Parisian street. In the relative remoteness of Montparnasse the sculptor could find studios that were essentially practical with nothing about them of the exotic, lavish or fashionable. Here he could work with air, space and peace with, in the case of Dalou and Bourdelle, prolific consequences in terms of sculpture. Bourdelle continued to work in the Impasse du Maine for forty-five years, amongst big oak benches and casts of the sculptures of antiquity.[16] Bourdelle's reputation reached its height in the twentieth century but he began the busts of Beethoven, which preoccupied him for many years, as early as 1887. He was com-

287. Paul Gauguin with cello, Anna La Javanaise, the painter Paul Sérusier (in fur cap) and friends in Gauguin's studio at 6 Rue Vercingétorix, Montparnasse. Photograph, 1894.

missioned in 1893 to design a monument to the dead of the Franco-Prussian War for the city of Montauban. Rodin supported the design in 1897 and the monument was inaugurated in 1902. But he also produced decorative sculpture for the Musée Grevin, the celebrated waxworks museum in Paris. In 1912 he executed a sequence of major reliefs to decorate the austere and innovatory building designed by Auguste Perret for the Théâtre des Champs-Elysées.

What is now the Rue Antoine-Bourdelle links the Rue Falguière to the west with the Avenue du Maine to the east near the Gare Montparnasse. South of the station off the Avenue du Maine there were studios in the Rue Vandamme and in the Rue Vercingétorix (Plate 287) where Gauguin in 1894 lived on the second floor of a new house at No. 6, between his Tahitian visits and after leaving the Rue de la Grande Chaumière.[17] Other occupants of the house included the son of Jean-Paul Laurens and the sculptor Maxime Reale del Sarte. It was here that Gauguin lived with Anna la Javanaise. Gauguin decorated his apartment in exotic style inspired by the artefacts of Java and Polynesia. His visitors included Edvard Munch, Strindberg and Degas. Gauguin's taste for the exotic had been fired by the foreign pavilions of the Exposition Universelle of 1889 where Buddhist and Javanese art excited his imagination, although this may have simply confirmed his impression of cultures whose art was available in Paris from 1886 when Guimet gave his collection of oriental art to the state (now the Musée Guimet), and by the 1890s oriental (and African) art was also visible at the Trocadéro Museum.

The opposite end of the Rue Antoine-Bourdelle emerges into the long Rue Falguière which accommodates more studios. Heading south across the Boulevard Pasteur it incorporates a further *cité d'artistes* beside No. 72, the Cité Falguière which survives unrestored (see Plate 283). It was also known as the Villa Rose and was run as a commercial enterprise.[18]

Towards the southern edge of Paris the population of studios grows increasingly rare and sparse. The Symbolist Alexandre Séon occupied 81 Rue de l'Abbaye Groult off the

288. (*a* and *b*) Studio complex at the Impasse du Maine. Sculptures by Bourdelle.

289. The Studio complex La Ruche, Passage Danzig.

Rue de Vaugirard. Further south still, at a point behind the southern abattoirs of the city where studios are least expected on the very fringes of Paris there stands, hidden in a garden, the extraordinary twelve-sided building known as La Ruche, the bee-hive, near the southern end of the Rue Dantzig at No. 2 in Passage Dantzig. This is amongst the most extraordinary of all of the *cités d'artistes* in Paris (Plates 289–93). The main entrance of this rotunda is flanked by caryatids beneath a balustrade. The staircase within leads to the upper two floors of studios whilst the ground floor studios each have a separate door, one for each face of the polyhedron of the plan. La Ruche was the brainchild of the painter-sculptor Alfred Boucher who bought an area of land here between the railway and the slaughterhouses in 1895. After constructing a few small studio-huts for artists, his ambitions were encouraged by the acquisition of various pieces of pavilions dismantled after the Exposition Universelle. The caryatids originated in the Indonesian pavilion. Twenty-four studios of an extraordinary wedge shape were con-

229

290. A wedge-shaped studio at La Ruche, photograph of *c.* 1906. An unknown sculptor with equipment, busts, casts and, on the wall, gloves, shoes and fencing equipment. The modelled sculptures are wrapped to retard drying.

291. La Ruche, Passage Danzig.

structed, to constitute the main building (Plates 290 and 292), their awkwardness off-set by their cheapness and the proximity of the community of artists established in this furthest reach of Montparnasse. The rents were extremely low (50 to 300 francs according to height),[19] and eventually Alfred Boucher located 140 studios on his stretch of land. He also planned a theatre, exhibition hall and teaching academy. La Ruche was officially opened by the Under Secretary of State for Fine Arts in 1902. The buildings are still occupied by painters and sculptors almost a century later and have had an illustrious history in the early years of twentieth century art for here worked Chagall, Soutine, Zadkine, Archipenko, Léger and many others unknown and uncharted in the history of art.

292. Studio of an unknown female artist at La Ruche in 1906. The walls are damp and the bed is placed on the balcony. Studies hang on the walls.

293. La Ruche studio, Passage Danzig.

La Ruche was erected upon the boundaries of Parisian art in the late nineteenth century. A *cité d'artistes* on the perimeter of the metropolis, cheap and inconvenient, pervaded at night by the sounds of the slaughterhouse, yet it was a haven for the unknown artist with few funds and no recognition. It was in addition a community where artists could meet in the studios and gardens. In this respect its function was magnificently fulfilled, for La Ruche was to nurture some of the most celebrated of twentieth-century painters, and the cramped, inconvenient proximity of the studios proved crucial to their development.

231

# 11. Provincial Postscript

Whilst the magnet of Paris could scarcely be resisted, its opportunities drawing thousands of painters, sculptors and printmakers into the city from all over France and from many foreign countries, there were some artists who kept their distance as best they could, dividing their time between the capital and their base beyond the city, sometimes far away in the provinces. Félix Bracquemond, a driving force in the revival of printmaking in France and a founder of the Société des Aquafortistes in 1862 lived at Sèvres, meticulously maintaining his contacts with Fantin-Latour, Manet and many other painter-printers and writers (Plate 294). His short post as director of art-works at the Sèvres porcelain studios had provided a reason to settle there but even when employed in Paris he continued to live at Sévres, where his wife Marie Bracquemond, a former pupil of Ingres, also painted and made prints.

Sèvres, however, is almost the suburbs of Paris. Other artists abandoned Paris for different reasons. Van Gogh moved to the south for the light, turning his back upon the scant opportunities that Paris had provided. Gauguin had become the central figure of a circle of artists in Brittany before leaving France for Tahiti, but it was to Paris that he returned his canvases for exhibitions and sales. Cézanne, drawn from the South to Paris by his childhood friend Emile Zola, having associated with the Impressionists, for a period alternated between Aix-en-Provence and the capital before settling in the south with only occasional visits to Paris. His independence was supported by his family wealth, and his commitment to plein-air landsape painting found the fields around Mont-Saint-Victoire as fulfilling as were the city streets to the painter of modern life or, in a different way, to the Salon painter.

The Impressionists Monet, Renoir, Sisley, Pissarro, spent much of their time out of Paris, in the suburbs and towns accessible from the Gare St Lazare and increasingly

294. Félix Bracquemond's studio with his *Portrait of Manet* visible at the left. Photograph of 1913.

295. Rosa Bonheur's studio at the Chateau de By, Thomery, Fontainebleau Forest.

further afield. The painters of the Fontainebleau forest had provided an important precedent, which was not lost upon the Impressionists. But the countryside was of equally vital importance for other kinds of landscape painter and the precedent of the Barbizon school was important here too. Jean-François Millet dressed as a peasant complete with clogs, his personal image the antithesis of the carefully tailored urban artist from the Avenue de Villiers or the Institut, and his paintings suggested an authenticity of experience close to the land that was denied to the city-dweller caught up in an artificial world of fashionable tastes. Something of this authenticity is promoted in the paintings of both Rosa Bonheur and Jules Breton both of whom spent as much time as possible out of Paris. Yet both were enormously successful artists within the Parisian art world.

Marie-Rosalie (Rosa) Bonheur lived at the Château de By at Thomery in the Fontainebleau forest (Plate 295). She was perhaps the most highly regarded of animal painters in her day. She won a first class prize at the Salon of 1848 and launched her successful career in its wake. Her success was such that she could afford to ignore the Salon: she exhibited twelve paintings there in 1867 but apart from this, submitted no works at all to the Salon between 1855 and her death in 1899, a period of 45 years. Yet her reputation grew inexorably, popularised through thousands of post-cards and engravings.

She purchased the Château de By in 1859 and moved in with her friend Nathalie Micas in 1860 (Plate 296). Here she constructed an immense studio, had her own zoo and dissected animals in a thorough study of animal anatomy. She left the Château only with reluctance and in 1865 even the Empress Eugènie travelled here to present Rosa Bonheur with the cross of the Légion d'Honneur. She was later, in 1894, the first woman promoted to the rank of *officier* in the Légion d'Honneur. In her great studio she produced enormous paintings, the most famous of which, *The Horsefair*, was sold to the American collector Pierpoint Morgan for the equivalent of £12,000. She sold more than 200 paintings direct from her studio.

296. The interior of Rosa Bonheur's studio at the Chateau de By, 1870.

Her garden gate gave direct access to the forest where she would paint and walk regularly accompanied by her dogs and her two pet monkeys. For security in the forest she at first carried a revolver and was later accompanied by her manservant. At her country estate she dressed as a man and she adopted male clothes to draw at the races and in slaughter-houses. According to one source she was known at Thomery as the 'little man with fine white locks'.[1] Even clad as a woman in Paris she was once arrested as a transvestite. Her biographer Stanton recounted that' 'to Rosa Bonheur, masculine dress was a simply a convenience, and, sometimes a necessity. When working on one of her large canvases, and perched on a ladder, it certainly was a convenience; and out of doors, it was often a real protection to her. With her there was no posing in the matter'.[2] In 1857 she had applied for and been granted a formal permit from the police permitting her to wear men's clothing.[3]

Rosa Bonheur was a vigorous artist of large-scale paintings of animals often in strenuous movement. She sold paintings without difficulty from her studio as and when she required money. Her success was such that she did not need to seek out purchasers, and like Meissonier, she could profit by undersupplying the buoyant demand for her work. She had little need to live in Paris, and had no need at all for its Salons.

Jules Breton on the other hand was more deeply involved with the city. His first major success came with *The Return of the Harvesters* in 1853. Admitted to the Légion d'Honneur in 1861, he was promoted to *officier* in 1867 and *commandeur* in 1885. The following year he was elected to the Institut. He served on the juries of the Expositions Universelles of both 1889 and 1900. His home however was at Courrières in the Pas de Calais, the landscape of which he had observed with rapture since his childhood days, and these were experiences simply unavailable in the city: 'under the purple light of the sky the distant fields stretched far away, still wrapped in the mists soon to be dissipated by the glowing disk of the sun.'[4] What worried Jules Breton about conventional painters was that they failed to study directly 'the sunlight, with its solemn splendours and its

234

thousand caprices; the relation of the parts to the whole, and variety of effect and execution, according to the sentiment of the subject'.[5] Breton began working from the direct observation of landscape under the influence of Diaz, and he greatly admired the Barbizon painters. He was wary of finish: 'nothing is more insipid than expressionless perfection. A touch of madness is better than death'[6], and he recognised that the direct sketch had qualities absent from a meticulously finished painting; in this he saw that the artist was confronted by a problem: 'The more beautiful his sketch, the heavier and more laboured will be every touch that he adds to it; and every effort which he makes to finish it will seem to remove it still further from the desired end.'[7]

Brittany impressed Jules Breton greatly and he described it in terms comparable to those used by Gauguin, for it was the opposite and the antidote to urban sophistication: 'This monastic rusticity, this mystic wilderness, evoked in my mind confused and far-off recollections'.[8] Like Gauguin, Breton responded to the primitive carving of calvaries in Brittany: 'they may be monstrous,' he wrote, 'but they are neither vulgar nor ridiculous; their dreaming ugliness has a sombre and even a menacing air'.[9] And in a passage which seems to be reflected later in Gauguin's paintings Jules Breton described the assembling processions of the Pardon of St Anne de la Palud: 'And from neighbouring heights, on every path, over the rocks, on the plains below which fade into the blue of the sea covered with boats — from all sides, in a word, come lines of pilgrims with banners at their head.'[10]

Jules Breton visited Brittany on several occasions. It had long been an area that attracted artists, especially from the summer heat of the city. But for Breton it was more than an escape of convenience from the city streets to the landscapes of Brittany or his native Courrières. Away from the galleries, museums, salons and juries, away from patrons, dealers, and critics, painting, though no less demanding, could perhaps address itself more directly to sensation and feeling, to the demands of the eye and imagination, than to the search for success. Breton was well aware of both contexts and both were vital to his art. This demanded time at the Institut and submissions to the Salon; it also demanded time alone in the fields. His work could be conventional or instinctive. 'How many times does it happen,' Breton reflected, that the artist 'does not perceive his success until afterward... For when a work is completed it is easy to analyze it and to explain the means by which the effect produced has been brought about.'[11]

*     *     *

The Impressionists provided a new view of the city of Paris, its figures, cabs and its architecture, splintered and dissolved into light. They showed a city in movement, inhabited and agitated by activity. Their techniques were evolved in the landscape in the forest at Fontainebleau, in the suburbs of Paris and on the edges of nearby towns at Eragny, Argenteuil, Marly-le-Roi and further afield to Rouen and Le Havre. As their careers progressed they travelled further exploring the Midi, Brittany and even London.

In their maturity they settled away from Paris and felt less need to engage in combat with the Salon by organising group exhibitions. As their art increasingly found respect, Monet, Renoir and Pissarro built studios well away from the city, studios in gardens full of light and air, pursuing their delectation of the senses and their astute perceptions of light and colour. Camille Pissarro constructed a studio at Eragny-sur-Epte, with roses twisting across the window, and maximum access to the brilliant light that bathed the trees and the fields (Plate 297). Claude Monet settled at Giverny, first moving there in 1883. It remained his base for the next forty-three years until his death in 1926. By contrast Degas remained in the city which had fascinated him and which provided the themes of his art for a lifetime. Degas was an urbane man; his fascination was with

297. Camille Pissarro in his studio at Eragny-sur-Epte, photograph from *c.* 1890, Archives des Amis de Camille Pissarro (photograph André Bonin), Pontoise.

people, city dwellers in particular. Monet's uninhabited fields did not attract Degas for he did not share Monet's voracious appetite for brilliant light. A letter from Degas to Jacque-Emile Blanche made this clear: 'I am writing to you from Halévy's house at Etretat, where the weather is fine, but more Monet than my eyes can stand'.[12]

Conversely Monet at Giverny explored composition on a colossal scale in paintings that were of necessity studio works. They were based upon direct observation of waterlilies in his garden, but even the garden was organised by Monet with long sustained attention to detail (Plate 298). He planned every part of it and had it executed to his wishes. In August 1897 he bought an adjacent strip of land in which he dug a pool diverting water from a nearby river to feed it. Here grew the waterlilies. In 1899 he demolished a cottage to build a second studio. With failing eyesight he executed whole series of immense paintings of nothing more than the pool, its lilies and sometimes a tree, as well as a multitude of smaller canvases of his Japanese bridge, his rose-covered pergola, irises by the water and waterlilies. A third studio was built for the big paintings. Plans existed in 1913 for a studio approximately 23 × 12 × 15 metres and by August 1915 construction was well advanced. The studio recalls that of Puvis de Chavannes with its mural scale paintings. Curtains control the top light. There is a comfortable sofa Everything else is bare, practical and devoted to the production of the paintings. It is devoid of all pretention. Monet with his enormous palette selects a brush to continue, despite his suffering eyes, the largest undertaking of his long career. He had often of necessity completed paintings in the studio, but these works are studio works from their inception. Monet had always shunned the ready-made formulae of Salon paintings subjects, handling of paint and composition, just as he had learned to survive without the Salon. In all of these respects his own work was demandingly original. At Giverny in

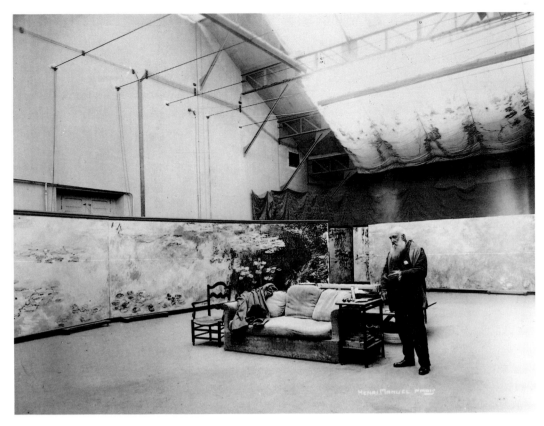

298. Henri Manuel, *Claude Monet working on his waterlily paintings 'Les Nymphéas' at Giverny*, photograph of 1924, Musée Marmottan, Paris.

his last years, Monet did not take less effort with his painting, he took more. He constructed a unique garden, and he built spacious studios in which his largest last compositions evolved, not from direct observation, but from watching the paintings themselves, for ultimately, in the studio, the painting took precedence, drawing upon memory and experience to construct uprecedented compositions. The horizon is taken off the top of the canvas leaving the lily-leaves and flowers alone to define the receding plane of the surface of the water. Through this translucent plain plunge the reflections of reeds, trees and the sky. There is no vanishing point and no horizon. In the blaze of light evoked by thick swirls of paint in which colour and drawing unite in controlled and energetic gestures, Monet presents his ambiguous picture space, flat yet receding, receding yet falling vertically away. The eye explores, its field of vision filled with colour and movement in which nothing is rigid or fixed, in which the only coherence is the light, the paint surface and the structure of the picture space. A life-time of insatiable and direct observation of the light in streets, fields, rivers and the sea informs these works. The studio was essential to them for their production goes beyond direct observation, demands long contemplation of the action of colour against colour and mark against mark.

The studio is no more than a container, a kind of equipment, a room in which to paint or sculpt, a necessary space. In its isolation the artist watches his painting, adjusts it, instinctively responsive to his pigments and colours, resolving their conflicts. In this way the studio is also an arena in which controlled yet instinctive and unpremeditated discovery unfolds.

# Notes

PART ONE

*1. Introduction*

1. M.O. Gréard, *Meissonier*, Paris, 1897, p. 126.
2. Ibid., p. 35.
3. Jules Breton, *The Life of an Artist*, translated by M.V. Sefrano, London, 1891, p. 140.
4. Ibid., p. 141.
5. Ibid.
6. 'The Lay Figure' in *The Studio*, vol. 16, 1899, p. 218.
7. Ibid.
8. George du Maurier, *Trilby*, in *Novels of George du Maurier*, London, 1947, p. 224.

*2. The Louvre*

1. See R. Rudorff, *La Belle Epoque*, London, 1972, p. 22.
2. Shirley Fox, *An Art Student's Reminiscences of Paris in the Eighties* London, 1909, p. 76.
3. Gréard, *Meissonier*, p. 110–11.
4. Albert André, *Renoir*, Paris, 1928, p. 30, cited in Michel Drucker *Renoir*, Paris, 1944, p. 125.
5. Rodin, *Art: Conversations with Paul Gsell*, University of California Press, 1984, p. 107.
6. Jacques-Emile Blanche, *Portraits of a Lifetime*, London 1937, p. 29.

*4. Beginnings*

1. George Moore, *Confessions of a Young Man* (written 1886). First published 1918. This edition Harmondsworth, 1941, p. 26.
2. Ibid, p. 27.
3. Ibid., p. 82.
4. Blanche, *Portraits*, p. 29.
5. Several studios were opened for female students including one at 51 Rue Vivienne. Other studios included those at 48 Faubourg St Denis (*c*.1880, for men), at 5 Rue Fromentin (*c*.1888), and in 1890 five large studios were in operation at 31 Rue du Dragon. In the early 1900s a women's studio was situated at 55 Rue du Cherche-Midi. For a discussion of the Académie Julian see Catherine Fehrer, *New Light on the Académie Julian* in *Gazette des Beaux-Arts*, Mai-Juin, 1984, pp. 207–15.
6. Fox, *Reminiscences*, p. 34.
7. Ibid., p. 52.
8. Ibid., p. 49–50.
9. Moore, *Confessions*, p. 27.
10. Ibid., p. 28.
11. Ibid., p. 30.
12. Marie Bashkirtseff, *Journal* (22 September 1887), Paris, n.d., p. 214.
13. Ibid., p. 213.
14. Ibid., p. 217.
15. Ibid., p. 218.
16. Ibid., p. 277.
17. Ibid., p. 257.
18. Ibid., p. 229.
19. Ibid., p. 291 (entry for 5 January 1880).
20. Ibid., p. 234.

21. Ibid., p. 292.
22. Theodore Stanton, *Reminiscences of Rosa Bonheur*, London, 1910, p. 303.
23. Clive Holland, *Student Life in the Quartier Latin, Paris* in *The Studio*, vol. 27, No. 115, 1902, p. 33.
24. John Rewald, Foreword to *Pissarro*, catalogue of the Arts Council of Great Britain exhibition *Camille Pissarro 1830–1903*, London, 1981, p. 9.
25. Blanche, *Portraits*, p. 35.
26. E. Durand-Greville, *Entretiens de J.J. Henner*, Paris, 1925, p. 52.
27. Horace Lecoq de Boisbaudran, *The Training of the Memory in Art*, London, 1911, p. xii.
28. Ibid., p. xxiv.
29. Ibid.
30. Ibid., p. 5.
31. Ibid., p. 38.
32. Ibid., p. 39.
33. Ibid., p. 97.
34. Ibid., p. 163.
35. Ibid., p. 57.
36. See John M. Hunisak, *The Sculptor Jules Dalou*, New York, 1977, p. 22.
37. Rodin, *Art*, p. 33.
38. Ibid., pp. 33–4.

*5. The Ecole des Beaux-Arts*

1. Fox, *Reminiscences*, p. 71.
2. W.C. Morrow, *Bohemian Life in Paris Today*, London, 1899, p. 40.
3. Du Maurier, *Trilby*, p. 229.
4. Fox, *Reminiscences*, p. 98.
5. Morrow, *Bohemian Life*, p. 56.
6. Ibid., p. 58.
7. Fox, *Reminiscences*, p. 74.
8. Ibid.
9. Morrow, *Bohemian Life*, p. 52–3.
10. Ibid., p. 53.
11. Fox, *Reminiscences*, p. 74.
12. Moore, *Confessions*, p. 22.
13. L. de Fourcaud, *Bastien-Lepage, sa vie et ses oeuvres*, Paris, n.d., p. 4.
14. Moore, *Confessions*, p. 24.
15. Morreau-Vauthier, *Gérôme*, Paris, 1906, p. 183.
16. Morrow, *Bohemian Life*, p. 54–5.
17. Moreau-Vauthier, *Gérôme*, pp. 186–8.
18. Fox, *Reminiscences*, p. 75.
19. Ibid., p. 90.
20. See A. Boime, *The Academy and French painting in the 19th. Century*, London, 1971. p. 54.
21. Fox, *Reminiscences*, p. 78.
22. See Ibid, p. 102–12.
23. Morrow, *Bohemian Life*, p. 54.
24. Boime, *The Academy*, pp. 49–52.
25. Henry Stacy Marks cited in Leonie Ormond, *George du Maurier*, London, 1969, p. 39.
26. Gréard, *Meissonier*, p. 299.
27. Morrow, *Bohemian Life*, p. 46..
28. Gréard, *Meissonier*, p. 299.
29. Fox, *Reminiscences* p. 103.
30. Lecoq de Boisbaudran, *The Training of the Memory*, p. 83. Hunisak, *Jules Dalou*, p. 23.

32. De Fourcaud, *Bastien-Lepage*, p. 6.
33. Fox, *Reminiscences*, p. 201.
34. Letter from Toulouse-Lautrec, 7 May 1882 cited in P.H. Huisman & M.G. Tortu, *Lautrec par Lautrec*, Paris, 1964, p. 36.
35. See Richard Ormond, *John Singer Sargent*, London, 1970, p. 94, note 20.

*6. Paris as Dwelling Place for Artists*

1. Rodin, *Art*, p. 15.
2. Breton, The *Life of an Artist*, p. 264.
3. Albert Wolff, *La Capitale de l'art*, Paris, 1886, p. v.
4. Ibid., p. vi.
5. Morrow, *Bohemian Life*, p. 322.
6. New York Graphic Society, The Complete Letters of Vincent Van Gogh, New York, 1958 (Letter of August-October 1887), vol. 3, p. 513.
7. Wolff, *La Capitale*, p. 285ff.
8. Breton, *Life of an Artist*, p. 288.
9. Moore, *Confessions*, p. 41.
10. Emile Zola, *Nana*, first published Paris, 1880. This edition Harmondsworth, 1980, translated by George Holden, p. 21.

*7. The Studio as Such*

1. Breton, *Life of an Artist*, p. 189.
2. Marius Vachon, *Puvis de Chavannes*, Paris, 1895, p. 7.
3. Breton, *Life of an Artist*, p. 190.
4. Holland, *Student Life*, p. 34.
5. According to Morrow in *Bohemian Life*, p. 315.
6. Holland, *Student Life*, p. 35.
7. Gréard, *Meissonier*, p. 213.

*8. The Image of the Artist*

1. Morrow, *Bohemian Life*, p. 41.
2. Gréard, *Meissonier*, p. 215.
3. Morrow, *Bohemian Life*, p. 69.
4. Durand-Greville, *Entretiens*, p. 29.
5. Ibid., p. 157.
6. Breton, *Life of an Artist*, pp. 188–9.
7. Gréard, *Meissonier*, p. 179.

*9. Plein-Air Practicalities*

1. Emile Zola, *L'Oeuvre*, first published 1886. This edition in *Emile Zola Oeuvres Complètes*, Paris, 1967, vol. 5. Quotation from p. 467.
2. Breton, *Life of an Artist*, p. 247.
3. Ibid., p. 248.
4. Ibid., p. 219.
5. Ibid., p. 247.
6. Ibid., p. 219.
7. Ibid.
8. Lecoq de Boisbaudron, *The Training of the Memory*, p. 30.
9. Ibid.
10. Ibid., pp. 30–1.
11. Thadée Natanson, *Peints à leur tour*, Paris, 1948, pp. 33–4.
12. Breton. *Life of an Artist*, p. 344.

*10. A Society Studio*

1. Gabriel Mourey, 'Some French Artists at Home' in *The Studio*, vol. 7, 1896, p. 27.
2. Wolff, *La Capitale*, p. 257.

3. Ibid., p. 287.
4. Ibid., p. 291.
5. Bashkirtseff, *Journal* (30 April 1882), p. 389.
6. Edmund and Jules de Goncourt, *Journal, Mémoires de la vie littéraire*, Monaco, 1956, vol. 14, p. 91.
7. Wolff, *La Capitale*, p. 295.
8. Gabriel Mourey, 'Some French Artisit at Home,' p. 27.
9. Ibid., p. 26.
10. Mantz, *Salon 1889*, p. 21, discussing Carolus-Duran's *Bacchus*.

*11. Salon Stars and Hopefuls*

1. Rodin, *Art*, p. 230.
2. Morrow, *Bohemian Life*, p. 72.
3. Paul Mantz, *Salon 1889*, Paris, 1889, p. 1.
4. Ibid., p. 3.
5. Ibid.
6. Marquis de Chennevières, 'Le Salon de 1880' (3ᵉ article), *Gazette des Beaux-Arts*, July 1880, p. 499, cited in MaryAnne Stevens, 'Innovation and Consolidation in French Painting', in *Post-Impressionism*, Royal Academy of Arts, London, 1979, p. 19.
7. See Boime, *The Academy*.
8. Letter from Renoir to Durand-Ruel, March 1881, translated from Lionello Venturi, *Les Archives de l'Impressionisme*, Paris-New York, 1931, vol. 1, p. 115.
9. *Equivoques, Peintures Françaises du XIXᵉ Siècle*, Musée des Arts Décoratifs, Paris, 1973, pp. 21–2.
10. *Equivoques*, p. 22.
11. Morrow, *Bohemian Life*, p. 74.
12. 'French Salon Accounts' in *The Art Journal*, 1885, p. 29.
13. Figures discussed in 'Salon of 1887', in *The Art Journal*, 1887, p. 318.
14. F.G. Stephens, 'Paris Salon' in *The Art Journal*, 1887, p. 252ff.
15. See Hunisak, *Jules Dalou*, p. 185; and Geraldine Norman, *Nineteenth-Century Painting*, London, 1977, p. 88.
16. Bashkirtseff, Journal (27 June 1880), p. 304.
17. Ibid.
18. Zola, *L'Oeuvre*, p. 206.
19. See Fox, *Reminiscences*, pp. 153–7.
20. Bashkirtseff, *Journal* (24 March 1880), p. 294.
21. Ibid. (1 May 1881) p. 338.
22. De Fourcaud, *Bastien-Lepage*, p. 10.
23. Fox, *Reminiscences*, p. 158.
24. Durand-Greville, *Entretiens*, p. 58.
25. Breton, *Life of an Artist*, p. 224.
26. Zola, *L'Oeuvre*, p. 296.
27. Fox, *Reminiscences*, p. 159.
28. Gyp, *La Fée Surprise*, Paris, 1897, p. 215.
29. Ibid., p. 217.
30. Zola, *L'Oeuvre*, p. 283.
31. E. de Goncourt, *Journal* (1 May 1882), vol. 12, p. 170.
32. Gyp, *La Fée Surprise*, p. 175.
33. Ibid., p. 223.
34. Zola, *L'Oeuvre*, p. 284.
35. Letter from Théodore Duret to Camille Pissarro, 15 February 1874, cited in John Rewald, *The History of Impressionism*, New York, 1961, p. 310.
36. Zola, *L'Oeuvre*, p. 135.
37. Blanche, *Portraits*, p. 58.
38. Bashkirtseff, *Journal* (12 May 1878), p. 273.
39. Ibid.
40. *Degas: Letters* (ed. Marcel Guérin), Oxford, 1947, p. 65 (Letter of 2 May 1882).
41. Lionel Robinson: 'French Art' in *The Art Journal*, 1886, p. 37.
42. Anon., 'The Paris Salon' in *The Art Journal*, 1885, pp. 191–2.

43. Ibid.
44. Stephens, 'Paris Salon', p. 252ff.
45. Anon, 'The Paris Salon', p. 191–2.
46. Lionel Robinson, 'French Art', pp. 19–23 (this quotation, pp. 22–3).
47. Ibid., pp. 22–3.
48. Anon., 'The Paris Salon', p. 192.
49. Sophia Beale, 'French Art' in *The Art Journal*, 1886, p. 129–32 (this quotation p. 129).
50. Anon., 'Art Notes and Reviews' in *The Art Journal*, 1885., p. 359.
51. Beale, 'French Art', p. 65–8 (this quotation p. 65).
52. This sequence of quotations from Gabriel Mourey, 'The Salon of the Champs-Elysées' in *The Studio*, vol. 8, 1896, p. 102.
53. Ibid., p. 103.
54. Anon., 'Studio Talk' in *The Studio*, vol. 11, 1897, p. 61.
55. Gabriel Mourey, 'The Salon of the Champs de Mars' in *The Studio*, vol. 8, 1896, p. 17.
56. In the year of the Great Exhibition of 1889, the Indépenants exhibited in the Salle de la Société d'Horticulture at 84 Rue de Grenelle on the left bank. Otherwise in the period 1887–1900, they exhibited on or near the Champs-Elysées. Le Douanier Rousseau made his debut at the Indépendants in 1886. It was unimaginable that his work would have been selected by any Salon employing a jury of professionally acclaimed artists.

*12. Vicarious Exposure*

1. Whistler's lithograph *The Long Gallery at the Louvre*, for example, was published in *The Studio*, vol. 3, 1894.

*13. Sales*

1. Gréard, *Meissonier*, p. 179.
2. Blanche, *Portraits*, p. 68.
3. Zola, *Nana*, p. 28.
4. New York Graphic Society, *The Complete Letters of Vincent Van Gogh*, vol 3, p. 515.
5. Gréard, *Meissonier*, p. 104.
6. Stanton, *Reminiscences of Rosa Bonheur*, p. 377.
7. J. & E. de Goncourt, *Journal* (23 May 1881), vol. 12, pp. 114–15.
8. *Degas: Letters*, p. 82.
9. Ibid., p. 94.
10. E. & J. de Goncourt, *Journal* (13 June 1892), vol. 18, p. 397.
11. Blanche, *Portraits*, p. 39.
12. E. & J. de Goncourt, *Journal* (30 March 1889), vol 16, p. 54.
13. Daniel Wildenstein, *Monet*, Lausanne/Paris, 1979, vol. 3, pp. 9–10.
14. Paul Gauguin: *Lettres de Paul Gauguin à Georges-Daniel de Monfried* (letter of 22 February 1899), Paris, 1918, p. 235.
15. Karl Baedecker, *Paris*, Leipsic, 1894, p. 250.
16. *Degas: Letters*, p. 247 (letter of 19 February 1892). For a discussion of the history of the Musée du Luxembourg see *Le Musée du Luxembourg en 1874*, Grand Palais, Paris, 1974 (ed. Geneviéve Lacambre)
17. Anon, 'Art Notes & Reviews' p. 259.
18. Ibid., p. 158.
19. Ibid., p. 259.
20. The Wallace Collection is now displayed in Manchester Square, London.
21. E. & J. de Goncourt, *Journal* (5 January 1887), vol 14, p. 184.
22. M.A. Belloc & M. Shedlock, *Edmond & Jules de Goncourt*, London, 1895, p. 79.

23. Ibid., p. 82.
24. E. & . J. de Goncourt, *Journal* (3 April 1887) vol. 14, p. 215.
25. T. Natanson, *Peints à la tour*, p. 172.
26. Ibid., p. 174.
27. *Degas: Letters*, p. 125.
28. See M. Berhaut, *Caillebotte l'Impressioniste*, Lausanne, 1968, p. 56.
29. 28 February 1897, ibid.
30. By Monsieur Hervé de Saisy, cited in ibid., p. 58.
31. Ibid.
32. Stanton, *Reminiscences of Rosa Bonheur*, pp. 380–1.
33. New York Graphic Society, *The Complete Letters of Vincent Van Gogh*, p. 515.

*14. Sculpture in the Making*

1. Rodin, *Art*, pp. 96–7.
2. Cited by Hunisak, *Jules Dalou*, p. 182, from G. Geoffroy, *Dalou in La Vie artistique*, tome VIII, 1903, p. 320.
3. Mantz, *Salon 1889*, p. 51.
4. See Hunisak, *Jules Dalou*, p. 93.
5. Rodin, *Art*, pp. 88–9.
6. Ibid., pp. 54–5.
7. Hunisak, *Jules Dalou*, p. 101.
8. Ibid, p. 92.

*15. Sites*

1. See Hunisak, *Jules Dalon*, p. 49.

*16. Public Painting*

1. Zola, *L'Oeuvre*, p. 335.
2. Now concealed by Chagall's ceiling painting.
3. M. Vachon, *Puvis*, p. 58.
4. E. & J. de Goncourt, *Journal* (30 December 1889), vol. 16, p. 193.
5. Ibid. (26 January 1889), p. 11.
6. Degas letter to Rouart (16 October 1883) in *Degas: Letters*, p. 74.

*17. The Great Exhibitions*

1. E. & J. Goncourt in *Pages from the Goncourt Journal*, edited and translated by Robert Baldick, London, 1980, p. 367, entry for 6 May 1889.
2. Ibid. (2 July 1889).
3. Anon, 'The Eiffel Tower' in *The Art Journal*, 1887, p. 128.
4. *Livre d'or de l'Exposition 1900*, Paris, 1900, vol. 1, p. 60.
5. Breton, *Life of Artist*, p. 341.
6. J. & E. de Goncourt, *Journal* (23 June 1889), vol 16, p. 94. See also Wildenstein, *Monet*, vol. 3, p. 21.
7. Breton, *Life of an Artist*, p. 344.
8. Wolff, *La Capitale*, p. 225.
9. Ibid., p. 228.
10. Ibid., p. 234.
11. Ibid., p. 215.
12. Ibid., p. 222.
13. According to *The Art Journal* the sale of 3 February 1884 included the following prices (sterling equivalent): *Argenteuil*, £500; *Olympia*, £400; *Bar at the Folies Bergère*, £234; *Nana*, £120; *The Balcony*, £120.
14. Wildenstein, *Monet*, vol. 3, p. 23, letter no. 1000 (to Emile Zola, 22 July 1899).
15. See *The Art Journal*, 1889, p. 307 ff which cites the prices inconsistently in pounds sterling and in francs. But also note that in 1889, the sum of 100,000 francs

was equivalent to £4,000. The prices have been converted accordingly which may distort the historically earlier prices. The sale was not finally concluded. The *Angelus* was sent on an American tour and finally bought by M. Chouchard, proprietor of the Magasins du Louvre for £32,000. He bequeathed it to the Louvre. See A.S. Hartrick, *A Painter's Pilgrimage through Fifty Years*, Cambridge, 1939, p. 6.

16. Pascal Forthuny, *L'Exposition Centennale* in *Livre d'Or de L'Exposition Universelle*, Paris, 1900, p. 137ff. This quotation p. 142.

*18. How are the Mightly Fallen?.*

1. Blanche, *Portraits*, pp. 67–8.
2. Rodin, *Art* p. 47.
3. Ibid., p. 143.
4. Gabriel Mourey, for example, in *The Studio* (vol. 8, 1896, p. 19), called him 'incontestably the greatest of living French artists'.
5. Wolff, *La Capitale*, p. 179.
6. Anon. in *The Studio*, 1896, pp. 203–4.
7. Woff, *La Capitale*, p. 219
8. Mantz, *Salon 1889*, p. 96.
9. Gabriel Mourey, *Puvis de Chavannes* in *The Studio*, vol. 15, 1899, p. 206.

**PART TWO**

*1. The Studios of Paris*

1. Zola, *L'Oeuvre*, p. 20.
2. Morrow, *Bohemian Life*, p. 25.
3. Ibid., p. 21.
4. Ibid., p. 225.

*2. The Grands Boulevards*

1. G. du Maurier, *Trilby*, p. 237.
2. Zola, *L'Oeuvre*, p. 214.
3. Augustus J.C. Hare, *Paris* (2 vols,), 1900, vol. 1, p. 23.
4. Zola, *L'Oeuvre*, p. 75.
5. E.J. de Goncourt, *Journal* (2 June 1883), vol. 13, p. 38.
6. Nadar was the pseudonym of Gaspard Félix Tournachon (1820–1910). He photographed many of the celebrities of his day including the artists Doré, Corot, Guys, Courbet, J.F. Millet, Daubigny, Manet, Delacroix, Daumier and many others. He was also a balloonist, draughtsman, writer and collector. See the catalogue of the exhibition *Nadar*, Bibliothèque Nationale, Paris, 1965.
7. Zola, *Nana*, p. 273.

*3. North to the Boulevard de Clichy*

1. See Hillairet, *Dictionnaire historique des rues de Paris*, Paris, 1979, vol. 1, p. 535.
2. Zola, *Nana*, p. 272.
3. Baedecker, *Paris*, p. 32.
4. Jean Renoir, *Renoir My Father*, London, 1962, p. 313.
5. Michael Drucker, *Renior*, Paris, 1944, pp. 125–6.
6. Gabriel Mourey, *A Dream-Painter — M.L. Lévy-Dhurmer* in *The Studio*, vol. 10, 1897, p. 4ff.
7. See Fox, *Reminiscences*, p. 206, who also records Benjamin Constant's final move to the Rue Ampère.
8. Degas in an undated letter to Alexis Rouart, cited in *Degas: Letters*, p. 118. It was to 19 bis Rue Fontaine that Degas for a period descended from his home at 6 Boulevard de Clichy to work in his studio. At No. 19, Toulouse-Lautrec lived at the home of Doctor Henri Bourges from 1887 to 1893 and used the studios at No. 19 bis. In 1896 Lautre had a room at No. 30, whilst at No. 37 Rodolphe Julian had a teaching academy operative from 1870. See Hillairet, *Dictionnaire historique des rues de Paris*, vol. 1, p. 535. The Surrealist André Breton was later to occupy No. 42 Rue Fontaine for many years (p. 775).

9. Moore, *Confessions*, p. 39.
10. *Degas: Letters*, p. 49.
11. Ibid., p. 36. Letter to Bracquemond, 8 August, 1873.
12. Degas cited in Durand-Greville, *Entretiens*, p. 18.
13. Hillairet, *Dictionnaire historique des rues*, p. 558, gives the address as 15 Avenue Frochot. No. 8 was occupied by the Institut member Ferdinand Humbert.
14. Gavarni and later Berlioz had occupied 43 Rue Blanche, and in a vast studio behind No. 96 the theatre director Antoine started his Théâtre Libre (Hillairet, *Dictionnaire historique des rues*, p. 200–1). Alfred Jarry's play *Ubu Roi* had its premier on 10 December 1896 at the Nouveau Théâtre at No. 15 Rue Blanche (p. 739).
15. In this area too is the Rue de Bruxelles where Zola occupied No. 21 from 1887 until his death in 1902 (Hillairet, *Dictionnaire historique des rues*, vol. 1, p. 247). The painter Félix Barrias was at No. 34. The fashionable Belgian painter Alfred Stevens was in nearby Rue de Calais at No. 15 (in 1883). According to the Goncourt *Journal* for 21 October 1893 Stevens confided: 'I hardly dare say it, but I have done 71 paintings since the month of January' (vol. 17, p. 183). In the Rue Chaptal, No. 9 is the site of the Goupil Gallery where Van Gogh worked, and at No. 20 bis the Théâtre du Grand Guignol was founded in 1896 at the studio formerly used by Rochegrosse (Hillairet, *Dictionnaire historique des rues*, vol. 1, p. 311).
16. Moore, *Confessions*, p. 22.

*4. The Boulevard de Clichy*

1. Andre Warnod, *Les Berceaux de la jeune peinture*, Paris, 1923, p. 23.
2. By 1889 Seurat had moved to nearby Passage de l'Elysées-des-Beaux-Arts, near Place Pigalle.
3. Morrow, *Bohemian Life*, p. 87.
4. Ibid., p. 87–8.
5. Ibid., p. 95.
6. Ibid., p. 88.
7. Ibid., p. 12.
8. G. Boethius, *Anders Zorn*, Stockholm 1954.
9. Morrow, *Bohemian Life*, p. 85.
10. Ibid., p. 38.
11. Ibid.
12. See *The Romantics to Rodin*, exhibition catalogue, Los Angeles County Museum, 1980, p. 285ff, and S. Lami, *Dictionnaire des sculpteurs de l'école française au dix-neuvième siècle*, vol. 3, p. 54ff.
13. J. &. E. de Goncourt, *Journal* (19 April 1883), vol. 12, p. 168.
14. Moreau-Vauthier, *Gérôme*, p. 138.
15. No. 63 was the Cabaret du Tambourin, No. 62, the Cabaret des Quat'z Arts from 1893, No. 53, the Cabarets Le Ciel and L'Enfer. Daumier had occupied No. 36 from 1869 to 1873, and the history-painter Francis Tattegrain was at No. 12 (Hillairet, *Dictionnaire historique des rues* vol. 1, p. 357–9).
16. See Louis Verneuil, *La Vie merveilleuse de Sarah Bernhardt*, New York, 1942, pp. 106–9. 11 Boulevard de Clichy was much used by artists including the 28 year-old Picasso in 1909 (see Hillairet, *Dictionnaire historiques des rues*, vol 2, p. 37–9).

17. Alice Meynell, *Mme Sarah Bernhardt* in *The Art Journal*, 1888, pp. 134–9. This quotation p. 138.
18. Ibid., p. 139.
19. Durand-Greville, *Entretiens*, p. 107.
20. Moore, *Confessions*, pp. 72–3,
21. Ibid., p. 73.
22. Ibid., p. 76. Degas' *Absinthe* was painted here, depicting the actess Ellen Andrée and the painter Marcellin Desboutin. Regular visitors to the café included the painters Forain, Raffaëlli and Zandomeneghi.
23. Gabriel Mourey, *Some French Artists at Home* in *The Studio*, vol. 7, 1896, special winter number, p. 25.
24. According to Moreau-Vauthier, *Gérôme*, p. 189.
25. Durand-Greville, *Entretiens*, p. 170.
26. The Chat Noir once occupied 12 Rue Laval (now Rue Victor-Massé)

*5. The Heights of Montmartre*

1. This has several times changed its name. Villa des Beaux-Arts was used as a street name until the name Rue Hégésippe-Moreau was conferred in 1890. The studio block at No. 15, the Villa des Arts, was opened by M. Guéret (Hillairet, *Dictionnaire historique des rues*, vol. 2, p. 112).
2. Fox, *Reminiscences*, pp. 204–6. He was at 27 Rue Pigalle in 1900.
3. Ibid., p. 202.
4. Mantz, *Salon 1889*, p. 31.
5. See B. Welsh-Ovcharov, *Vincent Van Gogh and the Birth of Cloisonism*, Art Gallery of Ontario, Toronto, 1981, pp. 28–9. See Hillairet, *Dictionnaire historique des rues* who gives the address as No. 63.
6. Anon., *Some Drawings by Steinlen* in *The Studio*, vol. 16, 1899, p. 25.
7. According to Hillairet, *Dictionnaire historique des rues* vol. 1. p. 284 and p. 750.
8. Warnod, *Les Berceaux*, p. 133ff.
9. Ibid., p. 133.
10. Jean Renoir, *Renoir*, p. 177.
11. Ibid., p. 259.
12. Ibid., p. 366. See also Hillairet, *Dictionnaire historique des rues* vol. 1, pp. 245–6.
13. Jean Renoir, *Renoir*, p. 240–7, and Huisman & Tortu, *Lautrec*, p. 87.
14. See Morrow, *Bohemian Life*, pp. 240–6.
15. Jean Renoir, *Renoir*, p. 89.
16. See Huisman & Tortu, *Lautrec*, p. 44.
17. Warnod, *Les Berceaux*, p. 25.
18. The clientèle later included Picasso, Severini, Modigliani as well as the writers Apollinaire, Jacob and Salmon. The Russian Futurist group *The Donkey's Tail* later took their name from Lolo's performance.
19. Jean Renoir, *Renoir*, p. 180 and 183.
20. The house originated in the seventeenth century. Valadon was discovered by Degas. Also but later associated with 12 Rue Cortot were the director André Antoine, and the painters Othon Friesz, Raoul Dufy, Maurice Delcourt and the artist Francis Poulbot, habitué of the Lapin Agile. See Hillairet, *Dictionnaire historique des rues* vol. 1, p. 394.
21. This square was detached from the Rue Ravignan and renamed in 1911. The Bateau-Lavoir was formerly a piano-makers; it was divided into studios after 1880. See Hillairet, *Dictionnaire historique des rues* vol. 1, p. 474.

*6. Gare St Lazare and Les Batignolles*

1. Moore, *Confessions*, p. 41.
2. This *Joan of Arc* by Paul Dubois, sited in 1900, is a replica of his monument at Reims.
3. In the Rue d'Amsterdam the poet Baudelaire occupied No. 22 in 1860 and had translated Edgar Allen Poe here. No. 24 housed Alphonse Daudet and the humorist writer and exhibitor Alphonse Allais died here in 1905. Numerous artists had studios at No. 77, amongst them Manet in 1879. See Hillairet, *Dictionnaire historiques des rues de Paris*, Vol. 1, p. 80
4. The Boulevard des Batignolles was formed in 1863. Manet occupied No. 34 early in his career before moving to the Rue St Petersburg (Rue Leningrad). See Hillairet, *Dictionnaire historique des rues de Paris*, Vol. 1, p. 156.
5. Moore, *Confessions*, p. 56.
6. *The Studio*, Vol. 7, 1896, special winter issue, p. 28.
7. In the Avenue de Clichy, at No. 3 was the Taverna de Paris from 1903, decorated by Léandre, Steinlen, Chéret, Willette and others. No. 9 had been the Café Guerbois, an important meeting place for Manet's circle before their move to the Café de la Nouvelles Athènes.

*7. Around the Arc de Triomphe*

1. Holland, *Student Life*, p. 35.
2. Wolff, *La Capitale*, p. 286.
3. Zola, *Nana*, p. 301.
4. Ibid., p. 312.
5. Ibid.
6. Degas considered that his cheif value was to military suppliers. See D. Haléry, *Degas Parle*, 1960, cited in the *Gazette des Beaux-Arts*, July-August, 1975, p. 27.
7. Gréard, *Meissonier*, p. 115 and p. 335.
8. Wolff, *La Capitale*, pp. 173–4.
9. Breton, *Life of an Artist*, p. 188.
10. Wolff, *La Capitale*, p. 180.
11. E. de Goncourt, *Journal* for 26 April 1881, Vol, 12 p. 112.
12. Wolff, *La Capitale*, p. 183.
13. Degas quipped that he was 'a giant among dwarfs': G. Rivière, *Mr Degas, bourgeois de Paris, Floury*, 1935, cited in *Gazette des Beaux-Arts*, July-August 1975, p. 31.
14. Wolff, *La Capitale*, p. 182.
15. Mantz, *Salon 1889*, p. 46.
16. Durand-Greville, *Entretiens*, p. 15.
17. Wolff, *La Capitale*, pp. 286–7.
18. Meynell, *Mme Sarah Bernhardt*, pp. 134–9. This quotation p. 138.
19. Hillairet, *Dictionnaire historique des rues* vol. 1, pp. 539 and 775.
20. S. Lami, *Dictionnaire des sculpteurs*, vol. 1, p. 60.
21. Mantz, *Salon 1889*, p. 14.
22. Anon. in *The Studio*, vol. 7, 1896, special winter number, p. 28.
23. Marie Bashkirtseff died at 30 Rue Ampère in 1884 aged 23 (Hillairet, *Dictionnaire historique des rues*, vol. 1, p. 79).
24. The street was detached from the Rue Alphonse-de-Neuville in 1926 and named after Roll who had lived at No. 17. The Rosicrucian J. Péladan occupied the building on the corner of the Rue Verniquet in 1903 (Hillairet, *Dictionnaire historique des rues*, vol. 1, p. 73).
25. Former 23 bis Boulevard Berthier was the art nouveau *hôtel* of the performer Yvette Guilbert, and Carrier-Belleuse was amongst the artists in the studio block at No. 31. See Hillairet, *Dictionnaire historique des rues*, vol. 1, pp. 188 and 738.
26. Blanche, *Portraits*, p. 153.
27. Ibid., p. 154.
28. Mantz, *Salon 1889*, p. 40.
29. Anon. in *The Studio*, vol. 7, 1896, special winter number, p. 29.

30. Anon. in *The Studio*, vol. 10, 1897, p. 126.
31. Mantz, *Salon 1889*, p. 54.
32. E. de Goncourt, *Journal* (27 March 1884), vol. 13, p. 100.
33. In 1910, Nadar the photographer had once lived at this address also. See Hillairet, *Dictionnaire historique des rues* vol. 1, p. 149.
34. See Lami, *Dictionnaire des sculpteurs*, vol. 2, p. 405ff.
35. Anon. in *The Studio*, vol. 7, 1896, p. 26.
36. Vachon, *Puvis*, p. 57.
37. Ibid., p. 48.
38. Mantz, *Salon 1889*, p. 12.
39. Ibid.
40. Ibid.
41. Fox, *Reminiscences*, p. 218.
42. Moore, *Confessions*, p. 38.
43. E. de Goncourt, *Journal*, for 12 February 1888, vol. 15, p. 77.
44. Zola, *Nana*, p. 351.
45. Blanche, *Portraits*, p. 32.

### 8. The Left Bank: The Latin Quarter

1. Holland, *Student Life*, p. 39.
2. Rodin, *Art*, p. 25.
3. E. de Goncourt *Journal* for 17 April 1886, in *Pages from the Goncourt Journal*, edited and translated by Robert Baldick, London, 1980, p. 337.
4. Rodin, *Art*, p. 5.
5. Ibid., p. 146. 68 Rue d'Assas was a group of studios forming a *cité d'artistes*. Paul Huet had worked there, as did the sculptor Paul Dubois. Falguière eventually annexed several of the studios.
6. No. 100 bis, a sculptor's courtyard studio was later occupied by Osip Zadkine (from 1928) and now houses the Zadkine Museum.
7. Blanche, *Portraits*, pp. 42–3.
8. Gavriel Mourey, *A Modern Portrait Painter: M. Aman-Jean* in *The Studio* 1896, pp. 197–9.
9. *The Studio*, 1896, p. 109.
10. Warnod, *Les Berceaux*, p. 152.
11. Ibid., p. 55.

### 9. The Rue Notre Dame des Champs.

1. Jean-Paul Crespelle, *La Vie quotidienne à Montaparnasse à la Grande Epoque 1905–30*, Paris, 1979, p. 10.
2. See Breton, *Life of an Artist*, p. 191 and p. 271.
3. This is also part of the Rue Jules-Chaplain (formerly passage Stanislas) and renamed after the medallist Chaplain in 1913.
4. Wolff, *La Capitale*, p. 257.
5. Moreau-Vauthier, *Gérôme*, p. 126.
6. Breton, *Life of an Artist*, p. 265.
7. Anon, *Art Notes & Reviews* in *The Art Journal*, 1885, p. 127, discussing seven paintings by Bouguereau exhibited at Goupil's Gallery in 1885.
8. Holland, *Student Life*, p. 40.
9. Ibid., p. 38.
10. Ibid., pp. 38–9.
11. Ibid., p. 38.
12. Zola, *L'Oeuvre*, p. 66.

### 10. Southern Reaches on Montparnasse

1. Holland, *Student Life*, p. 35.

2. A Musée de Montparnasse was formerly housed at 10 Rue de l'Arrivée, near the railway station. See Crespelle, *La Vie Quotidienne*, p. 29.
3. See ibid., p. 73. Later inhabitants included De Chirico and the poet Rilke. (See Hillairet, *Dictionnaire historique des rues* vol. 1, p. 744) and Jules Flandrin, Charles Guérin and Othon Friesz (see Warnod, *Les Berceaux*, p. 157).
4. A successful campaign to resist their demolition was mounted in 1972. See Crespelle, *La Vie quotidienne*, p. 93. A copy of President Georges Pompidou's letter guaranteeing their future as studios is still visible on the gatepost. The area is 2,000 metres square. Later occupants included Daniel de Monfried, Pierre Roy, Sudeikin and Modigliani.
5. More studios are to be found at 73 Boulevard Arago and round the corner at 45 Rue de la Santé. See Hillairet, *Dictionnaire historique des rues* vol. 1, p. 729.
6. The present Rue Antoine-Bourdelle was formed in 1913 by extending the old Impasse du Maine. It was renamed in 1930. The Symbolist poet Jean Moréas lived in this street.
7. Paul Mantz writing in *Le Temps*, 4 July 1878, cited in de Foucard, *Bastien-Lepage*, p. 23.
8. Castagnary writing in *Le Siècle*, 1 June 1878, cited in de Foucard, *Bastien-Lepage*, p. 23.
9. Wolff, *La Capitale*, p. 259.
10. Wolff writing in *Le Figaro*, 14 May 1879, cited in de Foucard, *Bastien-Lepage*, p. 26.
11. Wolff, *La Capitale*, p. 257.
12. E. de Goncourt, *Journal* for 28 March 1885, vol. 13, p. 217.
13. Breton, *Life of an Artist*, p. 346.
14. A. Theuriet, *Jules Bastien-Lepage, l'homme et l'artiste*, Paris, 1885, and de Foucard, *Bastien-Lepage*.
15. E. de Goncourt, *Journal* for 17 February 1888, vol. 15, p. 82.
16. Bourdelle occupied 16 Impasse de Maine. His studio and works were given to the City of Paris by Mme Bourdelle in 1948.
17. Gauguin had lived in the Rue Falguière at No. 74 between 1877 and 1880.
18. Later Foujita, Soutine, Lipchitz and Modigliani worked here. See Crespelle, *La Vie quotidienne*, pp. 90–2, and Hillairet, *Dictionnaire historique des rues* vol. 1, p. 770. This lane was formerly known as the Impasse Frémin until it was renamed after the sculptor along with the Rue Falguière (formerly Rue des Fourneaux) in 1910.
19. According to Hillairet, *Dictionnaire historique des rues* vol. 1, p. 759.

### 11. Provincial Postscript

1. Cited in Stanton, *Reminiscences of Rosa Bonheur*, p. 363.
2. Ibid., p. 366.
3. Reproduced in Ibid., p. 364.
4. Breton, *Life of an Artist*, p. 59.
5. Ibid., p. 144.
6. Ibid., p. 297.
7. Ibid., p. 295.
8. Ibid., p. 308.
9. Ibid., p. 309.
10. Ibid., p. 320.
11. Ibid., p. 293.
12. Degas letter of July 1882 in *Degas: Letters*, Oxford, 1947, p. 69.

# Index

# Street Index

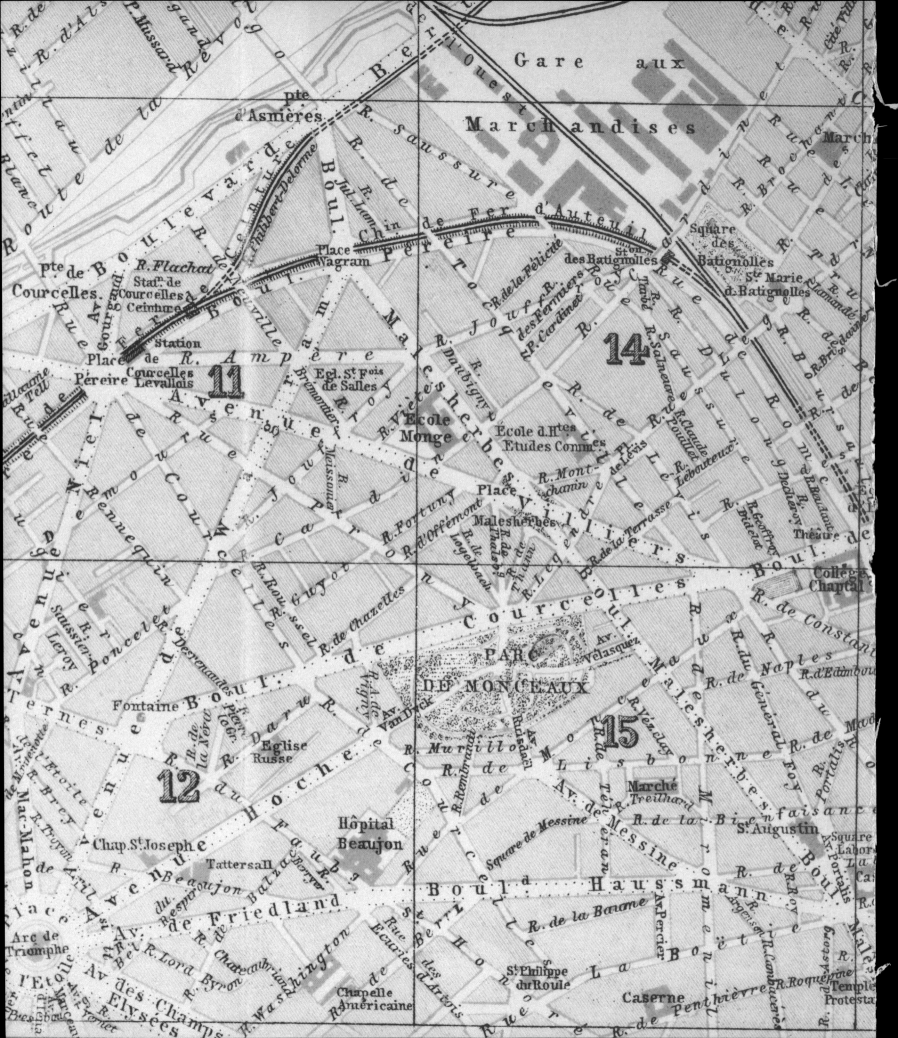